European Communism since 1989

European Communism since 1989

Towards a New European Left?

Kate Hudson
Principal Lecturer in Russian and East European Politics
South Bank University, London

palgrave

Published by PALGRAVE
Houndmills, Basingstoke, Hampshire RG21 6XS and
175 Fifth Avenue, New York, N.Y. 10010
Companies and representatives throughout the world

PALGRAVE is the new global academic imprint of
St. Martin's Press LLC Scholarly and Reference Division and
Palgrave Publishers Ltd (formerly Macmillan Press Ltd).

Outside North America
ISBN 0-333-77342-X

In North America
ISBN 0-312-22939-9

This book is printed on paper suitable for recycling and
made from fully managed and sustained forest sources.

A catalogue record for this book is available from the British Library.

Library of Congress Cataloging-in-Publication Data
Hudson, Kate, 1958-
European communism since 1989 : towards a new European left? / Kate
Hudson.
p.   cm.
Includes bibliographical references and index.
ISBN 0-312-22939-9 (cloth)
1. Communism—Europe.   2. Socialism—Europe.   3. Post-communism-
-Europe.   4. Communist parties—Europe.   5. Socialist parties—Europe.
6. Europe—Politics and government—1989-   I. Title

HX239 .H83   1999
335.43'094—dc21   99-042144

10   9   8   7   6   5   4   3
08   07   06   05   04   03   02

Printed and bound in Great Britain by
Antony Rowe Ltd, Chippenham, Wiltshire

In memory of my father
Tom Hudson
who inspired me with hope for the future of humanity

In memory of my father
Tom Hudson
who inspired me with hope for the future of humanity

Contents

List of Figures

List of Tables

Acknowledgements

During the process of writing and researching this book I have received the support and help of numerous colleagues, family members and friends, who have most generously and usefully given of their time, insights and critical comments.

I would particularly like to thank Redmond O'Neill, David Holland, Gus Fagan, Berhanu Kassayie, Nathalie Levallois, Mària Makai, Jimmy Jancovich and Patrick Theuret for their specific advice and help on the manuscript, and my colleagues Jeffrey Weeks and Morag Buchan at South Bank University for their warm encouragement.

Whilst responsibility for the content of the book is my own, the analysis contained therein is undoubtedly the product of collective and constant discussion over the last decade. During the course of my research, I have been privileged to benefit from the experience of many direct participants in the events this book addresses. Particularly formative for me has been my contact with the Hungarian Left Alternative in Budapest and the valuable discussion provided by their regular international conferences; I have also benefited from the exchange of ideas provided by the journals *Socialist Action Review, Labour Focus on Eastern Europe* and the French *Correspondances Internationales*.

KATE HUDSON

Part 1

The Long Evolution of the European Left

1
Introduction: 1989–99: Crisis, Splits, Renewal and Revival

As the Berlin Wall came down at the end of 1989, the conventional wisdom throughout the western world was that communism, as a significant political current, and socialism as an economic, social and political perspective – which had informed to one degree or another the philosophy of the great majority of the European labour movement for more then a century – was finished. Such views were inevitable, given the way in which the existence of the Soviet Union prior to 1991, and its conflict with the United States, had shaped most of the history of the twentieth century. As the historian Eric Hobsbawm put it:

> ... with the significant exception of the years from 1933 to 1945, the international politics of the entire Short Twentieth Century since the October revolution can best be understood as a secular struggle by the forces of the old order against social revolution, believed to be embodied in, allied with, or dependent on the fortunes of the Soviet Union and international communism.[1]

Seen in this historical perspective, the perceived 'threat' of social revolution had been the external menace which had forced the end of colonialism and the creation of the welfare state after the Second World War to stabilize the capitalist system – a system profoundly shaken by two world wars, fascism, and – by 1949 – the loss of a third of the world's population to an alternative social system calling itself socialist or communist.

In this long view, the events between 1989 and 1991 – from the fall of the Berlin Wall to the dissolution of the Soviet Union – constituted, literally, a turning point in world history. Francis Fukuyama went

3

further, declaring that the very process of historical change, seen by him as the era of competition between western free market capitalism and socialism, was over – because capitalism had 'won'.[2] In the field of economics, the monetarism and neo-liberalism, pioneered as government policy by Ronald Reagan and Margaret Thatcher, seemed set to sweep all before them. As the decade progressed, country after country opened itself, not only to the free movement of goods, but also to the free movement of capital, as globalization extended from the field of trade to that of international capital flows. The main beneficiary was the United States of America, as the post-Second World War direction of capital flows reversed, and the world's savings flowed from the poorest countries in the world to the richest.

At the same time, inequality between and within nations reached levels never before seen in world history. By a perverse twist of logic, reversing cause and effect, the social dislocation and political upheavals which resulted from the economic squeeze upon a continent like Africa, were taken by columnists in 'serious' British newspapers to argue that the end of colonialism might itself have been a mistake.

On the military plane, while the Warsaw Pact dissolved, NATO announced plans not only to expand into eastern Europe, but also to develop an increasing 'out of area' orientation pioneered by the Gulf War, explicitly posing itself as a world police force, reminiscent of nineteenth century colonialism. For the first time since its formation, the US-led military alliance launched offensive military operations on the continent of Europe – in the former Yugoslavia, first in Bosnia and then with the illegal 1999 bombing campaign against the Federal Republic of Yugoslavia. At its fiftieth anniversary summit in Washington, DC on 24th April 1999, NATO took the historic decision to extend its sphere of military intervention to the whole 'Euro-Atlantic region' – that is, the whole of western Europe, eastern Europe and the former Soviet Union. A proposal by France that such 'out of area' operations should need United Nations approval was rejected.

In the sphere of social policy, Newt Gingrich, as leader of the Republicans in the US Congress, claimed that extensive welfare provision and progressive taxation had been artefacts of the Cold War. He argued that, with the external 'threat' of communism banished, these internal concessions to the socialist threat should be dismantled.[3] The European Union's 1991 Treaty of Maastricht seemed to signal a similar move towards a more US-influenced model of social provision in western Europe. Finally, the entire political spectrum shifted to the right. The decade opened with European communist parties variously dissolving, changing their names and splitting. Many considered that even the ruling Chinese, Vietnamese and Cuban Communist Parties had also embraced capitalist economics, although more astute observers have noted that it would be a strange kind of capitalism which combined markets for food and consumer goods with the predominance of state and collective ownership of industry, socialist planning and communist party government.[4]

Social democratic parties embraced central tenets of the economic and social philosophy of Ronald Reagan and Margaret Thatcher. Tony Blair, leader of the British Labour Party, went further than most, implying that the very formation of the Labour Party at the turn of the century had split Britain's progressive liberal tradition and launching his 'project' of a return to nineteenth-century Gladstonian liberalism.[5] Writers like Anthony Giddens have set out to provide a theoretical basis for such enterprises, declaring bluntly that socialism has been dissolved and as 'Social Democracy was always linked to socialism. What should its orientation be in a world where there are no alternatives to capitalism?'[6]

Traditional west European conservative parties also felt the impact of 1989, as the far right and neo-fascist parties which had emerged in the context of mass unemployment in the European Union in the 1980s, made further inroads into their electorates. This sits uncomfortably with the analysis of Francis Fukuyama, who regarded 1989–91 as the definitive victory of liberal democracy over all possible alternatives. But a less superficial analysis would not find it at all surprising that mass unemployment and an undermining of social solidarity should be accompanied, as in the past, by the kind of angry despair on which racism, xenophobia and the far right have always fed. At the time of writing, in Italy, Gianfranco Fini's 'post-fascist' National Alliance had stabilized its share of the vote in national elections at roughly 15 per cent, whilst in Austria, Jörg Haider's Freedom Party regularly wins more than 20 per cent. In France, it remains to be seen whether the split in the far right National Front is anything more than a temporary setback in its electoral advance. Thus, in the decade after 1989, for the first time since the 1930s, the far right established a mass electoral base in some of western Europe's key countries. This has occurred to the extent that even 'respectable' parties of the right are, on the one hand adopting their own brands of racist rhetoric and, on the other, seriously discussing following the example of Silvio Berlusconi's Italian coalition with the far right in an electoral and governmental bloc.

Yet, notwithstanding these real and profound changes, and contrary to the conventional wisdom established by them, by the end of the decade it has turned out that the triumphalism of the right which had followed 1989, is already losing momentum.

Ten years ago, few would have predicted the headlines which filled the financial press of the world in August 1998. The *Financial Times'* Lex Column was typical: 'Das Capital Revisited' it exclaimed, as the world's stock markets gyrated, following the biggest default on debt in history as Russia's entire financial system collapsed – itself a product of the widening shock waves caused by the 1929-scale crash of the East Asia economies a year earlier. With that economic chain reaction continuing to unfold at the time of writing, Brazil being the latest domino to fall, confidence in the well-being of the new globalized economy fell to levels last seen in the aftermath of 1929. Fewer would have anticipated that by 1999 social democratic parties would be back in government in 13 out of the European Union's 15 national states including the four largest – Germany, France, Britain and Italy. Fewer still, would have thought that many of these parties in turn would face increasingly vigorous challenges from their left by parties often originating in a scarcely-observed process of political renewal launched by the left wings of what had been communist parties in 1989.

This book is dedicated to examining a single aspect of the way the world has actually turned out in the decade since 1989. It is one which has received little sustained attention, however, from the serious media or even from academic observers – that is, the emergence, consolidation and, more recently, advance of what can be described as a new European left. This can be defined as a converging political current of communist parties, former communist parties and other parties to the left of social democracy, which instead of disappearing – as predicted in 1989 – are playing an increasingly pivotal role in the politics of a series of European states. These range from Russia, where the left wing of what was the ruling Communist Party of the Soviet Union has re-invented itself to become by far the largest party in that country, through France, Italy, Germany and Sweden where, in 1999, social democratic governments depend for their parliamentary majorities on parties to their left, to the growing links of these latter with a series of Nordic left parties deeply critical of the recent shift to the right of social democracy in Scandinavia.

This book argues that although most observers of the European labour movement have been transfixed by phenomena like Tony Blair's transmutation of the Labour Party to the right, they have often missed the fact that something new has started to emerge to the left of these parties. In western Europe, the new European left is already coordinating its activity and discussions on an international level. It has drawn lessons from the demise of the communist regimes in the east, and in particular, it embraces a strategy of what it calls 'democratic socialism' – which differs from both social democracy and much of the theory and practice of the state socialist regimes in eastern Europe. It has sought to transform its political perspectives and alliances to accommodate the rise of white-collar employment, feminism, black communities and ecological struggles in Europe on the eve of the twenty-first century.

To the east, in Russia and most of eastern European, communist parties, and parties originating in the communist parties, have paradoxically won a degree of electoral support in democratic political systems which most observers would have considered inconceivable a decade ago. No common political framework of these east European parties exists outside the states of the former Soviet Union, and their links with the new European left in western Europe were tenuous or non-existent – though this started to change after NATO's bombing of Yugoslavia in 1999. However, their common roots in the pre-1989 communist parties, and the inevitable fact that, as in the past, the evolution of the labour movement and the left will be influenced by events in both halves of the continent, necessitate an analysis integrating developments in both eastern and western Europe. The rest of this chapter will provide a brief survey of these developments.

Towards a new European left

The Communist Party of the Russian Federation (CPRF), though originating as a small minority on the left of the former ruling Communist Party of the Soviet Union, with little influence between 1991 and 1993, has since become the largest party in terms of membership and popular vote in that country. In the second round of the presidential elections in Russia in June 1996, Gennady Zyuganov, the communist candidate, polled just under 30 million votes, or 40.4 per cent. In part, this advance can be attributed to the party's success in placing itself at the head of 'patriotic' opposition to the social and economic effects of the kind of capitalist economic reform which President Yeltsin has imposed.

The fragility of the Yeltsin regime was demonstrated in September 1998, when, following the collapse of Russia's financial system,

President Yeltsin, notwithstanding the enormous powers conferred on him by the constitution, was forced to accept Yevgeny Primakov, the favoured nominee of the communist-dominated Duma, as Prime Minster. The general perception by the autumn of 1998 was that, for the first time, Russia had a government which depended on the support of parliament. Although Primakov was subsequently removed in the context of NATO bombing Yugoslavia, the fact that a politician promoting a strategic alliance of Russia, China and India as a counter-weight to the United States, and including communists in his government, could so easily come to power in Russia, was a symptom of the continuing vitality of the left in that country.

Whilst Gennady Zyuganov's CPRF, is more 'communist' than most of the former communist parties in eastern Europe, the trend of former communist parties gaining unexpectedly massive electoral support was replicated in many other parts of the former Soviet Union, notably Ukraine, Moldova and in a specific form Belarus. Equally, in eastern Europe, having frequently failed spectacularly in the first elections after 1989, the former communist parties gained electoral support so rapidly that they were able to form democratically elected governments in Poland, Hungary, Bulgaria, Romania and, most recently, Albania, following some of the subsequent polls.

In western Europe, the right wing of the former communist parties either disappeared or, in the case of the Italian Communist Party, became social democratic parties after 1989. But, far from disappearing into the oblivion predicted by many observers, left-wing currents originating in the communist parties have subsequently emerged – alongside the greens and left social democratic parties in northern Europe – as the main challengers to social democracy from the left.

In Spain, Italy, eastern Germany, France, Sweden, Greece and Portugal, communist parties or their successors to the left of social democracy have established themselves as credible modern electoral mass parties. This has begun to make them a factor in the politics of national states, capable of influencing what party forms the government and exerting an external pressure on social democratic parties to consider more radical policies than their leaders might desire. In Sweden's September 1998 general election, social democracy's share of the vote fell by nearly 10 per cent – from 45.3 per cent to 36.6 per cent, its worst election result for 70 years. But the former-communist Swedish Left Party doubled its share of the vote to 12 per cent, becoming Sweden's third largest party in terms of votes. The Swedish social democratic government now depends for its parliamentary majority on the votes of Left Party and Green MPs. The Left Party stood on a platform of increased welfare spending, opposition to Swedish participation in European Monetary Union and a 35-hour working week.

In Italy, the 1996 general election gave the Party of Communist Refoundation, originating from the left wing of the former Communist Party and the post-1968 new left, 35 deputies. That was enough to hold the balance of power in parliament, making Romano Prodi's Olive Tree coalition government dependent on Communist Refoundation's parliamentary support. When that support was withdrawn following differences over austerity measures in Prodi's 1999 budget, the government fell and was replaced by one in which the prime minister was the leader of the right wing of the former Communist Party – Massimo D'Alema.

In France, the Socialist Party, led by the decidedly non-Blairite Lionel Jospin, swept to power on a relatively left social democratic platform in the June 1997 general election, in a coalition which included two ministers from the French Communist Party.

In the German general election of September 1998, confounding those who expected a 'grand coalition' of the German social democrats with Helmut Kohl's Christian Democrats, the social democrats in coalition with the Greens to their left, won an absolute majority in a parliament which also included the Party of Democratic Socialism – the successor to the former ruling communist party of East Germany. The latter, for the first time, passed the 5 per cent threshold which, in the German electoral system, determines which parties are formally recognized as official parliamentary fractions.

In the most recent Spanish general election, in May 1996, while the social democratic Spanish Socialist Workers' Party lost governmental power, the Communist Party-led United Left confirmed that it had carved out a significant share of the country's politics by taking more than 10 per cent of the vote.

Commenting on the conflict between the Party of Communist Refoundation and Italian Prime Minister Romano Prodi, the European edition of the forthrightly anti-socialist *Wall Street Journal* was driven to conclude that a new phenomenon had broken through into west European politics. In one of a number of articles, with the headline 'Italy's Emboldened Left Highlights Trend, Radical Coalition Partners at Odds With EMU', the *Journal* pointed out: 'There's a lesson in the Italian crisis for all of western Europe. The left wins the elections, but in power it has trouble controlling the radical left.'[7]

Indeed, not merely have these parties succeeded in consolidating an electoral space to the left of social democracy in most countries of western Europe, they have also confirmed their character as an international political trend by increasingly cooperating on a pan-West European level through a common group in the European Parliament – the United European Left-Nordic Green Left. Founded in 1994, this has become a substantial group in the European Parliament. The group includes four MEPs from the Spanish United Left, six from the French Communist Party, four from Italy's Party of Communist Refoundation and two from its Party of Italian Communists, two from the Portuguese Communist Party, three from the Greek Communist Party, two from the Greek Synaspismos, three from the Swedish Left Party, two from the Finnish Left Alliance and six from the German Party of Democratic Socialism.[8]

The new European left also comes together in a second west European-wide body linking the parties directly – the New European Left Forum. Founded in 1991, NELF meets twice a year and can be broadly defined as a grouping of democratic socialist (as opposed to social democratic) parties. Its members, spanning 17 countries include: the Left Alliance of Finland, the Swedish Left Party, the Socialist Left Party of Norway, the Socialist People's Party of Denmark, the Party of Democratic Socialism of Germany, the Democratic Labour Party of Estonia, the Green Left Party of the Netherlands, the United Left of Belgium, the French Communist Party, the Citizens Movement of France, the Swiss Labour Party, the Party of Communist Refoundation of Italy, the United Communist Movement of Italy, the Left and Progressive Party of Greece (Synaspismos), the ADISOK Party of Cyprus, AKEL of Cyprus, Initiative for Catalonia of Spain, the United Left of Spain and the Communist Party of Austria.[9]

Indeed, it is on this international plane, that the political distinctiveness of these parties is most apparent. An appeal by a number of these parties, launching a common platform for the June 1999 elections to the European Parliament, specified a number of distinctive themes. They called for 'a break with neo-liberal dogma' in favour of a strategy prioritizing economic growth, job-creation, a tax on international capital flows, an end to privatization of the public sector, increasing rather than reducing public spending, the reduction of the working week and whatever changes necessary to the statutes of the European Central Bank to achieve these objectives. They demand urgent measures to combat racism, including fundamental revision of the Schengen Agreement, which tightens the external boundaries of the EU against immigration and asylum seekers. They call for the cancellation of third world debt and, in the light of the end of the Cold War, argue that NATO has no role. They argue for a democratization of the European Union to achieve these objectives which are very much in line with the positions taken by the parties in their individual states – for example, their, for the most part, vigorous opposition to the Gulf War and to NATO's eastward expansion and to its military intervention in Yugoslavia.

The failure of most analysts of the European labour movement to take account of a process which has produced the largest electoral parties in much of the former Soviet Union and eastern Europe, a significant grouping of deputies in the European Parliament, and small but nonetheless real factors in governments of the left in key west European states, shows just how far much academic theory can lag behind reality.

To take just one example, Donald Sassoon has written an impressive and encyclopedic history of what he calls 'the west European left in the twentieth century', providing an enormous wealth of detail in a work of more than 900 pages.[10] This deals extensively with the shift of European social democracy to the right, but it virtually ignores its counterpoint in the emergence of the new European left. One can only conclude that this omission is due to the fact that the emergence of these parties simply does not fit into Sassoon's schema that 'Everyone is, in some shape or other, openly or covertly, a signed-up member of the capitalist club'.[11] But whilst political analysts may, for a time, be able to ignore those facts which do not fit comfortably with their theory, practical politicians, faced with the realities of the way people vote and the resulting parliamentary arithmetic, do not have the same luxury. Social democratic leaders from Rome, to Madrid, Lisbon, Paris and Berlin have to deal with the practical political problems posed for them by an electoral challenge on their left which shows no signs of dissipating and may, indeed, grow.

In essence, writers like Sassoon seem to have entirely missed the fact that the rightward movement of social democracy over the last decade has had the entirely predictable result of opening up a large political space to its left. As a result, the part of the political spectrum formerly occupied by the communist parties has not disappeared: it contracted in the period up to and following 1989, then stabilized and finally has started to expand.

To grasp the significance of this, it is not enough to look at the parties of the new European left's share of the total vote in each country. It is also necessary to consider their share of the votes cast for parties based upon the labour movement. By this yardstick, parties like the Spanish United Left, Italy's Party of Communist Refoundation, Sweden's Left Party and the German PDS are now winning up to a third of the vote of the social democratic parties. Thus, while these parties will not overtake social democracy at the polls in the present phase of European politics, they have made breakthroughs – sufficient to make them factors in mainstream politics, and sources of pressure from the left on the majority parties of their respective labour movements. Furthermore, they have started to attract supporters and voters, particularly among young people, extending beyond the traditional bastions of the communist parties among a section of the most militant blue collar workers.

Sassoon argues that the collapse of communism accelerated a trend towards homogeneity, the 'convergence principle', whereby all parties – whether traditionally of the left or right – supposedly accept:

> that market forces can be regulated but not eliminated ... that the growth of public spending should be curbed; that the welfare state can be defended but not extended; that privatisation may be unavoidable and, when it eradicates monopolies, desirable; that equality, though still appealing as a goal, may be tempered by the need to preserve incentives...[12]

While it is true to say that both social democratic parties and traditional conservative parties have converged around such a neo-liberal agenda, the analysis is incomplete and therefore misleading, because it omits to mention that the price paid for this convergence has been the consolidation of a new left wing of the European labour movement which is precisely fighting *against* any such convergence and winning electoral support for this stand.

The inadequacy of this theory stems from the fact that Sassoon effectively reduces the history of the west European left over the last decade, to that of one, albeit the largest, part of it. Sassoon's definition of the European left is defective, reducing it to 'the mainstream socialist, social-democratic and labour parties, including the former communist parties'. This definition includes right-wing social democracy, former Eurocommunist forces that have become social-democratic and former ruling communist parties that have embraced neo-liberal economic policies. That there has been a convergence of these currents with straight-forward capitalist parties is true, but, as has already been demonstrated, this does not comprise the entire spectrum of the west European left – notably excluding the left communist parties, leftwards moving social democrats and other left forces which include communists within them, which are undergoing a convergence of their own *against* neo-liberalism. Furthermore, even within some of the mass social democratic parties there are clear signs of a left reaction to neo-liberalism – undoubtedly fuelled by the vast social struggles which accompanied the attempts to cut social spending and deregulate labour markets under the terms of the Treaty of Maastricht in the run up to European Monetary Union.

The scale of social mobilizations defending employment, pension and other social acquisitions in countries like France, Italy and Germany in 1995 and 1996, was certainly a major factor in bringing about the electoral defeat of the parties of the traditional right in the subsequent elections in those countries. Equally, the debates engendered by the shattering defeat of the French Socialists whose share of the vote fell to 16 per cent in the 1993 general election, after vigorously pursuing a policy of austerity, the dissolution of the Italian Socialist Party in 1994 following its implication in numerous corruption scandals, and the ejection of the Spanish Socialists from office in 1996, having alienated their working class support through monetarist policies, all provided much food for thought.

In the light of those events, the move of the French Socialists to the left under Lionel Jospin prior to the last general election and the albeit temporary presence of a more traditionally interventionist social democrat like Oskar Lafontaine as Finance Minister in the first months of the new German government, fall into place. Although it is clearly too early to be able to discern a more general tendency on the level of western Europe, it is quite clear that these individual developments, at least, indicate that the thesis of a quasi-universal convergence of right and left in Europe around what is effectively a neo-liberal agenda, may be undermined by the reaction of social democracy's electorate to the social consequences of such a course. The prediction of many commentators that Tony Blair would become a model emulated by social democratic leaders across the continent may or may not be realized. But Jospin's clash with Blair's neo-liberalism at the very first summit of the European Socialist Party attended by them both and the role of Lafontaine in the first months of the German social democratic government were the expression of powerful pressures in a different direction. Moreover, the electoral consolidation of the new European left is a symptom of a new mood among western Europe's voters and a warning to social democratic leaders who wish to emulate Blair that the price of doing so might be to lose support to this challenge from their left.

From what has already been said, it is also clear that the new European left cannot be assimilated to any category of 'nostalgic' communist sects, living in the past, tied to a disappearing electorate and in irreversible decline. Indeed, it was recognition that this perspective – the dominant one after 1989 – had been confounded, which provoked such alarm from serious right wing commentators like the *Wall Street Journal*. Communist sects do exist, but they form no part of the new European left, which is interesting precisely because of the capacity which its component parties, irrespective of whether or not they retained the name communist, have shown for open political debate and renewal, taking account of the realities of European and world politics at the end of the twentieth century. This has manifested itself in the ability of these parties to open themselves to, and durably ally or even merge with the electorally insignificant, but very active, new left organizations which had expanded dramatically after 1968. Such groups participate in Spain's United Left, merged with the left wing of the Italian Communist Party to found the Party of Communist Refoundation, are included in the electoral lists of Germany's Party of Democratic Socialism and have recently even been invited to participate in common actions and debates initiated by the French Communist Party.

At the same time, while constituting a clearly demarcated political current, the new European left is increasingly engaged in seeking to forge alliances with the much larger social democratic parties. These range from agreement on individual issues to parliamentary backing for social democratic-led governments against the parties of the right, through to actual participation in such governments. The resulting alliances and coalitions are far from unproblematic, and the issue of on what principles they should be constructed is undoubtedly the key political debate now opening within the parties of the new European left. It has already produced splits in Spain and Italy and as this book goes to press, NATO bombing of Yugoslavia – backed by European social democratic leaders and condemned by the new European left – shows the basic contradiction between the policies of the social democratic and emerging democratic socialist traditions. But the very fact that they now influence who can and cannot form governments is testimony to the fact that the new European left has no intention of allowing itself either to be trapped in any sectarian or dogmatic ghetto, nor to lose their distinct identity as parties of democratic socialism, as opposed to the rightward moving trends dominant in the leadership of the parties of social democracy.

Thus the fall of the communist regimes in eastern Europe in 1989, and dissolution of the Soviet Union in 1991, did indeed open a new epoch in European and world history. Irrespective of the view taken of the previous regimes in those states, their disappearance led international capital to believe that it could dismantle not only communism but also social democracy and the welfare state upon which it was based.

As Larry Elliott and Dan Atkinson observe in their book, *The Age of Insecurity*:

> once the external threat was removed, once there was only one model of global development on offer, capitalism quickly forgot the accumulated history of a hundred years. No longer were welfare states seen as a bulwark against Communism, a worthwhile price for keeping the workers content and peaceful. All of a sudden – and despite the fact that the West was richer than ever before – welfare states became an intolerable burden on capitalism, siphoning off investment and energy with their insatiable demands for benefit payments. By the mid-1990s, it had become one of the axioms of Western thought that Germany was being being eaten away from the inside by the high non-wage costs – fringe benefits, sickness pay, unemployment insurance – doled out to its pampered workforce. Whereas in the 1970s, the seven- and eight-week holidays enjoyed by the Volkswagen workers at Wolfsburg were seen as proof positive of the German productivity miracle, by the late 1990s they were decried as the outward manifestations of Germany's Euro-sclerosis. John Sweeney, the head of the American trade union movement, put the move to a harsher form of capitalism well when addressing capitalism's annual talking shop – the World Economic Forum in Davos, Switzerland – in early 1997. In the 1950s and 1960s, Mr Sweeney said, some of the nastiness of capitalism was tempered. There was a fair share of the spoils for everyone. Now there was a lack of concern in boardrooms about the impact on workers of downsizing and falling real wages. 'Once we grew together; now we're growing apart', he said.[13]

This book argues that the emergence of the new European left in western Europe, the mass electoral support for former communist parties in eastern Europe, the electoral dominance of a Communist

Party in Russia (which advocates the reconstitution of the USSR and a planned economy through the ballot box) – and even the emergence of the most radical leadership of the American trade union movement since the Second World War, around John Sweeney – are all symptoms of the fact that the new, post-1989, anti-welfare face of capitalism is far from being welcome to a very large part of the population. What was commenced after 1989 was so damaging for so many people, that they have begun to do something about it. For that reason, increasingly serious attention should be paid to these new, radical left-wing trends in European politics which, until now, most observers have chosen to ignore.

2
The European Left before 1989: Washington, Moscow and Brussels

The development of mass labour movements – that is trade unions and parties based upon and organized around a predominantly working-class electorate – is a characteristic feature of all capitalist societies once they have reached a certain level of development. It flows from the fact that, as individuals, wage and salary earners are virtually powerless *vis-à-vis* those who own the large concentrations of capital necessary to set the modern productive process in motion.

From this imbalance of economic, and therefore also of political, power arises the phenomenon of a section of wage and salary earners coming together to create trade unions and political parties to represent their specific interests. By the latter half of the nineteenth century, virtually every west European country saw repeated – and finally successful – attempts to create trade unions and political parties and to extend the franchise beyond property owners in order to pursue objectives such as limitation of the working day and other social reforms. The creation of working class political parties in industrialized economies has only been avoided where dominance of the world capitalist economy provided resources sufficient to contain the working class electorate within a framework of purely capitalist parties – notably Britain in the second half of the nineteenth century and the United States after the First World War.

Inevitably, from the very beginning the issues arose as to what the new labour movements' objectives should be and how they should be achieved. The first attempt to draw these together into a common political framework at an international level was the creation of the First International in 1864. The new organization's statutes and programme were drafted in London by Karl Marx. It stood for the creation of independent working class political parties in every capitalist country and by the time of its dissolution in 1878 explicitly socialist parties existed in Germany, Switzerland, Denmark, Portugal, Italy, Belgium, Holland and North America.[1]

The second bid to create a common international framework of the left was the formation of the Socialist, or second, International in Paris in 1889 – the centenary of the French revolution. This organization was significantly influenced by Marxism and its early years saw a tremendous extension of working class political organization, on both the international field and in terms of numerical support and votes.

In the first decade of the twentieth century there was a series of disputes within the Second International over issues such as participation in governments with non-socialist parties, colonial policy and immigration, but these were contained within a common organizational framework. What could not be contained, however, was the decision of most of the main parties, in August 1914, to support their governments in the First World War. Given that German and French socialists, for example, were now supporting a war in which their members were killing each other, the International effectively ceased to function for the duration of the carnage.

A very small minority of the Second International, around the Russian Bolsheviks led by Lenin, groups around Rosa Luxemburg and Karl Liebknecht in Germany and others, broke away. They considered that the Second International was dead – having abandoned its commitment adopted in 1907 and subsequently reaffirmed to oppose world war by all possible means:

> Should war break out despite everything, it is the duty of Socialists to act for its rapid conclusion and to work with all their strength to utilize the economic and political crisis provoked by the war to rouse the peoples and thus accelerate the abolition of the rule of the capitalist class.[2]

Thus the First World War opened a division which was to dominate the European and world labour movements for most of the twentieth century. The split was made permanent when, instead of disappearing, the minority which had opposed the war began to gain mass support as it progressed. This culminated in October 1917 when the Russian Bolsheviks came to power – overthrowing capitalism in the largest country in the world. From that point the Russian revolution became the rallying point for all of those who rejected the dominant policies of the parties of the Second International. In 1920 they launched the

Communist, or Third, International which won the support of large minorities of the European labour movement in the immediate aftermath of the war. Large communist parties were created in a series of states. It looked for a time as if the Russian revolution might rapidly be extended into western, and in particular, central Europe. This was indeed the Bolsheviks' aim. Lenin, himself doubted whether, given the relative backwardness of Russia, the revolution could survive unless it advanced into the more advanced capitalist states. The goal of the Third International was to achieve this.

The origins of 'Atlanticism'

To grasp the subsequent development of the European labour movement, and why the Third International failed to achieve its objective, it is necessary to see it in a still wider context. Until the First World War, world history had been dominated for 400 years by the rise and expansion of western Europe. In 1914 western Europe imploded, never recovering its previous dominant position and, after both the first and second world wars, proved incapable of restoring even its own internal stability without external support. As Max Silberschmidt has pointed out, from 1917 until 1991 the entire development of Europe, including that of its labour movements, was shaped by the contest between, and impact of, two 'external' forces – the Russian revolution and the United States of America.[3]

The very entry of the United States into the First World War coincided with the threat of Russia's withdrawal following the overthrow of the Tsar in Febrary 1917. With Russia in turmoil, the balance of economic and military power would have been tipped in favour of Germany – the US's greatest economic rival. It was only the intervention of the United States that finally secured the defeat of Gemany and its allies. As Graham Ross put it:

> The European powers ... were unable to resolve the conflict either by a clear-cut victory or through a negotiated settlement. Instead they succeeded in destroying the stability of the European state system and thus undermined European global predominance. Only with the help of the United States were Britain, France and Italy able to defeat the central powers.[4]

In the aftermath of the war, on the basis of its own resources, western Europe was incapable of restoring its economic and political equilibrium.

The Russian revolution was followed by revolutions in Germany in 1918, Hungary in 1919 and mutinies and mass strikes elsewhere, amid widespread economic dislocation and rapid growth of the communist parties. The attempt to overturn the Bolsheviks by military intervention on the side of the white armies in the Russian civil war failed, although the Soviet counter-thrust into Poland was also blocked. A new crisis then erupted, in 1923, when France occupied the Ruhr because Germany defaulted on payments of the reparations imposed under the Treaty of Versailles.

The situation in western Europe, and in particular Germany, could only be stabilized when the United States intervened to underwrite the European economy. In 1924, the Dawes Plan was agreed under which a huge inflow of capital into Europe from the United States began. Germany immediately received a $200 million stabilization loan, and over the next five years received over $4 billion, almost half of which it paid out in reparations, thus securing a measure of stability and economic growth in western Europe as a whole and indirectly benefitting the US economy which needed to export the surpluses created by what had become the most productive economy in the world. As Adam Ulam describes the Dawes Plan:

> This led to the famous and somewhat insane circular flow of reparations and debt payments that continued until the Depression: Germany paid the victors in the war, they in turn paid instalments on their debts contracted in the United States and among themselves between 1914 and 1918, and the U.S. lent huge sums to Germany.[5]

On the basis of these US credits, the situation in western and central Europe was stabilized and the inroads of the communist parties against their rivals in the re-constituted Second International were checked. As van der Pijl has observed:

> Hitherto, the European liberal bourgeoisie had been able both to contain domestic working class pressures and to maintain a degree of autonomy *vis-à-vis* the United States, but the Russian Revolution threw them into the arms of Wilson and the universalist policy he had been cultivating for several years ... The revolution would not have been confined to Russia had it not been for the entry of the United States in the crucial final stage of the war and the tremendous power thus thrown into battle on the side of liberal capitalism ...[6]

This US economic underpinning of western Europe's post-war economic recovery was the starting point for a profound re-alignment of Europe politics – the rise of Atlanticism. Conservative parties and European social democracy alike bound themselves in an alliance with the United States as the only possible guarantor of economic stability and therefore also the bulwark against the spread of communism, which was regarded at that time as a tangible possibility.

Thus by the mid-1920s a kind of equilibrium had been established. On the one hand, western intervention against the Russian revolution had been defeated. On the other hand, that revolution had been confined to the most backward region of Europe by virtue of the intervention of the United States. This pattern was to be repeated on a still grander scale following the Second World War. But, in the meantime, the resulting stand-off was also the basis of the rise of Stalin's regime in what became the Soviet Union. The strategy of building 'socialism in one country' was adopted and the international communist movement was brought under the direct control of the leadership of the Communist Party of the Soviet Union (CPSU). Over the same period, and for the reasons outlined above, social democracy became the most pro-American political trend in west European societies. This set the basic division of the west European labour movement between minority, pro-Moscow, communist parties and majority, pro-American, social democratic parties, which was to persist until the 1970s.

The impact of the Second World War

From 1929 a new crisis erupted, revealing again the necessity of US resources to under-pin the economic and social stability of western Europe. Following the Wall Street crash in October 1929, American capital flows to Europe effectively ceased, inaugurating a new wave of social instability. In Germany, the country most severely affected, the Nazis came to power in 1933. In Spain, the civil war exploded in 1936. The sequence of events had begun which was to culminate in the Second World War.

In this context, the social democratic parties were either swept away by fascism in Germany and Spain, or saw significant radicalization in their own ranks under the impact of mass unemployment and the threat of fascism. In a series of countries, such as Britain and France, splits occurred on both the right and the left. Stalin responded to the crisis by a series of abrupt turns which deeply disoriented, and weakened the communist parties – a turn to violent ultra-leftism up to 1933 whereby the social democrats were labelled 'social fascists', then a shift in 1935 to the popular front tactic based on seeking an alliance with Britain and France against the threat of war from Nazi Germany, and finally the Stalin-Hitler pact on the eve of the Second World War.

The Second World War was the most gigantic conflict in human history, with more than 50 million people dying as a result. Its outcome was victory for both the Soviet Union and the United States, and the weight and moral authority of the Soviet Union – which bore the overwhelming brunt of the war with Nazi Germany and succeeded in defeating it – was transformed. In addition to the primary role of its armies, the Moscow-linked communist parties played the decisive role in most of the resistance movements, while the socialist party organizations, on the other hand, virtually disappeared in occupied Europe. The war resulted in the weak regimes in eastern Europe, many deeply implicated in collaboration with the Nazis, being overturned. Tito's communist partisans came to power in Yugoslavia and in 1949 the Chinese Communist Party came to power in the most populous country on earth. The Chinese revolution, in turn, opened an intense class struggle in Asia, with massive, and ultimately unsuccessful US wars against communist-led revolutions in Korea and then Vietnam.

The victory of the Soviet Union over Nazi Germany in the Second World War gave renewed impetus to the left throughout Europe after 1945. In France, in the election of 1945, 45 per cent of the vote went to the socialist and communist parties, compared to 38 per cent in 1936. In Italy, the communist and socialist parties received 40 per cent of the vote in 1946, compared to 15 per cent in the last elections before Mussolini seized power. In Britain, Labour Party membership reached 5 040 000 in 1947 compared to 2 630 000 in 1938. Revived socialist parties entered or formed almost every post-war government in western Europe.[7]

Within the labour movement, as a result of the prestige of the Soviet Union and the communist role in the resistance movements, the balance of forces had shifted to significantly strengthen the communists:

In France the vote was 29 per cent for the CP and 14 per cent for the SP in the elections of November 1946, compared to 18 per cent and 19 per cent respectively in 1937. In Italy, 20 per cent of the vote was for the PSI and 19 per cent for the PCI in 1946, but the former had only 860 000 members compared to the 2 068 000 for the CP In Britain Communist Party membership advanced from 18 000 in 1939 to 45 000 by 1945 and in Belgium the CP received 13 per cent

of the vote in 1945 compared to 4 per cent in 1939 – party membership rising from 9000 to 100 000 in the same period.'[8]

Even the relatively tiny British Communist Party won two parliamentary seats in the 1945 general election.

At the same time, European capitalism emerged from the Second
World War enormously weakened both economically and politically.
The Soviet Union was the occupying power in eastern Europe and the
communists were advancing in China. A critical lesson of the First
World War had been that social revolution was a real possibility in
the defeated powers without massive economic aid. The US had been
planning for the post-war settlement throughout the war. Its key goal
was to create a world economy in which the pre-war obstacles to the
free movement of American goods – and to US access to vital raw
materials – were eliminated and an international monetary system
organized around the supremacy of the dollar. As Gabriel Kolko
points out, quoting the interim report of the State Department's
Special Committee on the Relaxation of Trade Barriers of December
1943:

> A great expansion in the volume of international trade after the war
> will be essential to the attainment of full and effective employment
> in the United States and elsewhere, to the preservation of private
> enterprise, and the success of an international security system to
> prevent future wars.[9]

To achieve this, US economic leverage was to be used to force Britain
to open its empire and spheres of influence to American goods. As
Kolko put it: 'The United States could not afford, however, to compromise on the essential principle of breaking down the sterling bloc, for
that was the key to the reconstruction of the world economy after the
defeat of the axis.'[10] Stephen Ambrose comments on what were
regarded as the stakes:

> If the rest of the world nationalized its basic industries and/or
> closed its markets, America could avoid overproduction and a
> resultant depression only by nationalizing the means of pro-
> duction and distribution itself. American foreign policy after
> 1945 had as one of its guiding stars, therefore, the prevention of
> these evils – or, put positively, the creation of an open door
> everywhere.[11]

However, in addition to its economic objectives, the US also had to contend with the new political and strategic situation in the aftermath of the war. As it did not have the resources to deal with all of the problems it faced, it had to prioritize. Michael Schaller summarized the result of the US discussion on this:

> [George] Kennan told an audience at the National War College in September 1947 that 'only five centres of industrial and military power in the world' mattered 'to us from a standpoint of national security.' These included the United States, Great Britain, Germany and Central Europe, Soviet Union and Japan. These areas alone possessed the industrial strength needed for the 'type of amphibious power which would have to be launched' to challenge America. As only the Soviet zone was now counted as unfriendly, the challenge ahead involved keeping the remainder of Europe and Japan in the American camp 'First and foremost' Kennan argued, America needed to counterbalance the Soviet Union on the Eurasian landmass. 'That balance is unthinkable as long as Germany and Japan remain power vacuums.'[12]

Hence, in Europe, the US embarked upon the course of rebuilding the German economy, and later German rearmament, as a bulwark against the Soviet Union. The concomitant of this was the division of Germany and the division of Europe and once this course became clear, the Soviet Union established communist regimes in most of the occupied countries of eastern Europe.

The division of Europe

In 1947, the US president spelt out the Truman Doctrine, pledging US political, military and economic aid to any anti-communist government under threat. Clearly, in this developing 'cold war' situation, stabilizing western Europe was a key objective because 'total economic disintegration appeared to be imminent'.[13]

In March 1948, two weeks after the communists had come to power in Czechoslovakia, the US Senate endorsed the Marshall Plan, an economic aid programme designed to bring about west European recovery. Its aims were to rebuild a strong European economy integrated into a US-led world order, to thereby ease the social conditions which were leading to mass support for the communists, and to ensure the continued existence of the US export market, of which Europe was the largest part.

In essence, it was the economic arm of the Truman Doctrine and it made possible the rebuilding of west European capitalism – under the hegemony of the US – economically through the Bretton Woods institutions and militarily through the US military presence, formalized in 1949 by the establishment of NATO. However, the need to secure popular support in a region with a far more massive and politically organized labour movement than the US, and where Soviet military power was seen as an ever-present threat, also made a relatively social democratic policy of welfare provision and labour market regulation essential.

The US also encouraged the creation of the European Economic Community to further bolster European capitalism *vis-à-vis* the perceived threat from the east. As Perry Anderson has observed, objections on the grounds of the EEC's potential for economic competition were overridden by the White House and the State department:

> American politico-military imperatives, in the global conflict with Communism, trumped commercial calculation without the slightest difficulty. Eisenhower informed Pineau that the realisation of the Treaty of Rome would be 'one of the finest days in the history of the free world, perhaps even more so than winning the war.' Pregnant words, from the Allied Supreme Commander.[14]

Overall, the onset of the Cold War not only divided Europe into 'east' and 'west', but also deepened the political split in the west European labour movement. The leading circles of social democracy, again on the basis of the role of the US in rebuilding the west European capitalist economies after the war, backed the foreign policy of the United States. The trade unions and socialist parties went through a series of splits as left socialist political and trade union currents opposed to this 'atlanticist' orientation were excluded.

The Italian and French trade unions were split by US intervention, as was the Italian Socialist Party, and very strongly anti-communist leaderships were at the helm in the French Socialist Party (SFIO), the British Labour Party and the west German SPD. The communist parties, on the other hand, were clearly aligned with the Soviet Union. These parties dominated the labour movement in the economically weaker southern European countries – in Greece, Italy, France, Spain and Portugal, where strong social democratic parties had not emerged. US sponsorship of the dictatorships in Spain, Portugal and later Greece, further enhanced the influence of the underground communist parties in these latter countries. Social democracy dominated in the stronger northern European states, especially in Britain, Scandinavia and the Federal Republic of Germany.

The economic and political impact of the Vietnam war

From 1948 to the mid-1960s, the post-war economic boom provided the conditions for relative stability in the relationship between west European and US capital and the lines of divide in the labour movement remained relatively stable. Social democratic parties restored their dominance in the west European labour movement outside southern Europe but were unable to eliminate minority anti-US communist parties.

The end of the post-war economic boom at the end of the 1960s then created the conditions which would break up the relative stability of relations between the US, western Europe and the Soviet Union – and together with it the structure of the labour movement which had emerged on the basis of this over-arching inter-relationship.

The turning point in the relationship was the Vietnam war. Until Vietnam, the US, for the reasons outlined already, had been a net contributor to the west European economies. Under the strain of the Vietnam war, and in conditions where significant opposition to the war developed within the United States, the US economy no longer had the resources to continue to act as the motor of the world economy. Until the peak of the Vietnam war, and definitively from the world recession which followed in the middle of the 1970s, US economic growth and exports of capital had been the locomotive of the world economy. From that point US economic growth took place at the expense of the growth in western Europe and Japan, and the consequences were dramatic. The west European economies had grown much more rapidly than that of the US until the mid-1970s and their average level of unemployment was half that of the US. From then on, west European unemployment rose to more than double the US levels.

In succession, the devaluation of the dollar in 1971, then the huge increases in oil prices in 1973, and later Ronald Reagan's policies of high interest rates, all struck enormous blows against the economies of western Europe and Japan to the benefit of the United States. By 1976, the United States had been transformed from a net exporter of capital to the rest of the world into an importer of capital. This culminated in the enormous inflows of capital into the US which financed Reagan's military build-up in the 1980s, and transformed the US from the world's largest creditor nation into its greatest debtor nation.

Inevitably, this turnaround in economic relationships had profound political consequences. In this context, the attitudes of both European capital and social democracy began to change towards the US, in particular leading to attempts by some western European leaders, notably de Gaulle, to steer a course more independent of the US.

This shift was also reflected in the west European labour movement. As the post-war boom came to an end, an enormous cycle of struggles was commenced, in particular by trade unions – at the peak of their membership, as a result of the long boom – and by an emerging student movement, newly-radicalized by their revulsion for the American role in Vietnam. There soon followed the May 1968 general strike triggered by the student movement in France, a wave of strikes in Italy in 1969 and a series of trade union struggles in Britain which culminated in the fall of Ted Heath's Conservative government in 1974. A massive wave of social unrest ended with the fall of the Franco dictatorship in Spain and the toppling of the dictatorship in Portugal in 1975, amid mass strikes, demonstrations and major disaffection and radicalization in the ranks of the army.

The first sign of the shift in west European politics occurred among young people. The Vietnam war, and the accompanying shift in the relationship between western Europe and the United States, unleashed the most significant anti-US movement – against the Vietnamese war – seen in Europe until that point. This substantially outflanked not only the pro-American socialist parties, but also the communist parties, who were increasingly discredited as a result of the events which had recently taken place in eastern Europe. The widespread rejection, including within many communist parties, of the Soviet invasion of Hungary in 1956, was reinforced by the revelations of Khrushchev's so-called 'secret speech' – attacking Stalin's 'cult of the personality' and detailing his crimes – at the Twentieth Congress of the CPSU, and most particularly by the Soviet invasion of Czechoslovakia in 1968. The combination of these events, with the mass workers' struggles which followed 1968, substantially shaped the politics of the 'new left', but the 'new left' itself never succeeded in constituting a significant political alternative to the socialist and communist parties, in the field of mass politics.

In part, this was due to a radical mis-estimate of the real possibilities inherent in the new situation. Many on this 'new left' – which emerged to the left of not only the socalist, but also the communist, parties through these events – considered them to be the harbinger of revolution in western Europe. They were wrong, but the results were nonetheless spectacular – the destruction of southern Europe's dictatorships, the rise of mass opposition to the United States in western Europe and a process which, as will be seen, resulted in a massive realignment of the balance of forces in the west European labour movement to the benefit of the socialist parties and at the expense of the communists.

The anti-missiles movement

During the 1970s and into the 1980s, the new economic relationship between the US and the world economy, fuelled increasing competition between the US and western Europe – particularly its most powerful economy, West Germany. West European capital's response to this was to attempt to pursue a more independent course – though within definite limits determined by its military dependence on the United States within NATO.

The axis of this was the reinforcement, expansion and deeper integration of the European Community culminating in 1999 with the launch of the single European currency, which constitutes a fundamental challenge to the world role of the dollar. Expansion began with the adhesion of Britain to the EEC in 1975, then towards southern Europe, then north towards Scandinavia and finally, after the fall of the Berlin Wall, preparing for the integration of key east European states as a kind of economic border region. This has remained to this day very much within a framework of strategic subordination, made necessary until 1991 by military dependence on the US *vis-à-vis* the Soviet Union. But as early as the beginning of the 1980s, disputes over agricultural subsidies and steel were symptoms of rising tensions on the economic field.

The US response, under Ronald Reagan at the beginning of the 1980s, was to propose a common endeavour to ameliorate the contradictions between western Europe and the US, by expanding their fields of operation into eastern Europe. The means to this end was to increase the military pressure on the Soviet Union with a view to finally breaking its hold over eastern Europe. The key instrument for this was to be the deployment of Cruise and Pershing missiles in western Europe and the launch of the so-called 'star wars' strategic defence initiative in the United States. The significance of these weapons was that they greatly reduced the time necessary for nuclear weapons to be delivered against Soviet cities and made feasible the prospect of 'limited nuclear war' confined to the European theatre, but they were also expensive – both financially and politically. Under Reagan the US military budget was increased by 40 per cent, and was funded by inflow of capital from Japan, the third world and, to a lesser extent, western Europe.[15]

However, before the missiles could be deployed, a major obstacle had to be cleared. That was the immense opposition to the missiles on the part of the populations in the countries which had agreed to accept them. The movement against Cruise and Pershing missiles developed into the biggest mass movement in Europe since the second world war, with demonstrations involving literally millions of people, and the reinforcing of a new 'green' movement to the left of both the communist and the socialist parties of the time. This green movement has become a durable feature of west European politics and has provided one of the springs which have fed the later development of the new European left.

The driving force of the anti-missiles movement was straightforward. Previously, it was popularly assumed that the capacity of the United States and the Soviet Union to annihilate one another many times meant that no government would be mad enough to actually start a nuclear war. The prospect of 'mutually assured destruction' (MAD) was believed to mean that deterrence worked, but Cruise and Pershing missiles changed that – they made it possible to fight a 'limited' nuclear war in Europe. That prospect naturally elicited a reaction of extraordinary alarm on the part of the inhabitants of the country where such a war was likely to take place, as well as in the countries which had agreed to deploy the new missiles – because they too would be obvious targets. This movement penetrated deep into society bringing completely new sections of the population into its ranks. It had a considerable impact on both the communist and socialist parties, so that one of the first actions of the British Labour Party following its defeat in the 1979 general election, was to lead a mass demonstration against the missiles.

The United States and its NATO allies devoted enormous resources to defeating the anti-missiles movement and they were ultimately successful – although they did pay a price in terms of the emergence of a new radical force in west European politics. That victory for Ronald Reagan and his allies then set the scene for the events which were to culminate in 1989. Given that the Soviet economy was only half the size of the US which, moreover, benefitted through the 1980s from inflows of capital to the tune of $100 billion a year, this escalation of the nuclear arms race threatened to break the Soviet economy. In addition, the strategic position of the Soviet Union had suffered incalculable damage as a result of the deepening of its conflict with China following the end of the Vietnam war and US exploitation of that split through a *de facto* Sino–US alliance against the Soviet Union. Moreover, this was at a time when the Soviet and east European economies has ceased to catch up with the west, and growing discontent was developing with an economic model which prioritized heavy industry over living standards and thereby delivered a lower level of living standards than could otherwise have been achieved. The combination of the increased dynamism of the west European economies, under the impetus of EEC integration, the ability of the US to fund its military build-up at the expense of its allies and the sheer impossibility of meeting the demands of a new spiral of the arms race, finally led to the shift in Soviet policy which brought Gorbachev to power. It was Gorbachev's decision to seek a new accommodation with the US, in part by withdrawing the Soviet guarantee of military backing for the east European regimes, which was to inaugurate their collapse in 1989.

Towards European integration: Eurosocialism and Eurocommunism

These shifting relationships had a direct impact upon the labour movement: for the first time since 1914, resistance to the US was not monopolized by pro-Moscow communist parties. Under the impetus of the rise of working-class struggles after 1968, the European socialist parties made a turn to the left which was accompanied by the step by step shift from Atlanticism to an orientation to European integration as a means of competition with the US. Through the 1970s and 1980s the socialist parties became the strongest backers of European economic integration in west European society, providing key leaders of the entire project like European Commission President Jacques Delors.

From this perspective, the key to prosperity and social democratic reform could no longer be alignment with the US – which was striking blows against the west European economies – but the pushing forward of the economic integration of the European Community. In this way, the theory ran, the European working class would ultimately benefit from the improved performance of European capital. The prospect of modernization and integration into the EEC was particularly attractive as an alternative way forward in southern Europe, following the fall of the dictatorships. It provided the strategic cutting edge for social democracy's drive to break communist hegemony in the labour movements of Spain, Portugal, France and Italy.

Symbolized by such leaders as Mitterrand in France, Craxi in Italy and González in Spain, this Eurosocialism, as opposed to Atlanticism, became the dominant trend in west European social democracy. In a situation where the US was undermining – not boosting – the west European economies, Eurosocialism represented the biggest strategic re-orientation of European social democracy since the First World War. The results were spectacular: often utilizing an extremely radical rhetoric, including against the US, from the end of the 1970s through the 1980s, the socialist parties overtook the communists in France, Spain, Portugal and Greece and substantially expanded their governmental role in Italy. They were assisted in this by the strategic impasse in which the communist parties found themselves – as a result of the decline in the prestige of the Soviet Union following the Prague spring, and also because of the way significant sections of them responded to the new situation in Europe through their own turn to Eurocommunism. In Spain and Italy, at least, this sometimes made them appear to be to the right of the socialist parties. As a result they lost ground to the socialists in the electoral and trade union fields, and to the new left and the Greens among young people and the intelligentsia.

Eurocommunism emerged as a political force from the mid-1970s, as a response to the same factors which had led to Eurosocialism, and gained the ascendancy in the communist parties in Italy, Spain and, for a time, France, as well as the smaller west European parties like the Communist Party of Great Britain. The West German Communist Party (DKP) was an exception, taking its line from the totally pro-Soviet Socialist Unity Party (SED) of the German Democratic Republic.

The Eurocommunists' key goal was to distance their parties from the Soviet leadership and thereby rehabilitate themselves in a west European political order which had kept the communists out of government for the entire period following the immediate post-war crisis. This was a cardinal point of US post-war policy, for they considered that communist parties linked to the USSR and opposed to NATO were, in effect, a fifth column in western Europe. Eurocommunism aimed to make clear that its goal was the reform, not overthrow of the capitalist order in western Europe, by demonstrating that its first loyalty was to the existing order in its own country and not the Soviet leadership. The latter meant a political, though not organizational, rapprochement with social democracy. This began on the ideological plane with the abandonment of the theoretical goal 'the dictatorship of the proletariat', posed as a move to break with the identification of the west European communist parties with the regimes in eastern Europe and the Soviet Union. The problem, however, was that the response of the voters to the Eurocommunists moving towards the politics of social democracy was to question the basis of their existence as distinct political parties. Hence by conceding ground to the Eurosocialists, the Eurocommunists tended to accelerate rather than halt their loss of political ground.

Debates on the right in the 1970s considered whether Eurocommunism was purely tactical, 'essentially only window dressing', as Jacques Chirac put it in 1977, or whether Eurocommunists were actually 'social democratic turncoats' – the view of the new left in Italy and France.[16] Neither were quite correct. It was true, as it turned out, that the Eurocommunists were on a trajectory towards social democracy, but it was a long path which had originated decades earlier in the requirements of Soviet policy and diplomacy for alliance with the west European states against Nazi Germany and the dissolution of the Communist International in 1943. But, of course, the critical contrast with the popular front in the 1930s, or indeed communist participation in post-war governments in France and Italy, was that these were carried out at the behest of and in pursuit of the diplomatic objectives of the Soviet leadership before and after the war. Eurocommunism, on the other hand, constituted a break with both the Soviet leadership and the Soviet Union.

The first public statement of principles, endorsed by more than one communist party without the agreement of the Soviet leadership, was the Joint Declaration of the Italian and Spanish Communist Parties, of 12 July 1975. As well as endorsing multi-party democracy and individual and collective freedoms, the declaration stressed the importance of 'the national unity of democratic and progressive forces, isolating the socially conservative and reactionary ones', in order to find a way out of the crisis of European capitalism.[17]

The forces with which 'points of convergence and agreement' were sought, were 'socialist, social democrat, Christian democrat, Catholic, democratic and progressive'. In other words, they sought to ally themselves with what they saw as more progressive sections of the bourgeoisie in order to aid ailing western European capitalism, and to avoid 'the attempts of certain capitalist groups to impose an openly reactionary and authoritarian solution to the crisis'. The problem soon became apparent, at least in Spain and Italy: that what the 'progressive sections of the bourgeoisie' wanted was support for policies which – by negatively affecting the living standards of the communist electorate – would cut into its vote.

The second Joint Declaration came four months later in November 1975, from the French and Italian parties, making similar points and also emphasizing 'united initiatives by the popular forces and the left forces' in the European Parliament, and for the 'democratization of the orientations and modes of operation of the European Economic Community and for the progressive building of a democratic, peaceful and independent Europe'.[18]

Ultimately, the result of the Eurocommunist phase, was that it so minimized the political space between the communist parties and the socialist parties that it was no longer clear what, if any, the fundamental differences really were. Although it was an expression of independence from the politics of the Soviet leadership, as subsequent developments were to confirm, Eurocommunism did this by moving to the right towards classical social democratic politics, rather than to any left-wing critique of Soviet orthodoxy. Moreover, it meant that the major radicalizations which did develop in western Europe, notably the anti-missiles movement, largely by-passed the communist parties.

All of these developments were then considerably accelerated by the collapse of state socialism in 1989. European social democracy moved further to the right and Eurocommunism merged with social democracy. Paradoxically, however, these developments also opened up a vacuum on the left wing of the European labour movement which, as we have seen, was filled by other currents originating primarily in the communist movement.

3
Eastern Europe: The Road to 1989

The predominant role of the United States and Soviet Union, in shaping the destiny of Europe for most of the twentieth century, took a directly military form as a result of the Second World War. In terms of casualties and sheer physical destruction the war was fought overwhelmingly, first on the territory of the Soviet Union itself and, secondly, in eastern Europe. As Richard Overy put it: 'In the course of human history there has probably been no more terrible place than Eastern Europe between 1941–45.'[1] Even today, any visitor to the region is struck by the all-pervasive legacy of what was the greatest blood-letting in human history.

Whereas the liberating armies in the west were led by the US, in the east they were led by the Soviet Union. The resulting division of the continent was not, as is sometimes supposed, an amicable accommodation between Stalin, Churchill and Roosevelt at Yalta in the winter of 1945. It was, on the contrary, determined by the fact that, while US policy-makers never accepted a Soviet sphere of influence in eastern Europe, the political and military balance at the time was such that they were incapable of reversing the outcome of the war in the east – their goal was to contain it and ultimately roll it back.[2] The Soviet leaders, on the other hand, having already suffered three devastating invasions from the West – led by Napoleon in the nineteenth century, and then by Germany on two occasions in the twentieth – were unwilling to withdraw their troops without guarantees that they would not face another. No such guarantees were forthcoming, however, and the division of the continent was codified in what was, in reality, a 'cold' stand-off between the Soviet and US military machines.

The origins of the division of Europe

Capitalism in eastern Europe was already far less developed than in the West. Many of its ruling classes were deeply discredited by their pervasive collaboration with the Nazis before and, even more so, during a war which had been waged, not simply against the German army, but also against its Hungarian, Romanian, Croatian, Ukrainian and other allies. The chief political forces which actively resisted the Nazis in most east European countries were led by the local communist parties. Thus, in comparison with the west, most of eastern Europe emerged from the Second World War more devastated, with weaker ruling classes, more left wing workers' movements and with the determining military power in the hands of the Soviet Union.

The weakness of the capitalist social formations in eastern Europe has deep historical roots. As Perry Anderson has traced with detailed scholarship, it goes back to the legacy of the Roman empire whose eastern limit was effectively the Elbe.[3] The lasting legacy of Roman rule in western Europe was strong towns within the feudal mode of production which ultimately emerged out of the clash between classical antiquity and successive Germanic invasions. As a result, the great crisis of feudalism in the fourteenth century led to the disappearance of serfdom in most of the region by 1450, the further rise of the towns, and, via the interlude of feudal absolutism, the economic development out of which capitalism for the first time emerged – making western Europe the most economically dynamic part of the world until the end of the nineteenth century.

In eastern Europe, which had been primarily outside the Roman empire and where, in consequence, developed towns did not exist on anything remotely like the scale of the West, the crisis of feudalism had quite different results. It led, not to the ending of serfdom, but to a second and deeper enserfment of the rural population, and the subordination of the towns to the feudal order to a degree unknown in the West. As Anderson puts it:

It was fundamentally this weakness of the towns that allowed the nobles to adopt a solution to the crisis which was structurally barred to them in the West, a manorial reaction that slowly destroyed all peasant rights and systematically reduced tenants to serfs, working on large seigneurial demesnes.[4]

As a result of the original weakness of urban development, later reinforced by the second wave of feudalism, eastern Europe never developed the unique combination of elements which created the dynamic towards capitalism in the other half of the continent. Indeed, such was the underdevelopment of the region that the commercial classes in the towns were frequently of different nationality to the local peasantry. Germans, for example, formed the commercial class in towns developed along the trade routes of German colonization into eastern Europe and western Russia over the preceeding 500 years or more. Much of eastern Europe remained ruled by absolutist dynasties right up to the end of the First World War.

The east European capitalist states were created by the Treaty of Versailles in 1919, but, with the exception of Czechoslovakia, they were unable to achieve the levels of capitalist economic development on which west European parliamentary democracy was based – until it too collapsed after 1933. As a result, social democracy, which historically has only been able to stabilize itself within western parliamentary democracies with the economic resources to concede substantial social reforms, proved incapable of sinking deep roots in eastern Europe. Even before the First World War, left wing developments, like the Russian Bolsheviks, were much stronger in the eastern than in the west European labour movements.

In the inter-war period, again with the exception of Czechoslovakia, it was typically the communist parties – not social democracy – that had the leading role in the east European labour movements. This position became more pronounced, as these countries slipped into various degrees of authoritarianism, forcing the left to operate underground. Communist-influenced workers' movements competed for popular support with various shades of authoritarian populist, anti-semitic and fascist forces. Communist predominance on the left was further reinforced during the war, while many of the local ruling classes threw their lot in with Hitler – making their position untenable once the Soviet army arrived.

Soviet aims in eastern Europe

The original aim of the Soviet Union was not to establish communist regimes in eastern Europe. In the period between 1944 and 1947, the occupation authorities generally sponsored coalition governments in which communist ministers controlled the key security posts but which also included 'bourgeois' parties committed to capitalist economic development. Apart from Yugoslavia, where the communist partisans came to power independently in 1945, the decisive break with capitalism in most of the rest of eastern Europe came only with the launching, by the United States, of the Marshall Plan for western Europe from 1948. In response, the Soviet leadership adopted a course of eliminating the non-communist parties from power between 1948 and 1950, generalizing nationalizations and introducing planned economies. From 1951, five- and six-year plans were developed and the eastern European economies were integrated increasingly with that of the USSR.

At the same time, military cooperation was enhanced to create a buffer zone between the USSR and NATO, which had come into existence in 1949. Even after this, as David Horowitz put it: 'the main thrust of Soviet policy in Europe during the years 1952–55 was to obtain a settlement which would mean German neutrality.' However, the US, 'following the strategy of the Truman administration wished to avoid any serious negotiations with the Soviet Union until the West could confront Moscow with German rearmament within an organised European framework as a *fait accompli*.'[5] Gorbachev attempted to revive the proposal for German neutrality in exchange for Soviet withdrawal more than 30 years later and met with a similar response.

It should be noted that, following the immediate post-war seizure of former German property, and the transfer of plant and equipment from eastern Germany to the Soviet Union – which did not remotely compensate for the colossal destruction of the Soviet economy by German armies – the net economic balance between the Soviet Union and eastern Europe was one whereby the Soviet Union, by supplying cheap energy and raw materials, subsidized the more developed economies of eastern Europe. Apart from the period immediately after the Second World War where physical capital in the form of factories and machinery were actually removed from eastern Europe and taken to the Soviet Union, the Soviet Union was a net subsidizer of its east European satellites, through the provision of cheap energy, but also through the CMEA pricing policy: '...the Soviet Union paid more than what would have been the market price for its substantial net imports of manufactures from its partners, since their prices did not make adequate allowances for quality differentials...'[6] Indeed, the loss of this Soviet subsidy was a factor in the economic slump which followed the re-introduction of capitalism from 1989. In this sense, the Soviet occupation cannot be understood as a simple analogy with capitalist colonialism. The Soviet leadership insisted on a monopoly of political and military control in eastern Europe, not in order to economically exploit the region, but to maintain a military buffer against NATO and to ensure that no precedent of political pluralism was set within the communist movement which might have repercussions within the USSR itself.

The achievements of the communist parties

In the period immediately following the war, the communist parties enjoyed significant popular support for two reasons. One was the superior economic performance of the Soviet Union, albeit from a far more backward starting point, compared to eastern and even western Europe in the 1930s. As David Lane observes: 'The economic effects of Soviet developmental policy were positive and compared favorably with capitalist type economies. Western estimates for annual rates of economic growth for the period 1928–40 range from 8.8 per cent (Nutter) to 13.6 per cent (Seton); for the more backward areas the figures were 9.2 per cent (Nutter) to 14.1 per cent (Hodgman).'[7] These figures easily outstrip the figures for the European or American economies in comparable periods of development, and their impact upon public opinion was enhanced by the contrast with the post-1929 slump in the United States and Europe. This achievement of the Soviet planned economy was real and gave it enormous attractive power. Second, as captured fleetingly in the scene at the end of the film *Schindler's List* when the Soviet tank appears over the horizon of the concentration camp, signifying liberation, the war in eastern Europe had been between the Soviet Union and fascism – those were the only two sides in material existence. As a result, when, for example, the Yugoslav communist leader, Marshall Tito, toured eastern Europe following the war, he was greeted by crowds of hundreds of thousands of people – and the Yugoslav partisan's prestige was second only to that of the Soviet leadership. Thus, there was at the outset widespread good-will towards the communists and what many saw as their modernizing, egalitarian project for reconstructing these impoverished countries, devastated and brutalized by the experience of Nazi occupation and home-grown dictatorship.

In the period of the first five-year plans, eastern Europe achieved similar levels of growth to the Soviet Union in the 1930s. The countries were industrialized to a significant degree and priority was given to funding welfare programmes unprecedented in countries on similar levels of development – free healthcare, education and childcare, subsidized housing and utilities, full employment, leisure and sporting facilities. Whilst the economies were able to provide and sustain increasing living standards, a fairly stable balance existed in those societies, where people tolerated the politically repressive system because, overall, their lives were much improved.

However, the high levels of growth which characterized these economies in the 1950s, based on industrialization, began to slow in the 1960s, and even more so in the 1970s. By the second half of the 1970s, economic growth was also slowing in the Soviet Union so that, for the first time, it stopped catching up with the United States and started to fall behind. At the root of this growing problem of economic stagnation was that these economies had exhausted the phase of 'extensive' economic growth. That is, they had proven to be extremely efficient at generating high levels of savings to fund capital investment, and in mobilizing – and educating to very high levels – a new workforce, drawn principally from, firstly, the large reserves of labour on the land and, secondly, the integration of women into the workforce – more rapidly even than in western Europe and the United States.

But once this stage of extensive economic growth had exhausted itself, they faced great difficulty in effecting the transition to a more 'intensive' phase – which would have to be based upon rapidly increasing the productivity of labour and capital.

Reasons for economic decline

While very high levels of capital investment were sustained right into the 1980s, the return in terms of productivity growth constantly diminished. The critical reason for this was the difficulty in motivating the workforce. Some economists argued that this was because of the absence of the 'whip' of sackings and mass unemployment in a non-market economy. However, the post-1989 experience of falling productivity amid sharply rising unemployment, powerfully undercuts that theory. In fact, there were three principal reasons for the failure to rapidly increase labour productivity, once the first phase of industrialization had been completed.

1. Firstly, the Soviet and east European economic planners had deliberately given the primary place in their economies to the development of heavy industry. For the Soviet Union this was literally a question of survival, for without a heavy industrial sector it would

have been incapable of producing the armaments which made victory in the Second World War – and stalemate in the Cold War – possible, and it would have been overwhelmed by Germany or, later, the United States. However, as the *Socialist Economic Bulletin* has pointed out, internationally the most rapid growth in productivity in the post-war period has not been in the heavy industrial sector but in the sectors of consumer durables and consumer services.[8] Therefore, persisting in prioritizing heavy industry, long after the Soviet Union had established itself as the second most powerful military force in the world, and then applying this model to eastern Europe, locked the region into an economic structure in which the most dynamic sectors in terms of productivity growth were grossly under-developed.

2. Secondly, the failure of the Soviet and east European planners to give sufficient priority to the production of consumer goods, high quality food and consumer services (like plumbing, electricians, shops, and so on) had a significant impact on the workforce. No matter what financial incentives were introduced, the generalized shortage of consumer goods and services, together with their low quality, meant that the workers had relatively little incentive to increase their earnings and productivity, because what they could buy was extremely limited. The entire sectors of the economy orientated to the production of food, consumer goods, and consumer services – that is the sectors necessary for rising living standards – were massively underdeveloped relative to the level of development of these economies. This was the root of the demoralization, waste, and so on, which increasingly affected the workforce.

3. Thirdly, the decision for political, not economic, reasons to sharply reduce, and in the case of the Soviet Union to eliminate, the proportion of the workforce engaged in self-employed or very small-scale private enterprise such as shops, consumer repairs, food outlets, and so on, made the problem much worse. Moreover, there is no inherent reason – as the Soviet Union demonstrated at the beginning of the 1920s and China and Vietnam more recently – why an overall planned economy with public ownership of the industrial core and banking system cannot co-exist with a market and small-scale private enterprise in the consumer goods and services sectors of a non-capitalist economy.

At the same time, the lack of insertion of the Comecon economies into the international division of labour meant that their pricing systems bore less and less relation to real costs – which, apart from anything else, made effective planning increasingly difficult. The irrationality of the pricing mechanism was exacerbated by the bureaucracy's attempts, through the latter half of the 1970s and the 1980s, to buy social peace by maintaining artificially low prices for basic foods, transport, housing and other necessities. These constituted a sort of additional structure of the welfare state, so that while consumer durables and high quality food were in short supply, a kind of rationing system ensured that basic necessities were available at prices which the entire population could afford. The removal of this social safety net, through price liberalization after 1989 (1991 in Russia) was a key factor in the collapse of living standards which accompanied the reintroduction of capitalism. The alternative within a planned economy would have been to restore accurate pricing, but to maintain the social safety net by other, more economically transparent mechanisms, such as social security payments.

This basic economic imbalance – between overdeveloped heavy industry and underdeveloped consumer production and distribution – was a key factor in undermining support for the communist regimes because it meant that living standards were lower than was merited by the real capacities of the centrally planned economies. Swedish living standards were never possible in the Soviet Union, but many of the shortages of consumer goods were not inevitable in the society which successfully launched the world's first spacecraft. On the level of economics, at least, as the Chinese economic reform has shown, there was a viable alternative within a planned economic framework – that is a plan which redirected resources into the consumer sector of the economy and which allowed a degree of private enterprise at the level of small-scale production of consumer goods, shops and so on.

Had the population had a say in some democratic process of establishing the priorities of the planning process, this problem might have been resolved, but they did not. As for the Soviet leadership, the priority to heavy industry was central to its entire strategy of 'socialism in one country'. This aimed, on the basis of the resources of the Soviet Union, to have the industrial capacity not simply to match the West on the military field but to catch up with – and in Khrushchev's famous phrase 'overtake' – the advanced capitalist countries.

This required replicating within the Soviet economy, and later the Soviet bloc organized through Comecon, all of the key sectors of the international division of labour. This created enormous inefficiencies. As John Williamson notes: 'Czechoslovakia is reputed to have produced domestically some 65 per cent of all categories of industrial goods... – a higher proportion than Japan, despite Japanese GDP being at least 20 times as large. Similarly, East Germany produced a wider range of industrial products than did West Germany'.[9] Instead of specializing in their fields of maximum efficiency and utilizing the international division of labour and importing goods produced more efficiently elsewhere, whilst protecting themselves via the powerful mechanism provided by planning and public ownership, the aim was to replicate the entire world economy within a very small part of it. This was always an impossible utopia, which would mean enormous and unnecessary sacrifices for the population.[10]

From the point of view of the population, sacrifices were understandable and accepted with incredible stoicism in periods of national emergency and war. When they continued, however, in the form of shortages of consumer goods, for decade after decade, in circumstances where the Soviet Union had become the second most powerful country in the world, they became more and more deeply resented.

The failure of attempts to reform

A number of east European countries, particularly Poland, sought a way out of this impasse at the beginning of the 1970s by borrowing from the west to invest in export-oriented manufacturing in the context of some relaxation in western trade restrictions against the region. However, as this was rapidly followed in the mid-1970s by the first synchronized recession in the world capitalist economy since the 1930s, together with the explosion in oil prices, demand for east European goods did not meet expectations. In fact, the experiment was a disastrous failure. Together with further borrowing to finance subsidies of popular consumption, it left key states with gigantic debts to the west – by 1990, $41 billion for Poland, $14 billion for Hungary and $11 billion for Bulgaria. As a result, the burden of interest payments on these sums was added to the internal contradictions of bureaucratic planning in eastern Europe. At the same time, the west gained a crucial lever for putting pressure on the regimes.

The bureaucracy in Poland concluded that the only way out of the situation was to sharply increase domestic prices, but this in turn provoked a far bigger problem. The Polish working class began three gigantic waves of struggle against price increases, including massive strikes, in 1971, 1976 and 1980, which forced the government to back down and culminated in the creation of the ten million strong independent trade union, Solidarity. The net result was to shatter the legitimacy of the regime which, after all, was supposed to represent the working class. After the inter-regnum of martial law from 1981, this breach was the decisive one in the whole of eastern Europe, for as the Polish leadership proved incapable of finding an alternative way out, the leading circles of underground Solidarity, during the period of martial law, established links with the west and became an advocate of the reintroduction of capitalism.

Other experiments with limited market reform, in Hungary, for example, were equally ineffectual, although a Polish-scale social explosion was avoided elsewhere. The severity of the economic problems, combined with popular dissatisfaction over living standards, unnecessary state repression, and a lack of solutions by the ruling elite, meant that in eastern Europe the system had been weakening for more than a decade before 1989. In this period, currents began to emerge within some of the leading circles of some of the regimes, advocating a reversion to capitalism, but these remained a minority while Soviet military intervention remained a real possibility.

The problems which emerged in eastern Europe in the 1970s and 1980s were extremely serious, but they did not constitute a full-blown crisis of communist rule because the centre of the system, the Soviet Union, remained relatively stable, and capable of enforcing its will throughout the region. It had weathered workers' demonstrations in Berlin in 1953, a crisis in Poland in 1956 and an armed uprising in Hungary in 1956. Only a crisis at the centre could fundamentally destabilize the system in eastern Europe. Only when the Soviet military backing was removed from the east European states did they actually topple, and, even then, rapid and radical overturns only really occurred in those in the best positions to be integrated into the west European economy: Poland, Hungary, the German Democratic Republic and Czechoslovakia.

The reasons for the crisis of the Soviet system

To understand what precipitated the 1989 crisis in eastern Europe and the dissolution of the Soviet Union in 1991, it is necessary to grasp why the overall strategy of the Soviet leadership suffered fundamental defeat during the 1980s – provoking crisis at the heart of the Soviet system. What changed from the 1980s, and brought Soviet economic problems to a head, was that two factors which had been powerful objective supports for the Soviet Union, had now ceased to exist. The first had been the breakdown of the international division of labour during the 1930s and the major conflict between the chief capitalist powers prior to 1945, which meant that the Soviet Union had not had to face a unified capitalist world economy, during that period. The second was that, just when the US had succeeded in creating the conditions for a unified world economy under its own leadership in 1945, it was immediately confronted by a series of revolutions and wars in Asia – in China, Korea and Vietnam.

Following the entry of China into the war, Korea produced a stalemate – the first time in history that the US was not victorious in a war. Vietnam became the first war that the US actually lost. Its political consequences were momentous: domestic public opinion – the so-called 'Vietnam syndrome' – meant that the US was unable to stop Cuban troops tipping the scales against the South African apartheid regime in the Angolan war and could not use its own military forces to save its allies, the Shah of Iran or Somoza in Nicaragua. It was hardly surprising, therefore, that from the 1950s to the 1970s, US leaders feared that *they* might lose the Cold War. They concluded that they would not have been fought to a standstill in Korea, nor defeated in Vietnam, had those countries not benefitted from Soviet economic and military assistance. It was decided that the only way to prevent more dominoes falling was to break the Soviet Union. This could not be done militarily without risking the nuclear annhilation of the United States, but the arms race provided a mechanism to place an ever-increasing burden upon the Soviet economy in the hope that it would eventually crack under the strain. The economic means to achieve this were provided by the extension of globalization to the flows of capital as well as goods, which meant that the US could draw upon the resources not only of its own economy, but also those of its allies. The political opening was created by the conflict between the Soviet Union and China and the ability of the US to exploit it.

The fatal flaw in the strategy of socialism in one country, on the economic plane, was that it was not competing with capitalism in *one* country – had that been the case, the Soviet Union would still exist. In reality, the Soviet Union confronted – from the 1960s through to the 1980s – not merely the US, but an entire world economy organized under its leadership. This was decisive, because while the the US economy, in the mid-1970s, was only a little more than double the size of the Soviet economy, the world capitalist economy as a whole was more than seven times bigger. Even the maintenance of military parity with the US alone, placed a huge burden on the Soviet economy. To match the US militarily required a far higher proportion of output, more than double, to be allocated to defence by the smaller Soviet economy. In that sense, every increase in military spending by the US, required effectively more than double the effort from the Soviet Union. However, Ronald Reagan's arms race, which finally broke the Soviet economy, would not have been possible for the US alone – it would have placed an unacceptable burden on the American population. Even the Vietnam war had required an effort so great, that the US had been forced to place a burden on its allies in Europe and Japan, which finally destroyed the post-war Bretton Woods world financial order. Reagan's military build up would have been impossible without drawing upon the resources of Japan, western Europe and the third world on an unprecedented scale. Only an inflow of capital into the US, which rose to more than $120 billion a year in the 1980s, allowed Ronald Reagan to break up the stability of the Soviet economic system. As has been pointed out: 'It might be asked what would have been the performance of the Soviet economy in this period if it had been receiving capital injections of $100 billion dollars a year.'[11]

The political conditions which made it possible for the US to focus its, and other peoples, resources on a new stage of the arms race with the Soviet Union, were those produced by the Sino-Soviet conflict. Prior to the Chinese revolution, it had generally been assumed that conflict between communist states was inconceivable. The founding document of the communist movement, Marx and Engels' *Communist Manifesto*, after all, concludes with the call upon working people of all countries to unite.[12] But once more than one communist state came into existence, a second fatal flaw became apparent in the theory of socialism in one country – namely, which country takes the lead? This was a supplementary factor in the erosion of support for the communist regimes in eastern Europe. The Soviet leadership would not tolerate local leaderships with any degree of political independence, even within a common communist framework. The result was the split with Tito, as early as 1948, followed by a wholesale purge of east European communist leaders deemed too independent.

The division with China, however, given that country's size and strategic importance, was of a different order of importance. Although it originated in Chinese criticism of the Soviet leadership from the left, by the late 1970s, with the end of the war in Vietnam, the United States was able to exploit the conflict between Moscow and Beijing, to conclude a *de facto* alliance with China – effectively stabilizing the situation in Asia for the first time since the Second World War. This, in turn, allowed Ronald Reagan to focus US power on the arms race with the Soviet Union. As Fred Halliday pointed out: 'Had the USA faced even a low key Peking–Moscow alliance, Washington would have felt much less confident about launching the Second Cold War than it did.'[13]

The denouement came rapidly, with the failure of mass opposition to prevent the deployment of Cruise and Pershing missiles in western Europe. Given that the Soviet Union could not sustain another spiral of the arms race, the majority of the Soviet leadership concluded that the only way out was a new degree of accommodation with the west. The man charged with its execution, Mikhail Gorbachev, was elected general secretary by a margin of one vote in the Politbureau of the CPSU. Gorbachev's goal was to carry out a limited reform of the Soviet economy, not introduce capitalism, and to gain the breathing space necessary for this, by easing tensions with the west.

Gorbachev rapidly became a hero in western capitals as he set about seeking to reduce tensions with the US: firstly, by reducing the Soviet intervention into various regional conflicts; secondly, by signalling that the Soviet Union would not intervene to back the communist regimes in eastern Europe – which brought about their collapse; thirdly, by acceding to German unification; and finally, by embarking upon the full-scale Soviet withdrawal from eastern Europe. By 1990, the Soviet delegation to the United Nations Security Council was casting its vote in favour of the resolutions which authorized the biggest US military action since Vietnam – the Gulf War.

Washington's response to Gorbachev was logical – every concession was accepted, without for an instant relaxing the pressure for more. The unification of Germany, which overturned the entire post-war settlement in Europe, was a case in point. The original Soviet position, that any unified Germany should be neutral, was rejected out of hand by Washington and Bonn. The Soviet Union ended up withdrawing from a Germany which became united within NATO – and which inevitably then went on to decide, for the first time since the Second World War, that its forces could be deployed outside its own borders. The Soviet strategic position in Europe had collapsed.

Internally, Gorbachev's economic reforms took the economy from stagnation to crisis, and – together with his foreign policy – they deeply divided his own party. His political liberalization created the openings for the emergence of the political forces which were finally able to exploit the ensuing crisis to depose him and dissolve the Soviet Union at the end of 1991. The western governments, who had considered the balance sheet of his period in office to have been a positive one, nevertheless went on to welcome Yeltsin to undertake the next stage of the process – the dismantling of the Soviet planned economy.

The verdict of Russian voters on Gorbachev is clear: he is one of the least popular politicians in the country, with a polling rating between 1 and 2 per cent. After all, he started out as leader of the second most powerful state in the world, yet when he left, that state no longer existed.

The fall of the regimes in eastern Europe, followed two years later by the dissolution of the Soviet Union and of the CPSU, constituted a turning point in world history: the United States had won the Cold War and the main pole of attraction for those opposed to the US had disappeared. Whilst it had been clear to left-wing socialists, trade unionists and leaders of national liberation struggles, that Soviet leaders such as Brezhnev and Chernenko bore little resemblance to the likes of Ho Chi Minh and Fidel Castro, nevertheless, they had considered that their crimes were compensated for by the continued existence of the Soviet Union – which was, after all, the most powerful objective ally of any struggle in conflict with the US. After 1989 and 1991, that counterpoint was shattered, and the international labour movement was shaken to its very foundations.

4
Russia: An Undecided Outcome

with Redmond O'Neill

It is only possible to understand the present political situation in Russia and, in particular, the revival of a party originating as the anti-capitalist, and even anti-Gorbachev, minority of the Soviet Communist Party, in the context of the social and economic consequences of the dissolution of the Soviet Union and the reintroduction of capitalism from the end of 1991. This has unleashed a political struggle whose outcome will, as in the past, have momentous consequences for the world and, indeed, for the shape of the international and European labour movements – even if this reality has not yet come home to most western observers, particularly on the left.

The simple fact is that the capitalist economic reform which began formally in Russia with price liberalization in January 1992 has produced the greatest peacetime industrial collapse of any economy in history. All of the subsequent political developments, particularly, the survival, revival and then rapid rise of the most anti-capitalist wing of the former Soviet Communist Party, are only comprehensible if this overall context is firmly grasped. Moreover, the role of western institutions in formulating the key stages of the reform process is well-understood in Russia, and this, together with western governments' backing for President Boris Yeltsin – even when his tanks were storming Russia's elected parliament in October 1993 – has shaped popular attitudes to the West. As will be shown, the evolution of the Communist Party of the Russian Federation (CPRF) – at the time of writing the leading party in terms of both votes and membership in Russia – has been to a considerable degree shaped by the population's response to this situation.

The tragic effects of the economic reforms on Russian society are well-documented. In 1997 the United Nations Development Programme

(UNDP) published a report on 'Human development under transition'. Its conclusions, with regard to Russia, are worth reporting at some length:

> The attempted 'shock therapy' reforms launched in January 1992 ushered in a period of economic decline of unprecedented proportions ... Partial price liberalisation in January 1992 unleashed an inflationary process in which consumer and producer prices rose by over 2500 per cent in less than a year. The resulting dislocation and fall in personal incomes were reinforced by the gradual reduction in subsidies for rent, transport, and other necessities of life.[1]

In a phenomenon characterized by the UNDP as 'hyper-stagflation': 'GDP declined continuously every year since 1990, and it declined by 20 per cent in 1994 ... Industrial output declined 4.7 per cent in 1995, bringing the total fall to 53 per cent since 1989 ... National Income fell by over 40 per cent between 1991 and 1996.'[2] The impact on living standards has been devastating: 'In the Soviet era it was generally recognised that 10 per cent of the population were living in poverty.'[3] Whereas by 1997: 'The number of people living below the poverty line has been variously estimated at around 90 per cent ... or between 25–34 per cent on the basis of a much lower national poverty line of ... \$50 [per month – KH].'[4] One of the reasons for this was that between 1990 and the end of 1994 the price index for paid services like housing, transport and domestic utilities rose by over 6000 per cent.[5]

Indeed, the social and economic collapse in Russia as a result of capitalist economic reform has been so awful that economic data alone do not convey the full picture. Statistics have shown the enormous hardship now confronting the overwhelming majority of the population, including – amongst many other indicators – a significant decrease in life expectancy, the increase of heart, digestive and infectious diseases, the late or non-payment of wages and a dramatic increase in homelessness and unemployment. Expectations of high levels of foreign investment have not been fulfilled, indeed, in the period between 1991 and 1998, the annual outflow of capital from Russia, much of it the illegal proceeds of the deeply criminalized privatization process, has far exceeded the total inflow of capital in the form of investment, foreign aid, IMF credits and other loans.

In the context of this disastrous social and economic decline, it is hardly surprising that support for the parties linked to the band of reformers most closely identified with the West, privatization and shock therapy, has almost completely collapsed. Russia's Choice, the party set up by Yegor Gaidar, one of the architects of price liberalization, for example, stood at one per cent in a poll conducted by the National Public Opinion Centre, on 20–25 November 1998.[6] Even right wing politicians, and out and out mafiosi, now tend to adopt a rhetoric of opposition to the free market and the West, to have any chance of securing election. The popular response to the NATO bombing of the Federal Republic of Yugoslavia from March 1999 also consolidated anti-western feeling, with 92 per cent of the population opposed to the NATO aggression.

'Revolution from above'

Distrust of a free market model of development is not new in Russia. There was no majority support either for western-style capitalism or for the dismantling of the Soviet Union even at the time when the process was initiated. As Kotz and Weir observe: 'A referendum on preserving the Union won with 76.4 per cent of the vote only nine months before the Union was dismantled'.[7] Indeed opinion polls in Russia show that popular support for social security, egalitarianism and collectivist social and economic values remains far more extensive within society than even votes for the communist parties would indicate. As Peter Gowan points out, in 1996 polls showed that an absolute majority of the population thought big industrial enterprises should be state-owned rather than privatized.[8]

The explanation for the post-1991 free market experiment lies according to Kotz and Weir, in the fact that the system was actually dismantled in a 'revolution from above' by the 'ruling party-state elite of the USSR' in pursuit of increased wealth and power.[9] In fact, as with other communist parties referred to in earlier chapters, a wide range of both pro and anti-capitalist forces emerged from the ruling bureaucracy and therefore it included those who wanted to reform and improve the system and those who wanted to reform and dismantle it. The appearance of monolithism was shown to be merely a facade, and as Urban and Solovei point out:

> the diverse political-ideological factions that openly surfaced among the CPSU activists in the U.S.S.R.'s twilight years were grounded in long-standing differences of opinion which had been concealed from public view by the Soviet party-state's enforced code of unanimity.[10]

Furthermore, whilst it was always evident that many would join a ruling party for careerist and self-interested reasons, the rapid emergence of a number of communist parties immediately after the collapse of the previous regime demonstrates, again as Urban and Solovei observe, that there were many within the CPSU and notably within the lower and middle levels of the Soviet bureaucracy, who were genuinely committed to a socialist perspective.

The most significant developments took place at the top of the party, however. Political conflict up to 1990 largely took place between three sections of the CPSU leadership: the opponents of extensive market reform, such as Yegor Ligachev; Gorbachev reformers; and those moving towards support for capitalism who, led by Yeltsin, eventually left the CPSU altogether. Undoubtedly Gorbachev was elected with the expectation that he would modernize the economy, probably along the same lines that Andropov had commenced in the early 1980s, of investment and anti-corruption measures. But, although commencing the 12th Five-Year Plan in 1985 with just such policies, by 1988 it became apparent that Gorbachev's reforms were unleashing forces that were going to lead to fundamental change if they were not restrained.

Yeltsin seized the political initiative from Gorbachev who vacillated between the reformers and hardliners. When the hardliners attempted to halt what they perceived to be a process of disintegration by declaring a State of Emergency and removing Gorbachev from power in August 1991, their indecisiveness reflected their minority position in the CPSU leadership, and Yeltsin was able to overturn the coup, restore Gorbachev and emerge as master of the political situation. On 6 November 1991, Yeltsin banned the Russian Communist Party, and the CPSU on Russian territory, even though it was not directly implicated in the coup attempt. At the end of 1991, Yeltsin initiated the dissolution of the Soviet Union and proceeded rapidly towards full free market reform.

The balance of political forces in the early Yeltsin years

Initially, there was very little opposition within the Russian parliament to Yeltsin's economic policies. Even the parliamentary speaker, the economist Ruslan Khasbulatov, who was to rapidly emerge as a key oppositionist, initially supported shock therapy.[11] However, the disastrous results of the economic reforms, commenced in January 1992, soon ended the quasi-unanimity. During the first two years of Yeltsin's leadership, until the elections of December 1993, the parliamentary opposition to Yeltsin's policies shifted from being a small minority to being the majority position. Yeltsin had put Yegor Gaidar in charge of economic policy which he drew up with the International Monetary Fund (IMF). The IMF's plan for Russia focused on raw material production and energy, which would have the effect of orienting the economy away from industrial production and manufacturing and towards primary production. It called for drastic cuts in subsidies to consumers and for the statutory right to a job to be abolished. The IMF estimated that under its proposals, within two years industrial output would fall by one-fifth, consumer expenditure by one-eighth and unemployment would rise to over 10 per cent.

Nevertheless, the shock therapy strategy was chosen – to achieve a very rapid transformation of the economy into a capitalist market system, attempting simultaneous change in all spheres of the economy. The main planks of shock therapy were price liberalization, privatization, macroeconomic stabilization through tight monetary and fiscal policies, complete abolition of central allocation of resources and the removal of barriers to foreign trade and investment.[12] In February 1992, controls on the prices of the vast majority of goods were removed, leading to hyperinflation, the eradication of savings and massive economic hardship.

This was the social and economic context into which the Communist Party of the Russian Federation (CPRF) emerged at its founding congress in February 1993, following the lifting of Yeltsin's ban by the Constitutional Court. Delegates at the founding Congress represented some 450 000 members of the local party organizations of the former Russian Communist Party, who had decided to reconstitute themselves after the ban was lifted. The political context into which the CPRF emerged, was a split – through shock therapy – in the constituencies which had brought Yeltsin to power. Those who had supported him expecting higher living standards and greater social justice began to peel away, eventually leaving the hard-core free market liberals influenced by the IMF. As a result, Yeltsin lost his majority in the Russian parliament, and his persistence with shock therapy policies led to a series of confrontations between Yeltsin and parliament, through which the CPRF was to become increasingly influential. From January 1992, shock therapy created a new alignment in Russian politics into three main groupings: firstly, economic liberals, led by Gaidar and supported by Yeltsin, who called themselves 'democrats' but considered that their economic goals took precedence over democracy; secondly, the centre led by Vice-President Rutskoi and Parliamentary Speaker Ruslan Khasbulatov, which included industrial managers – tending to support the introduction of the market, but oppose shock therapy, because of its negative impact on Russian industry, democrats – for democracy and against the break up of the Soviet Union, and moderate nationalists; thirdly, the communist–nationalist alliance in the National Salvation Front, which wanted to stop shock therapy, reconstitute the Soviet Union and stop making concessions to the west. By the beginning of 1993, each of these three groups had the support of roughly a third of the parliamentary deputies.

Yeltsin's attempts to seize power

Prior to October 1993, the parliamentary resistance to Yeltsin was led by the centre forces, which were usually, but not always, backed by the left and part of the nationalists. Yeltsin aimed to destroy the centre ground and polarize Russian politics, forcing people to choose either shock therapy or the old regime. His two attacks on parliament during 1993 were undertaken with this goal in mind. His first attempt was in March 1993, where he announced on television that he was imposing a period of special rule, having consulted western leaders beforehand and obtained their approval. However, this attempt at a coup was condemned by Rutskoi, Khasbulatov and Zorkin, who was Chair of the Constitutional Court. The army also made it clear that they would not intervene to back Yeltsin's unconstitutional coup.

Thus Yeltsin was forced to back down but reasserted himself again in September 1993. When the Parliament failed to pass his budget, Yeltsin announced that he was dissolving parliament and ruling by decree for three months to push through his economic programme and hold elections for a new lower house. Yeltsin's aim was to rewrite the constitution giving supreme power to the president and to win elections by intimidating the opposition. Parliament pointed out that constitutionally Yeltsin could not dissolve it and offered simultaneous presidential and parliamentary elections, which Yeltsin rejected. The constitutional court declared that Yeltsin had violated the constitution and in retaliation Yeltsin suspended the court. Thus a head-on confrontation ensued between Yeltsin and the parliament.

For two weeks the parliament, occupied by the deputies, was under siege on Yeltsin's instructions by interior ministry troops, until eventually on 3 October pro-parliament demonstrators broke through the police lines and ended the siege. This popular victory was followed by an ill-advised attempt, encouraged by Rutskoi, to take the offensive. First the demonstrators captured the mayor's office, and then attempted to take over the main television centre at Ostankino.[13] They walked into a well-prepared trap in which the demonstrators were massacred by heavily-armed troops hidden in the building. This in turn provided the pretext for Yeltsin to order the army to attack parliament with tanks. The official death toll was 147, but there were fears that the actual figure was considerably higher.[14]

The victory for the parliament in lifting the siege was therefore turned into a victory for Yeltsin by the precipitate action of a section of the demonstrators, which Yeltsin immediately attempted to turn to his advantage in the forthcoming parliamentary elections, scheduled for December 1993, along with a referendum on the new constitution. In the region of 60 000 arrests were made, many were beaten. Press censorship was introduced and a state of emergency was declared in Moscow, during which all opposition newspapers were seized or their premises occupied, while television programmes which did not reflect the views of the government were cancelled and most of the opposition parties were temporarily banned. Yeltsin ordered police to clear the capital of 'unregistered aliens' and 20 000 people were expelled from Moscow.

The rise of the CPRF

Although Yeltsin had physically triumphed over the parliament in October, the December 1993 elections were actually a disaster for him. Yeltsin had succeeded in his aim of knocking the centreground out of Russian politics, but the result was not a swing to Yeltsin. The biggest votes went to the extreme nationalist Liberal Democratic Party of Zhirinovsky on the one hand, with 23 per cent of the vote, and to the CPRF with 12 per cent and its allies the Agrarians with 8 per cent on the other. The party of government, Russia's Choice, in spite of all its advantages, won just 15 per cent. The referendum on the constitution was passed although the veracity of the result was suspect. A government commission appointed by Yeltsin to look into it later confirmed that the result had been rigged.

Although under the new constitution the power balance was now heavily weighted towards the president, Yeltsin was nevertheless dealt a huge blow by the election results, which *Time* magazine described as 'the stunning victory of Yeltsin's ultranationalist and communist opponents'. However, Yeltsin continued with his reform programme – there was no fundamental change in economic policy. As a result, the economic collapse deepened, thus ensuring that opposition to Yeltsin would grow. The key issue was which forces would lead the opposition

– the ultra-right or the communists. This was the critical political battle in Russia between December 1993 and the next elections, two years later.

Zyuganov had already succeeded in establishing the CPRF as the unchallenged leadership of the left, and all attempts to set up a social democratic alternative, including by Gorbachev and the 60 million strong former official trade unions' leadership, had failed utterly. Other, more extreme communist groups, notably the Russian Communist Workers' Party, had boycotted the election and denounced Zyuganov for participating in it. Zyuganov, on the other hand, had stuck firmly to his course of seeking power by constitutional means. He had gone on television during the siege of parliament to urge protesters not to be provoked into bloodshed and had followed this up by throwing the party totally into the election campaign. On both counts he had been vindicated. Now he faced the test of the battle with Zhirinovsky and other anti-communist nationalists for leadership of the opposition.

This did not start auspiciously. For the first seven months of 1994, Zyuganov established an alliance with the new government led by Victor Chernomyrdin. His aim was to try to split the government between Chernomydin, seen as more tolerant of the parliamentary opposition, more patriotic and less directly under the control of the West, and the free market reformers, amongst whom Anatoly Chubais gained increasing influence. The element of rationality in this was that Chubais and Gaidar, following the US, took the view that parliament and the left had to be confronted by any means necessary. Chernomyrdin, on the other hand, wanted the support of the parliamentary left in order to neutralize the opposition. But he stuck firmly to the economic programme of the previous government. Yet, by a narrow majority, the CPRF decided to vote for his first budget. This deeply disoriented the left wing electorate and all of those desperate for a new economic policy.

It looked for a time as if they would be eclipsed by the right wing nationalists – whose racism and anti-semitism were totally undisguised. To their right, still more sinister forces started to emerge, such as Alexander Barkashov's paramilitary Russian National Union, which uses the fascist salute, stands for the elimination of Jewish people and demands that recruits show three generations of pure Russian descent.

By this time, the biggest demonstration of the political calendar in Russia, Liberation Day, commemorating the May 1945 victory over Hitler in the Second World War, had become an annual protest by the opposition. The marchers tended to be divided 50:50 between communists and nationalists. However, as the year progressed, and Chernomyrdin stuck to the IMF line on the economy, Zyuganov came under massive pressure from within his party to change course – this included a vigorous public debate in the communist-aligned press – *Sovetskaya Rossiya*, *Pravda* and the pro-Communist, but also virulently nationalist, *Zavtra*. Three currents emerged within the CPRF. The largest, around Zyuganov, represented about 40 per cent of the party, standing for a strategic alliance of patriotic forces against shock therapy and western interference in Russia, and thus constantly sought to find a 'patriotic' section of Russian capital to ally with – hence the backing for Chernomyrdin. The second, at that time about 30 per cent of the party, totally opposed the vote for the budget and gave greater priority to supporting workers protesting against its effects. The third was basically Brezhnevite, against any private ownership, and also strongly patriotic. Later, within the expanded parliamentary fraction of the party, a basically social democratic minority group of deputies also emerged.

By September 1994, with mounting opposition to the government's policy as wage and pensions arrears mounted, the 60-million strong former official, and very moderate, trade unions called a national day of protest. The CPRF changed line and came out for a campaign of no confidence in the government. It also supported the trade union protest – which was significant because such actions had not really figured in Zyuganov's strategy previously. As a result the CPRF rapidly regained momentum.

Between two and three million workers joined the protest on 27 November 1994. The same day, parliament carried, by 194:54, a constitutionally-invalid vote of no-confidence. On this line the communists greatly strengthened their position, in particular becoming the majority party among Russia's coal miners – who had backed Yeltsin in 1990 and 1991 – and dominating the so-called 'red belt' linking south-western Russia with the eastern Ukraine – the biggest coal and steel-making complex in the world.

Moreover, they also started to win the battle against the right-wing nationalists and fascists for leadership of the opposition. In this, Zyuganov's approach of building a 'patriotic alliance' was decisive. Thus between the 1993 and the 1995 parliamentary elections the CPRF made two major strides – it won over the miners and it defeated the right wing nationalists. The results were seen in the December 1995 parliamentary elections. The CPRF vote nearly doubled to 22 per cent,

Zhirinovsky's vote halved to 11 per cent, the government party, Our Home is Russia, polled 10 per cent, and Yavlinsky's liberal Yabloko 7 per cent.

Thus Zyuganov achieved his strategic aim of taking the leadership of the opposition away from ultra-nationalists like Zhirinovsky and linking it instead to the CPRF. Nevertheless, the CPRF has been subject to much criticism from other communist and left forces within Russia and internationally for the nationalist ideas which Zyuganov entwined with his perspective of a patriotic alliance. For whilst the concept of a patriotic alliance, on the one hand, enabled the CPRF to build a broad movement to oppose the dismantling of the Russian economy and society, the particular nationalist elements unnecessarily introduced into it also, on the other hand, exposed some leaders of the CPRF to well-founded charges of Russian nationalism.

Clearly, Zyuganov emerged as the most significant leader of the CPRF because of the strategic decision that the CPRF should lead the opposition to Yeltsin on the patriotic basis that integration into the world capitalist economy on IMF terms would destroy Russia. Although this, contrary to the views of much of the west European left, is clearly the correct strategy for opposing the restoration of capitalism, Zyuganov is also criticized harshly for his theoretical justification of this strategic step. Rather than theorizing this in Marxist terms – which would not preclude a broad-based patriotic coalition – that a capitalist Russia would not develop an economy like those of Germany or France, but would become a semi-colonial country and therefore that the patriotic struggle against such a process, as in any semi-colonial country, would be progressive – Zyuganov has also attempted to theorize this position through a number of his own writings. These focus, 'on the long-standing question of Russia's supposed superior uniqueness and exceptionalism as against the rest of European, and indeed Western, civilization'.[15]

It is not the case, however, that the majority of the CPRF support Zyuganov's eccentric theorization of the situation, but they do support the broad thrust of the patriotic alliance approach. This is not well-understood in the West, where academic observers frequently try to fit Russian politics into a preconceived framework modelled on western Europe, but is clearly an appropriate strategy in contemporary Russia. Russian perceptions cannot but be shaped by the scale of the catastrophe which struck them after 1991, including not simply massive social and economic deprivation, grotesque inequality, rampant crime including at the highest levels of government, the dissolution of what had been their country, the Soviet Union, the destruction of their parliament by force and the role of western governments and the IMF in supporting those responsible for all of this.

In such circumstances, where as a result of policies formulated by Western advisors great extremes of wealth and poverty were now apparent in a previously egalitarian society, a reaction against the West was inevitable – particularly in a country which less than 10 years previously had been one of the world's two superpowers. Indeed, opinion polls indicate that more than 60 per cent of Russians believe that the West is seeking to bring the country to its knees. If, in these circumstances the left did not advocate saving the country from national as well as economic and social collapse, then people would simply turn to extreme right wing nationalists and fascists. The election results of 1995 demonstrated that the CPRF's patriotic alliance had been the correct strategy to defeat the far right.

The 1996 presidential elections

The extent to which Russian politics had become polarized – and the leading opposition role of the CPRF within that – was clearly demonstrated in the presidential elections of June/July 1996 which in its second round became a two-horse race between Yeltsin and Zyuganov – indeed, for a period it looked entirely possible that Yeltsin might lose. A new twist in the economic problems of the government reinforced this possibility. As output collapsed firms could not pay both their taxes and their employees, and many paid neither. As a result the government's income slumped and it too stopped paying the army, teachers, nurses, scientists and other government employees; typically arrears would be up to six months pay. At the same time government borrowing sent interest rates into the stratosphere on occasion reaching 200 per cent on six-month bonds (GKOs). These provided rich pickings for the criminalized network of commercial banks, but crowded out all possibility of raising funds for investment in the productive economy. As the presidential election approached, the financial system was on the verge of meltdown.

Facing the prospect of seeing Yeltsin replaced by Zyuganov, the US urged the IMF to step in with a $10 billion loan, France and Germany also stumped up more than $3 billion between them. On this basis a vast effort was made to repay back wages and pensions in the months before the vote. The powerful regional governors were induced in their great majority to rally round Yeltsin through help in meeting their own financial shortfalls. At the same time, in addition to a frantic media campaign from the blatantly biased TV companies with endless films about the horrors of communism, Yeltsin adopted the tactic of tacitly sponsoring an alternative 'opposition' candidate, General Alexander Lebed. Lebed violently denounced the 'corruption' of the regime and demanded an iron fist to solve the country's problems – while less publicly firmly supporting privatization and being the only major politician in Russia to openly back NATO expansion. His campaign was well funded and he received unprecedented television coverage for an 'opposition' candidate in the week before polling. Even so in the first round Zyuganov came within 3 per cent of Yeltsin.

The CPRF went into the election as part of the Peoples' Patriotic Union – encompassing a range of forces initially including the Russian Communist Workers' Party, former Soviet Prime Minister Ryzhkov's Power to the People and some anti-communist forces like former Vice President Rutskoi. The totally dominant partner, however, was the CPRF. General Lebed announced his support for Yeltsin in the second round of the election, swinging a substantial number of voters to Yeltsin, and he subsequently joined the government for a few months. The result of the second round was that Yeltsin was returned with almost 54 per cent of the vote, while over 40 per cent backed Zyuganov – about 5 per cent voted against both candidates.

Following the presidential election, the crisis of government finances and non-payment of wages resumed with a vengeance while Zyuganov concluded a new alliance with Chernomydin for which he began to come under increasing criticism. As before, his assessment was that the government was split between puppets of US imperialism like Chubais and more nationally-oriented capitalists like Chernomyrdin, which was in fact correct. But he also argued that the CPRF should therefore support Chernomyrdin against the Chubais wing of the government, through voting for his budget, while the CPRF consolidated its position before a Chubais-led onslaught. This line, however, was opposed by the left wing of the communist movement, both inside and outside the CPRF, who argued that the negative impact on the working class of supporting Chernomyrdin's anti-working-class budget far out-weighed any tactical advantages gained by temporarily keeping Chubais down.

The result of this was that during the budget vote, only 54 CPRF deputies carried out the party line and supported the budget. Subsequent calls to discipline the rebels came to nothing, and the communist-oriented press began to be more critical of Zyuganov's line towards Chernomyrdin. By the time of the 1997 budget the mood had shifted still further to the left. The worsening economic situation – output fell a further 6 per cent in 1996 – led simultaneously to an increasing radicalization of the population as poverty deepened. Millions participated in a trade union day of action against non-payment of wages on 27 March 1997 – workers in many areas were owed several months back pay – and many workers resorted to more desperate direct action, in some areas setting up local 'salvation committees' taking on the functions of local government. The parliamentary fraction voted to oppose the budget, in spite of Zyuganov's obvious displeasure – although 29 deputies on the more social democratic wing of the parliamentary fraction voted with the government. Subsequently the left has been strengthened within the CPRF relative to both the social democratic wing and Zyuganov's own grouping.

This shift tallied with the mood in the country. In the first regional elections since Yeltsin had imposed his own appointees in most areas, after the destruction of parliament in October 1993, the government lost a series of supporters and the CPRF gained a crucial foothold and governor positions in some key parts of the country – a significant advance in a country the size of Russia.

Meanwhile the financial crisis was becoming acute. As a result, while previously the privatization process had essentially been a carve up between the main financial groups, an attempt was made to raise more money from privatization to ease the government's financial problems. The consequence was the 'war of the bankers' as the banks fought over who would get what. Chubais became a prominent casualty, when at the end of 1997, he was exposed as having received $90 000 from a company linked to one of the beneficiaries of the privatization of the state telecommunications company.

The lasting legacy of this period was deep divisions within the financial oligarchy, while Yeltsin's health visibly deteriorated and the issue of the succession was increasingly posed. From the summer of 1997 the financial situation grew ever more desperate. Wage and pension arrears mounted again and workers, lacking any real economic leverage, engaged in actions like blocking roads and the trans-Siberian railway, the east–west artery across Russia, hunger strikes, and a permanent picket of parliament by coal miners. The ultimate dead-end of the IMF strategy of turning Russia into an exporter of energy and raw materials, was revealed as the economic slump which hit Asia that summer sent oil prices down by 40 per cent in a year.

Financial collapse

At the same time, the financial turmoil in Asia had made foreign investors increasingly nervous about Russia. The crunch came with the forced devaluation of the rouble and default on Russia's domestic debt in August 1998. The devaluation sent the prices of food and consumer goods imports, on which Russian cities now depended, up by 40 per cent slashing living standards. The banks simply refused to pay their depositors, which is legal in Russia – thus stealing billions for both the Russian population and foreign investors. Virtually all private banks were technically bankrupt.

A new political crisis erupted immediately. President Yeltsin sacked the then Prime Minister Kiryenko and appointed Chernomyrdin in his place. This time the CPRF put up a bitter struggle against him – rejecting him twice. Yeltsin was left with three alternatives. He could dissolve parliament and call fresh elections – but that would have simply resulted in the electoral annihilation of all parties associated with government. He could dissolve parliament without calling election – in effect a coup – but polling in the army showed that 97 per cent of soldiers and officers would disobey orders to fire on the population. The only alternative was to back down – which he did, replacing Chernomyrdin with the former head of the foreign intelligence service, Yevgeny Primakov, a choice favoured by the CPRF.

As a result of this defeat, the Yeltsin regime was severely weakened. Yeltsin retained the power to sack Primakov, but until the NATO bombing of Yugoslavia in spring 1999 the government now depended for the first time since 1991 on parliament's support. Primakov rapidly appointed Victor Gerashchenko as head of the central bank – the man described by Jeffrey Sachs as the worst central banker in the world for his defence of Russian industry against shock therapy until he was sacked by Yeltsin. The new government, which included a leading communist in charge of the economy, announced strong action to stem the financial crisis. In February 1999, Primakov was even talking about freeing space in the prisons to make room for corrupt business leaders. In the field of foreign policy, the new government departed from Yeltsin's approach by forming a bloc with China, to denounce US bombing of Iraq in December 1998 in the strongest possible terms. Primakov also totally opposed NATO's bombing of Yugoslavia until Yeltsin took advantage of increased US support in that context to remove the Prime Minister from office.

While backing Primakov's first budget, the CPRF made clear that it regarded itself as independent of the government. Overall, it is clear that the outcome of the struggle in Russia is far from being resolved. The CPRF is very much a product of that struggle and is in no sense a frozen, monolithic party, as the conflicts mentioned above show. It wants to change the constitution to make Russia a parliamentary, rather than a presidential, republic, and believes that if it comes to power at the ballot box, there is no force inside or outside Russia which could stop it taking office. Nuclear weapons prevent foreign military intervention and the army is neither able nor willing to repress the population. The army is also more sympathetic to the communists, though also to Lebed, than it is to the neo-liberals whose policies have all but destroyed it – and no other wing of the security forces could take on the regular army.

The CPRF certainly now has an opportunity to extend its support into the big cities where it has been weakest until now – in part because living standards there were subsidised by cheap imports which are no longer available because of the devaluation of the rouble. In this increased radicalization, and in the years since its re-establishment in 1993, the CPRF has clearly emerged as the mass party of the working class, the leader of the left and the leader of the broad opposition to Yeltsin and IMF reform policies. Furthermore, as it maintains an anti-capitalist position, it is far to the left of any of the mass political forces that have emerged from the former ruling parties in central and eastern Europe. Its basic positions are for the restoration of the Soviet Union, the halting of privatization, the re-introduction of price controls on energy and transport, the protection of Russian industry from western competition, and opposition to NATO expansion. It has recently become supportive of the Chinese economic reform as an alternative to the IMF's strategy for Russia. It is committed to the achievement of these goals through 'constitutional means', through the electoral process.

Whether the CPRF will be able to maintain its leading position in the broad opposition to Yeltsin is, however, uncertain. The emergence of a second powerful opposition force, during the summer of 1999, in the shape of an alliance between Primakov and Moscow's Mayor Luzhkov, may well present a challenge to the ascendancy established by the CPRF in the mid 1990s.

Part II

The Recomposition of the West European Left since 1989

5
Introduction

The physiognomy of the west-European labour movement from the latter half of the 1970s to 1989, had largely been marked, on the one hand, by the rise of Eurosocialism and, on the other, by the decline of the communist parties. As we have seen, the latter's response – in the form of Eurocommunism – had simply accelerated their decline. The impact of 1989 upon this process was initially two-fold. First, it deepened the communists' crisis. Most of those parties which had not already done so, split. On the one hand, the Eurocommunist currents concluded that the entire enterprise of building communist, as distinct from social democratic parties, had been a mistake. On the other hand, the parties' left wings started a process of rethinking their entire political strategy, but from a standpoint which remained firmly anchored on the left, and in competition with, European social democracy.

For the Eurocommunist right, the historian Eric Hobsbawm put it succinctly: 'It was in 1920 that the Bolsheviks committed themselves to what in retrospect seems a major error, the permanent division of the international labour movement.'[1] Spanish Eurocommunist Santiago Carrillo, for example, drew the logical conclusion from this view and joined the Spanish Socialist Party in October 1991. He stated: 'the communist movement as such has completed its historical cycle and it makes no sense trying to prolong it.' In the unique conditions of the complete collapse of the the Italian Socialist Party, the Italian Communist Party (PCI) became Italy's section of the Socialist International – changing its name to the Democratic Party of the Left (PDS). Its general secretary foreshadowed the shift as early as the summer of 1988, proclaiming that the party's models should be Willy Brandt and Olaf Palme.[2]

On the left, the process of building independent left-wing parties or alliances – like the United Left in Spain, Communist Refoundation in Italy, the French Communist Party, the Portugese Communist Party, the Party of Democratic Socialism in Germany – was consolidated. On a visit to London in March 1997, German PDS leader, Gregor Gysi neatly summed up these parties' view of the difference between themselves and social democracy: 'Asked the difference between the German Social Democratic Party (SPD) and the PDS, he said that the SPD stood for democratic capitalism, while the PDS stood for democratic socialism'.[3]

Thus in a certain sense, European labour movement politics became simplified after 1989. Eurosocialism reigned supreme within the socialist parties and was reinforced by the absorption of Eurocommunism. Its only remaining rivals for the allegiance of voters on the left were the Greens, the left socialist parties of northern Europe, and, most importantly, the left-wing currents which emerged from the crisis of communism. The latter had made their own implicit assessment of the Soviet experience by making their goal *democratic* socialism.

Britain stands out as a somewhat special case, for the 'broad church' character of the British Labour Party means that most of those who would elsewhere have been in Green, left socialist or left communist parties, are instead loosely organized as the Labour left. Even so, defined by its politics, rather than organization, today's Labour left must be classified as closer to the Spanish United Left or the German PDS than to Tony Blair. Indeed, according to former British Liberal Democrat leader, Paddy Ashdown, Blair himself would like to see them outside the the Labour Party altogether.[4]

In 1989, it looked very much as if the political life of what was to become the new European left, would be extremely short, but reality, as demonstrated in chapter one, turned out to be quite different. To understand why, we must examine the critical choices made by west European political leaders and employers after 1989, and the population's response to their consequences.

What was to become the European Union had emerged from the 1980s facing a major crisis of perspectives. Guy de Jonquières, international business editor of the *Financial Times*, had already outlined its dimensions in November 1988:

> The 1980s have brought a rude awakening for Europe. After the prolonged paralysis and political indecision induced by the 1973 OPEC oil shock, Europe is being jolted by the discovery that many of the

comfortable certainties of the post-war era have been swept away, to be replaced by discontinuity, turbulence, and accelerating change. In almost every domain – political, economic, social and industrial – structures, policies and rules which have long underpinned Europe's own internal relationships and those with the rest of the world are starting to come under mounting strain.

The pressures are becoming so intense that they seem unlikely to be accommodated merely by selective tinkering with the status quo. Increasingly, Europe is being obliged to grope its way forward in search of a new model on which to base its future development ...

When the 1992 programme [for the single European market – KH] was launched three years ago, the primary motivation was economic. The plan was conceived as the best hope – perhaps even the chance – of revitalising European economies afflicted with sluggish growth rates, high unemployment and declining international competitiveness which were stubbornly refusing to respond to national policy prescriptions. It amounted to a belated acknowledgement that Europe must adapt to mounting pressures generated by structural changes generated in the world economy and international markets – or risk being engulfed by them.[5]

Towards a US model?

The 1980s had, indeed, been a time of setbacks for west European capital. During the 1960s, the European Community had the second highest GDP per capita in the world, and had been catching up with the USA. During the 1980s, it began to lose ground against the US and was simultaneously overtaken by Japan. From 1986, the EEC's trade balance began to deteriorate. During the 1960s, unemployment in western Europe had been roughly half the level of the United States. In the 1980s, it averaged a little less than 10 per cent, compared to 7.2 per cent in the US and 2.5 per cent in Japan.

These raw figures reflected the impact on the European economy of the change in international economic relationships after the Vietnam war. The US dollar devaluation in 1971, the oil price rises from 1973 and 1979, and the huge absorption of the rest of the world's capital into the United States under Ronald Reagan, undermined economic growth in western Europe. The impact of these events was magnified by the increasing competitive challenge from Japan and the Newly Industrializing Countries in East Asia. By the end of the 1980s, European leaders had arrived at the conclusion that if nothing was done about this situation the west European economy was going to suffer irreparable damage. Their response is well-known – the acceleration of the drive towards economic and monetary union (EMU), but what is not so well-understood is the full scope of this project. EMU, as formalized in the 1991 Treaty of Maastricht, aims to address not simply the fact that a European capitalist economy, fragmented into national markets, cannot hope to withstand the pressure of East Asia and the United States. It was preceded by a careful appraisal of all of the disadvantages of the European economy *vis-à-vis* its chief rivals.

The first conclusion was certainly that the economies of scale necessary to be competitive in a globalizing economy, required a market at least the size of what has become the European Union. That, in turn, required a single currency. German manufacturers, in particular, pointed out that the effect of currency swings in the 1980s was bigger than that of the tariff barriers which had been abolished by the Treaty of Rome when the Common Market was set up in the 1950s. A single market would tend to break in periods of economic recession without a single currency. Moreover, for companies to take advantage of the potential economies of scale provided by a single market they would have to be consolidated into much larger units on a European level.

Secondly, Europe possessed much stronger trade union movements and working-class-based political parties than either the US or Japan. These had succeeded, in the particular conditions of the post-war period, in achieving a more regulated labour movement and a far more extensive welfare state than in either of Europe's main competitors. Indeed, the 50 per cent higher level of investment achieved by the Japanese – as compared to the west European economies throughout the 1980s – could, on this interpretation, be put down to the difference of spending on the welfare state. In 1990, the EC devoted 20.8 per cent of its GDP to fixed capital formation compared to Japan's 32.6 per cent. On the other hand, in the same year, final government spending made up 18.1 per cent of European Community GDP, compared to just 9 per cent of Japan's. The conclusion of leading circles of business and governments was clear – transfer as much as possible of those resources from welfare provision to private investment.

As the EC's 1991–92 annual report observed: 'The Community, and the whole world, is facing a shortage of savings ... A saving surplus can only be realised if the considerable public dissaving [i.e. spending – KH] in the Community and the other major Western countries is reversed.'[6]

Thirdly, while a country like Germany had closed the productivity gap with the US in many sectors of manufacturing industry, the same did not apply to the economy as a whole. In particular, the productivity of European agriculture, large parts of the retail trade and financial services lagged far behind that of the USA. Therefore, these sectors also required rationalization.

In other words, the project of European integration involved not merely the goal of creating single market and currency, but also making the west European economy and society more like that of the United States, and in the field of welfare provision, also Japan. The problem with this project was that it was likely to meet gigantic social and political resistance from those at whose expense it would be carried out. This was likely to involve not simply the trade union and labour movements, but also the small farmers, shopkeepers and business sectors who would be eliminated by a major rationalization of those sectors. As a result, until the end of the 1980s, the course of European integration remained piecemeal and relatively timid.

1989 changed everything. No longer potentially threatened by communism from the east, European employers felt they had a once-in-a-lifetime opportunity to take on the domestic forces resistant to what they saw as the indispensable rationalization and integration of the west European economy. A memorable editorial in the *Wall Street Journal* spelled out the new thinking, not just in Europe, but in boardrooms throughout the world:

> Speaker of the US House of Representatives Newt Gingrich stood in front of reporters last week and announced that the progressive tax system was an artefact of the Cold War ... We would widen the field further: the long legislative run of Democratic liberalism was an artefact of the Cold War ... When the Berlin Wall fell in 1989, we all knew that the world had changed utterly ... The long era of public paternalism which emerged throughout the West during the Cold War is being swept aside.[7]

The Japanese economist Makoto Itoh noted why this should be the case:

> In retrospect, global capitalism seemed to have been in a defensive position since the Russian Revolution. Its territory was actually much narrowed after the Second World War. East European countries, China, North Korea, Cuba, Ethiopia, Vietnam, Kampuchea and

Nicaragua, for instance, opted for a socialist regime. Within capitalist countries, welfare policies, concessions to the demands of trade unions, as well as the burden of defence expenditures were regarded to be necessary costs to guard a free capitalist economic system against revolutionary socialism.[8]

Robin Blackburn, editor of the *New Left Review* in Britain, made a similar observation: 'Though other factors are certainly at work, it is interesting to note that welfare and social provision were often at their most generous in those European states bordering the former Soviet bloc, and were often introduced at a time when the prestige of the Soviet Union was at its highpoint, in the early postwar period.'[9] Indeed, it was ironic that after 1989, deep inroads were made into even the Scandinavian welfare systems, which had been held up as the model alternative to state socialism in eastern Europe.

The Treaty of Maastricht

1989 thus put 'global capitalism' very much back onto the offensive. In Europe the result was very rapid progress towards the conclusion of the Treaty of Maastricht in December 1991. This set out a strictly monetarist framework for economic and monetary union. It established strict limits on the levels of total public debt (60 per cent of GDP) and government budget deficits (3 per cent of GDP) – whose achievement would require major public spending cuts in most EU states. It also provided for the insulation of key areas of economic policy from democratic accountability, by giving the projected independent European Central Bank control of monetary policy, within a framework which specified that price stability took precedence over such things as economic growth, employment and living standards. The Maastricht framework outlawed not merely socialist incursions upon the free market (that had already been done by the Treaty of Rome) but the Keynesian economic policies which had previously been the leitmotif of west European social democracy.

As a result, West European politics in the 1990s was to be dominated by the struggle for and against the consequences of the implementation of the Treaty of Maastricht. Its first stages were not encouraging because the Maastricht provisions were made more onerous by the shift in the balance of power within the EU resulting from unification. As the strongest economy in Europe, Germany was the chief contributor to the European Union budget. Its trade surplus effectively subsidized the rest of the Community, while its industry benefitted from the relative exchange rate stability provided by the European monetary system. With unification, this balance changed dramatically. Indeed, the Maastricht Treaty provisions were set so rigidly because Germany had no intention of subsidizing the weaker EU economies.

The first crisis came rapidly as the European Monetary System collapsed in August 1993, essentially because, in the context of recession, the rest of the EU simply could not tolerate the levels of interest rate set by the German Bundesbank in order to attract the funds necessary to soften the impact of unification upon east Germany. The deadline for the start of monetary union was put back from 1997 to 1999. In order to meet it, virtually every EU government had already embarked upon a programme of public spending cuts and labour market deregulation in a context where EU unemployment averaged more than 10 per cent.

In June 1992, the Italian Socialist Party Prime Minister, Amato, launched an austerity programme, reducing spending on health care and pensions, cutting local spending and controlling public-sector pay. A similar programme in the Netherlands cut subsidies to education, housing and public transport. In Spain, with the highest levels of unemployment in the EU, the Socialist government of Felipe González introduced a plan to cut unemployment benefits. Under the French Socialist governnment at the beginning of the 1990s, the *franc fort* policy – linking the French and German currencies at an exchange rate at which France could not compete – ensured that unemployment never fell below 10 per cent, and the government destroyed its support through trying to reduce the resulting deficit through public spending cuts. Similar policies were introduced throughout the EC. Public opposition to these policies mounted rapidly, in the context of the highest levels of unemployment in the advanced industrial world.

The political consequences of the Maastricht Treaty

The social and political results were dramatic, and as the Maastricht deadline approached, and governments launched more and more desperate efforts to carry out spending cuts, trade unions launched the biggest waves of struggles seen in western Europe since the period following May 1968. Germany saw a series of major strikes starting with the public sector strike which paralysed the country in May 1992. In Italy, on 12 November 1994 one and a half million people demonstrated in Rome against the government's plans to cut welfare benefits and state pensions – a third of the marchers were pensioners. Most spectacularly of all, in November 1995, the French trade unions launched what developed into a wave of strikes and demonstrations, lasting for more than three weeks, against the conservative government cuts.

The reaction to the consequences of Maastricht was equally clear on the political field, and a pattern emerged. The mainstream Conservative Parties suffered massive splits in their social base. Italian Christian Democracy was virtually destroyed – dramatically losing support to the former fascist National Alliance in the south and the right wing separatist Northern League in the north. The French right lost a significant part of its electorate to the National Front whose vote rose to 15 per cent, becoming the largest party among small shopkeepers and the unemployed. Following a dramatic breakthrough for the fascist Republican Party in the 1991 European elections in Bavaria, the governing Christian Social Union made a sharp shift to anti-immigrant rhetoric. In Belgium, the extreme right wing nationalist Vlaams Blok won 11 parliamentary seats in 1991 and became the biggest party in Antwerp.

On the left, wherever they were in government, the Eurosocialist parties generally suffered reverses ranging, from serious to catastrophic. In the 1993 French election, Mitterrand's Socialist Party saw its vote fall to just 16 per cent having dominated the previous parliament. In the 1994, Italian general election, the Socialist Party was annihilated. In the 1993 general election in Spain the Spanish socialists lost their parliamentary majority and went on to be ejected from office in 1996. In the 1995 general election in Belgium the Socialist Party lost a third of its seats.

It was in this political context that the parties which had emerged out of the crisis of communism, to the left of social democracy, arrested their decline and began to advance. The Italian Communist Refoundation increased its vote from 5.6 per cent in 1992, to 6 per cent in 1994, to 8.6 per cent in 1996. The German PDS increased from 2.4 per cent in 1990, to 4.4 per cent in 1994, to 5.1 per cent in 1998 on an all-Germany basis, and over 20 per cent in parts of the former GDR. The United Left of Spain increased from 4.7 per cent in 1986, to 9.1 per cent in 1989, to 9.6 per cent in 1993, to 10.5 per cent in 1996.

At the same time, given their electoral consequences, the neo-liberal Eurosocialist currents within social democracy were significantly weakened in a number of countries. When the French Socialists, in alliance with the communists, were unexpectedly returned to power in the

1997 general election it was on the basis of manifesto commitments to reduce the working week from 39 to 35 hours with no loss of pay, to create 700 000 new jobs and public statements calling into question the rigidity of the Maastricht criteria. More generally, the increased weight of the new European left in Italy, France, Sweden, Spain and Germany had the potential to put pressure on social democracy from the left.

Left realignment and the emergence of the new European left

A new openness to a range of different left ideas had emerged out of the debris of 1989 – with the new European left parties and alliances incorporating significant parts of the new left which had emerged outside the communist movement after 1968 – particularly in Italy and Spain. This has led the chair of the PDS, successor to the ruling East German Socialist Unity Party, to state at their 1995 conference:

> Moreover, together we want to tap and use the ideas of communists such as Rosa Luxemburg, Karl Liebknecht, the old Leon Trotsky or Antonio Gramsci. It is undisputed for us that we commemorate those communists who were persecuted and killed by fascists. Yet it is also our duty to honour those who were killed by Stalin.[10]

The United Left

The first major manifestation of this left realignment which was to forge the new European left had occurred in Spain in the 1980s. The Communist Party of Spain (PCE) had been legalized in 1977, following the end of the Franco dictatorship, but had swung to the right in the late 1970s, espousing Eurocommunism. The PSOE under González – receiving funding from the German SPD and the Socialist International during the 1970s – was able to position itself as the more radical force. The PSOE won around three times as many votes as the PCE in general elections in 1977 and 1979, polling 30.5 per cent in 1979 as opposed to 10.8 per cent for the PCE. The disintegration of the right led to a PSOE victory in the 1982 elections. The PSOE won 46.1 per cent of the vote, gaining an absolute majority in parliament, elected, as Sassoon points out, 'to modernize the country, solve the economic problems and establish a welfare state'.[11] With the PCE winning only 4 per cent of the vote, the PSOE no longer ran the risk of being outflanked on its left and became one of the first socialist parties to embrace neo-liberalism, prioritizing a reduction in inflation which was paid for by a rise in unemployment from 17 per cent in 1982 to 22 per cent in 1986.[12]

This early shift to the right of the Spanish socialists in government created the political space for a left to emerge which would oppose the PSOE's anti-working-class policies. Shortly before the 1986 general election the PCE put together a coalition called the United Left (IU), intended to fill just this space. However, the IU was not merely the result of an attempt to consolidate electoral forces. It was born out of a mass campaign during the first PSOE government on NATO membership. Before entering government, the PSOE had opposed NATO membership and had promised a referendum on membership, changing its position when in government. A broad committee, including communists, pacifists, feminists, human rights groups, Christians and the far left coordinated a vigorous campaign, which in spite of massive media saturation and huge political pressure for a 'yes' vote, actually won 43 per cent of the vote against NATO. It was this campaign which provided the basis for the founding of the IU in 1986, and although it made little advance on the PCE's result of 1982, it remained the foundation for the IU's relaunch in February 1989 and a more than doubling of its votes in the general election of October 1989 with 9.1 per cent, and 'provided the major success story of the general election'.[13] This support had increased, by the general elections of 1996 to 10.5 per cent.

The IU was the forerunner of the new European left, its early development the result of the particular conditions in Spain following the demise of the dictatorship, and the early collapse of the PCE, as a result of the Eurocommunist policies of the late 1970s. The next wave in this trend emerged more directly as a result of the collapse of communism.

The Party of Communist Refoundation

By 1989, the Italian Communist Party had moved through its Eurocommunist phase, exemplified by the 'Historic Compromise', where, as Tobias Abse has put it, '... the Christian Democrats made the history, the Communists made the compromise.'[14] Indeed, as Sassoon points out: 'To all intents and purposes, the PCI had become a mainstream social-democratic party before the collapse of the Berlin Wall.'[15]

In November 1989, Occhetto attempted to bring the form of the party in line with this reality and proposed that the PCI be dissolved and that a new 'constituent phase' be entered, which would lead to the foundation of a new party, which 'would not be Communist but "socialist", "popular" (i.e. less class-oriented), "democratic" and "progressive". It would be committed to the realisation of a left-wing alternative and would hope to be not only an integral part of the European Left but also a full member of the Socialist International'.[16]

The 'constituent phase' was entered at the PCI's Special Nineteenth Congress in March 1990, and at the Twentieth Congress in January 1991 the Democratic Party of the Left (PDS) was launched with the support of the majority of delegates. This was accompanied, however, by the setting up of the Movement for the Refoundation of Communism (MRC), a grouping committed to the refounding of a communist party which attracted those from within the PCI who had opposed the move to social democracy. Adopting the name Partito della Rifondazione Comunista (PRC) during 1991, PRC was also joined by Democrazia Proletaria (DP), a parliamentary party originating in the Italian new left of the late 1960s and early 1970s, adding several thousand mainly young activists and working-class militants to the new party. By the end of 1991, PRC had a total membership in the region of 150 000. In the general elections of 1992, PRC polled 5.6 per cent, rising to 6 per cent in 1994 and 8.6 per cent in 1996. Between them, PRC and the PDS in 1996 reached around the 30 per cent mark that the PCI had last achieved in the late 1970s.

The Party of Democratic Socialism

The German Party of Democratic Socialism (PDS) was formed at an emergency Congress in December 1989, as the direct organizational successor to the ruling Socialist Unity Party (SED) of the German Democratic Republic. In the elections of March 1990, the PDS came third behind the CDU and Social Democrats (SPD), with 16.4 per cent of the vote,[17] demonstrating that it had maintained a solid base of support. In the local elections of 6 May 1990 in the east German *Länder*, the PDS won more than 10 000 seats in regional, city and local assemblies.[18]

The Congress of December 1989 adopted the definition of the SED-PDS as:

> a modern socialist party in the tradition of the German and international labour movement. It proclaims itself to be part of the tradition of Marx, Engels, Lenin and of the democratic, communist, social democratic, socialist and pacifist movement.[19]

From its inception, the PDS 'cast itself as a party which had purged itself of Stalinism but not of socialism',[20] and continues to do so: in

1996, 'Gregor Gysi claimed that the greatest success of the PDS since 1989 has been what he views as the PDS' "anti-Stalinist course of socialist renewal"'.[21] Polling 2.4 per cent in the Bundestag elections for the former GDR in 1990, the PDS has steadily increased to 4.4 per cent throughout Germany in 1994 and 5.1 per cent in 1998. The PDS polls up to 20 per cent or more in parts of the new eastern *Länder*, and from 1998 had two ministers in the state government of Mecklenburg-West Pomerania.

The French Communist Party

The French Communist Party (PCF) demonstrates a quite different route to a rather similar political perspective. Having passed through a Eurocommunist phase in the 1970s and by the 1980s returned to a pro-Moscow orientation, a defining moment for the PCF was the point at which it broke with the Soviet leadership. Whilst the PCF had supported Gorbachev's early initiatives, by the late 1980s it was distancing itself from the direction of the reforms and identifying more closely with the Portuguese and Cuban communist parties. The clear break came over the Gulf War in 1990, as it did for many parties, and helped to set the future direction of the PCF. Gorbachev supported the US operation in the Gulf, whereas the PCF was not prepared to back American imperialism. In its opposition to the war, the PCF worked in a committee – Appel des 75 – with a range of left forces, including Trotskyists, ecologists and anarchists. David S. Bell correctly points out that this would previously have been an unthinkable alliance for communists, but sees it as 'another index of communist decline'.[22] In fact, this was to indicate a new orientation of the PCF towards other left groups which, far from being a grasping at straws during a period of crisis, has been consolidated within the more open political practice and debate of the PCF during the 1990s.

The significance of the Gulf War

The Gulf War was a defining moment for the left because it forced parties to take a pro- or anti-imperialist position. It certainly clarified the ultimate logic of Gorbachev's trajectory and served as a factor in the realignment of the internatonal left. In Britain, for example, both the Eurocommunist CPGB, which was in the process of trying to dissolve itself, and the more orthodox CPB, supported Gorbachev's reforms. Both participated in the Committee to Stop War in the Gulf with a range of Trotskyist, pacifist, Labour left and other groups.

During the course of the campaign, the CPB stopped supporting Gorbachev's line and openly broke with it in their daily newspaper the *Morning Star*. The CPGB, on the other hand, did not change its position. The anti-Gulf War Committee served as a basis for a realignment of the far left in Britain in the following period.

On an initiative by Ken Livingstone, a left Labour MP, a Socialist Forum emerged from the anti-war alliance, which drew together left communists, left Labour, trade unionists, the anti-racist movement and others into a working alliance to campaign around common issues. The CPGB dissolved itself in 1991 and its successor organization, the Democratic Left, moved through 'radical democracy' to Blairism.

The second phase of realignment

The next phase of this emerging realignment was further developed through opposition to the austerity programmes, initiated in order to conform to the Maastricht criteria for EMU, and in particular this began to further radicalize the Scandinavian left parties, bringing them into a shared political framework with the parties mentioned above.

The forces to the left of social democracy in Scandinavia originated in orthodox communist parties, but began their transition to recognizable new left positions as long ago as thirty years before the collapse of communism in 1989, beginning with Aksel Larsen's split from the Danish Communist Party in 1959.[23] Although there were numerous national specificities to these parties, Stuart Wilks argues that by the mid-1960s, 'a distinctive Scandinavian new left had already emerged', offering an alternative to both social democracy and orthodox communism. The Danish Socialist People's Party was formed from a majority split from the Danish Communist Party in 1959. It was followed in 1960 by the formation of the Norwegian Socialist People's Party, which was a split from the Norwegian Labour Party. In 1975 the Norwegian SPP was renamed the Socialist Left Party. Both the Danish SPP and the Norwegian SLP rapidly replaced the communist parties as the main political parties to the left of social democracy. They are both green socialist parties, committed to feminism, anti-racism and social justice, and emphasize both parliamentary and extra-parliamentary activity. Whilst Norway remains outside the EU, the Norwegian Socialist Left Party maintains close relations with the European organizations which link the Scandinavian left parties with other European new left forces.

In Sweden, the Communist Party modernized itself during the 1960s, drawing closer to feminism and environmentalism in the 1970s and remained the main left party, renaming itself Left Party Communists in 1967 and Left Party in 1990 (see Table 5.1). According to party vice-chair, Johan Lönnroth, the Left Party is 'a party standing on four legs – socialist, internationalist, green and feminist.'[24] Its programme, adopted in 1996 states that: 'The Left Party strives for the abolition of capitalism. We fight against the division of society into ruling upper classes and oppressed lower classes.'[25] It also states its commitment to combatting racism. The Left Party is also opposed to Swedish membership of NATO and NATO expansion and whilst participating in the European parliament, the Left Party is against Swedish membership of the European Union and works for its withdrawal and argues for a referendum on EMU membership. In its 1998 general election platform, it highlighted its opposition to privatization, its commitment to full employment, a 35-hour week with no reduction of wages, increased public sector investment and environmental protection. It also made a clear argument for strengthening the Left Party electorally, to help it

Table 5.1   Results of Swedish general elections, 1948–98 (per cent of votes)

	1948	1952	1956	1958	1960	1964	1968
SAP	46.1	46.1	44.6	46.2	47.8	47.3	50.1
VPK	6.3	4.3	5.0	3.4	4.5	5.2	3.0
C	12.4	10.7	9.4	12.7	13.6	13.2	15.7
FP	22.8	24.4	23.8	18.2	17.5	17.0	14.3
M	12.3	14.4	17.1	19.5	16.5	13.7	12.9
Greens							
Others	0.1	0.1	0.1		0.1	3.6	4.0

	1970	1973	1976	1979	1982	1985	1988	1994	1998
SAP	45.3	43.6	42.7	43.2	45.6	44.7	43.7	45.3	36.4
VPK/VP	4.8	5.3	4.8	5.6	5.6	5.4	5.9	6.2	12.0
C	19.9	25.1	24.1	18.1	15.5	12.4	11.4	7.7	5.1
FP	16.2	9.4	11.1	10.6	5.9	14.2	12.2	7.2	4.7
M	11.5	14.3	15.6	20.3	23.6	21.3	18.3	22.4	22.9
Greens					1.7	1.5	5.5	5.0	4.5
KD								4.1	11.8
Others	2.3	2.3	1.7	2.2	2.1	0.5	3.0	2.3	n/a

SAP = Social Democratic Labour Party; VPK = Left Party – Communists, renamed Left Party (VP) in 1990; C = Centre Party; FP = Liberal Party; M = Moderate Party; Greens = Environmentalist Party, KD = Christian Democratic Party.
Adapted from: *Elections since 1945: A Worldwide Reference Compendium* (London: Longman, 1989).

move politics towards the left, and 'to fight right-wing politics whether carried on by the Conservatives or the Social Democrats'.[26]

The Left Party succeeded in its aim, for in the elections of September 1998, support for the Social Democratic Party fell from 45.3 per cent to 36.6 per cent, (see Fig 5.1 and 5.2) forcing it to look to the Left and Green parties for support for a minority government. The dilemma which faced Italy's Party of Communist Refoundation in the autumn of 1998 – whether to support the centre-left government's spending cuts or risk seeing it ousted by the right – may well come to face the Swedish Left Party in the months and years ahead. Swedish social democracy has moved considerably to the right, even undergoing what Johan Lönnroth describes as 'Blairification', so the issue will be whether the Left Party can push the government to the left, or whether the Left Party will itself end up following the social democrats to the right.

The Finnish Left Alliance was founded in 1990 as the successor to the Finnish People's Democratic League, which was formed as an electoral front for the Finnish Communist Party.[27] It is Finland's fourth largest party, with 14 000 members, over 300 000 voters, 19 MPs out of 200 in the Finnish parliament, two members of the European parliament, over 1130 municipal councillors, many leading trade unionists, and since

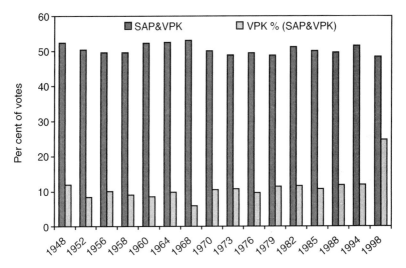

SAP = Social Democratic Labour Party; VPK = Communist Party 1921–67; renamed Left Party – Communists in 1967; renamed Left Party (VP) in 1990.

Figure 5.1   Election performance of the Swedish left, 1948–98

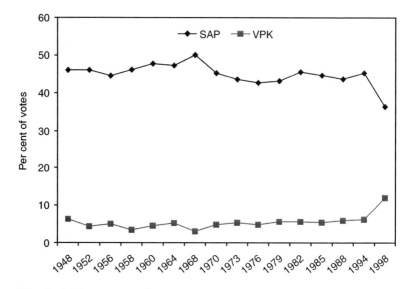

SAP = Social Democratic Labour Party
VPK = Communist Party 1921–1967; renamed Left Party – Communists in 1967;
renamed Left Party (VP) in 1990.

Figure 5.2   Election performance of socialist and communist parties in Sweden,
1948–98

1995 has two ministers in the Lipponen coalition government. The Left
Alliance describes itself as representing:

> the so-called Third left, which tries to combine labour movement
> traditions with the ideas of postindustrial democratic movements.
> Ideologically the party is a pluralist one: it gathers political left wing
> humanists, socialists, Marxists, feminists and ecologists – and simply
> leftwinger people.[28]

The basic goal of the party is described as a socially and economically just
and environmentally sustainable society, and whilst LA does not define
itself as a traditional socialist party, its aim is to limit 'societal power
based on capital ownership'. The LA formed the Nordic Green Left group
in the European parliament with the Swedish Left Party and the Danish
Socialist People's Party which cooperates with the United European Left
group. In 1991, LA was one of the initiators of the New European Left
Forum.

As the political transformation of these parties from orthodox communism towards more radical left and social movement politics – particularly feminism and environmentalism – had generally begun some decades before equivalent changes in their sister parties in western Europe, the Scandinavian left was less affected by the collapse of communism in 1989 than those parties still primarily identifying as communist with strong links with the CPSU. The catalyst which brought these parties back into a more militant anti-capitalist framework and back into cooperation with parties they had previously intended to wash their hands of, was the Maastricht Treaty. As Scandinavian social democracy moved to the right and began to implement cuts in the highly advanced welfare systems of these countries, these left parties moved into the breach, clarified their position on the left, and as has been seen clearly in the case of the Swedish Left Party, were able to increase their electoral standing on this basis.

An increase in support for the parties to the left of social democracy also took place in the Netherlands in the general election of May 1998, which saw a swing of 10 per cent from right to left. Whilst the Labour–Liberal coalition headed by Wim Kok – who had suddenly increased his left profile during the election campaign – was victorious with an increased number of seats for the two main coalition partners, the left opposition to the neo-liberal policies espoused by this coalition also increased its electoral support.[29] The Green Left – comprised of former communists, christian radicals and pacifist socialists – increased its representation from five to 11 seats, and the Socialist Party – a formerly Maoist party – which increased from 140 to 223 seats in the municipal elections of March 1998 increased from two to five parliamentary seats. The extreme-right party, the so-called Centre Democrats lost all three of their seats, and the Christian Democrats continued to decline.

Overall, the European labour movement after 1989 saw the disappearance of Eurocommunism, the first crisis and reaction against Eurosocialism as it tried to push through the Maastricht programme and the stabilization and then modest advance of the new European left.

6
France

The French Communist Party (Parti Communiste Français, PCF) has survived its supposed terminal decline and, on entering the tenth year since the collapse of communism, was able to point not only to its representation in the French government, but also its considerable role in forging the left alliance which defeated the right in the elections of 1997, and its contribution to building new left cooperation on a European-wide basis. Between 1989 and 1999, the PCF has undergone considerable changes, politically and structurally, being more open to arguments and ideas from both inside and outside the party – most recently demonstrated by its decision to structure its electoral lists for the 1999 Euro-elections with alternate male and female candidates. A target 50 per cent will be non-party members, but will share the PCF's views on the direction of Europe.

Yet the PCF has also, in some respects, maintained a remarkable continuity. It remains a Marxist party, based on the working class and has fought off attempts by reformers to shift it out of the class-politics framework. Although it has not recovered the level of electoral support it received before the rise of the Socialist Party (PS), it has, nevertheless, consolidated a stable level of support (see Table 6.1). Under the leadership of Robert Hue, it has attempted to shake off the tendency towards political sectarianism which it periodically manifested and its relative success in this field is demonstrated by the breadth of its national and international political intiatives. Like other left parties cooperating with social democratic parties in government, it justifies its participation on the basis that it pushes the government to the left. As the PCF was discredited by its period in the rightwards moving PS government in the early 1980s, there is some concern that the PCF will also on this occasion engage in excessive compromise and support policies unacceptable

Table 6.1 Results of French general elections, 1945–97 (seats)

	1945	1946	1946	1951	1956	1958	1962	1967
French Communist Party (PCF)	159	153	168	103	150	10	41	73
French Section of the Workers' International (SFIO)	139	129	93	104	95	40	66	
Socialist Party (PS)								
Federation of the Democratic and Socialist Left (FGDS)								121
Union of the Socialist and Democratic Left (UGDS)								
Radical Socialist Party	29			94	58	13	39	
Democratic and Socialist Union of the Resistance (UDSR)	31				33			
Rally of the Left Republicans (RGR)	60	53	59					
Popular Republican Movement (MRP)	150	167	160	85	73	57	55	0
Republican Party of Liberty (PRL)	39	35	42					
Independent Republicans	14	23	23	98				
Gaullist Union			9					
Rally of the French People (RPF)				118	21			
Union for the New Republic (UNR)						188		
UNR/ Democratic Union of Labour (UDT)							219	
Democratic Union for the Republic (UDR)								200
Rally for the Republic (RPR)								
Peasant and Social Action Party	11	9	8	0				
National Centre of Independents and Peasants					12	132		
Poujadists					52	0		
Independent Republicans (RI)							33	42
Centre of Progress and Modern Democracy (PDM)								41
Centre for Democracy and Progress								
Reformers Movement								
Union for French Democracy (UDF)								
Movement of Left Republicans (MRG)								
UDF/RPR joint								
National Front (FN)								
Other	14	17	7	23	16	25	12	9

Table 6.1 continued

	1968	1973	1978	1981	1986	1988	1993	1997
French Communist Party (PCF)	34	73	86	44	35	27	23	38
French Section of the Workers' International (SFIO)								
Socialist Party (PS)			103	285	206	260	54	241
Federation of the Democratic and Socialist Left (FGDS)	57							
Union of the Socialist and Democratic Left (UGDS)		102						
Radical Socialist Party								12
Democratic and Socialist Union of the Resistance (UDSR)								
Rally of the Left Republicans (RGR)								
Popular Republican Movement (MRP)								
Republican Party of Liberty (PRL)								
Independent Republicans								
Gaullist Union								
Rally of the French People (RPF)								
Union for the New Republic (UNR)								
UNR/ Democratic Union of Labour (UDT)								
Democratic Union for the Republic (UDR)	292	183						
Rally for the Republic (RPR)			154	88	76	127	247	134
Peasant and Social Action Party								
National Centre of Independents and Peasants								
Poujadists								
Independent Republicans (RI)	61	55						
Centre of Progress and Modern Democracy (PDM)	33							
Centre for Democracy and Progress		30						
Reformers Movement		34						
Union for French Democracy (UDF)		0	124	63	53	129	213	108
Movement of Left Republicans (MRG)			10	0	2	9	6	
UDF/RPR joint					147			
National Front (FN)			0	0	35	1		1
Other	10	13		11	21	23		1

Adapted from: *Elections since 1945: A Worldwide Reference Compendium* (London: Longman, 1989).

to the left. The judgement of its supporters on its new record in government will, no doubt, be delivered at the next legislative elections.

The PCF was the largest left party in post-war France until the 1970s, outpolling the Socialist Party (Parti Socialiste, PS) for the last time in the legislative elections of 1973 (see Figure 6.1). The PS was formed in 1971 as a regroupment of non-communist left forces by François Mitterrand, and it proceeded over the next 10 years to surpass the PCF and play a significant role in its reduction to a marginal position in French politics. Mitterrand pursued a strategy of left unity with the PCF intending to simultaneously strengthen the PS's left credentials through association with the PCF and in particular its war-time resistance record, and win away the PCF's voters. In 1972 the PCF and the PS signed the Common Programme which included many of the policies of the PCF, including further nationalization of industry, increased wages and welfare benefits, and improved union rights.

The PCF was not united, however, in enthusiasm for the Common Programme. As Ross and Jenson observe, 'From the outset of the party's turn towards a united front there had been a substantial internal opposition to the dilution of workerist purity which the new strategy was bound to bring.'[1] Unlike the PS which did not have a trade union base, the PCF was strongly grounded in the labour movement. This was the party's

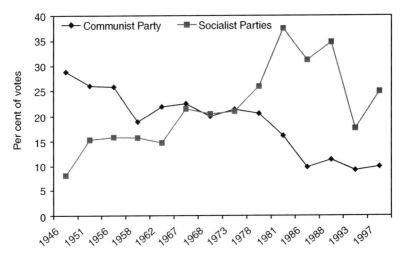

Figure 6.1 Election performance of communist and socialist parties in France, 1946–97

greatest strength and the reason for its survival and redevelopment, but it did periodically result in the very narrow interpretation of class. This internal tension increased with the turn to Eurocommunism in the mid-1970s and led ultimately to an alliance between pro-Soviet elements in the leadership who opposed Eurocommunism and those who opposed the united front.

In 1977 the balance within the party shifted in favour of this grouping when the PS performed better than the PCF for the first time in the municipal elections of that year. In the summer of 1977, the PCF broke with the PS and adopted a renewed 'militant autonomy' position,[2] intensely critical of the PS, and reorientated away from Eurocommunism towards a closer relationship with the CPSU leadership. The left, which had seemed set to win the legislative elections of 1978 was now defeated although the PCF won 20.6 per cent of the vote.

In the period before the next legislative election, the PCF's pro-Soviet turn had become more evident – in 1979 the party's daily paper, *L'Humanité*, provoked widespread disapproval by describing the social-ist regimes of eastern Europe as 'globally positive'.[3] The PCF also, along with a number of other more orthodox parties, supported the Soviet intervention in Afghanistan in 1979 and subsequently opposed the introduction of Euromissiles – intermediate-range nuclear weapons sited in western Europe. In 1980, the party co-hosted a conference on peace and disarmament with the ruling Polish United Workers' Party, to support the line of the CPSU. As David S. Bell observes, '...the French had decided to choose their "camp" and it was the "Socialist camp" as distinct from the "imperialist camp" led by America, which had, they said, "gone onto the offensive"'.[4]

By the legislative elections of 1981, the PS had regained all its lost ground and the PCF suffered a humiliating loss of votes with a big transfer of its own erstwhile supporters to its rival. Mitterrand won the presidential election, and the PS won 37.5 per cent of the vote in the legislative elections, with the PCF securing only 16.1 per cent. These results transferred into an absolute majority in the parliament for the PS but, nevertheless, hoping to disarm the PCF and more importantly its trade union confederation, the Confédération Générale du Travail (CGT), Mitterrand offered the PCF four ministries – which they accepted.[5] It is noteworthy, however, that Mitterrand chose the PCF ministers that he wanted – he did not leave it to the PCF leadership to select their representatives. Indeed, it has been observed that Mitterrand chose ministers that would help to weaken and split the party.[6]

This did turn out to be the case, for the former ministers were key players in the attempt in 1990 to turn the PCF towards the PS and abandon its class position. However, the PCF's participation in government did not halt its electoral decline, not least because the PS government fairly rapidly abandoned its traditional social democratic course and shifted towards a harsh austerity programme and a renewed commitment to the EMS. Contradictions also surfaced over the differing foreign policies of the two parties, particularly over the issue of peace and disarmament – the communist ministers supported the government's approval of the Euromissiles, whereas the party remained hostile to them.[7] The PCF also welcomed Jaruzelski's declaration of a state of emergency in Poland to deal with the Solidarity crisis.[8] The PCF eventually withdrew its ministers from government in 1984 in belated protest at the effects of Socialist policies on the working class, although the ministers themselves were reluctant to withdraw. The PCF continued to register electoral decline, polling only 11 per cent in the European elections of 1984.[9]

The problem for the PCF, was that in its phase in government in the early 1980s, it had not adopted an independent stand within the government on questions of domestic policy. The ministers did not really act as 'communist ministers', or attempt to push the government to the left – instead they gave total support to the government regardless of the social cost of its policies, including the deindustrialization of the early 1980s. In theory, the party mobilized against these policies, but its opposition was utterly ineffectual. The party itself failed to save the industrial 'red belt' – the name given to the traditionally communist voting outer ring of Paris – which, particularly the northern and eastern suburbs of Paris, became an industrial wasteland, seriously impacting on the PCF's electorate. Political opposition and mobilization was also ineffectual in central France, for example in St Etienne and the former engineering areas, resulting in a huge loss of support for the PCF.

The PCF's 25th Congress – the first to be held after the experience in government – in February 1985, affirmed the continuity of party policy[10] in its turn away from the PS, and the party's general secretary, Georges Marchais, offered a fairly orthodox assessment of national and international politics and emphasized support for the socialist countries: condemning the Socialist government for its austerity programme; asserting that 'the crisis was a capitalist one, even if the socialist countries were undergoing problems arising from historical conditions';[11] and underlined the significant advances made by the socialist countries.

There was considerable dissatisfaction within the PCF over the break-up of left unity and the reorientation towards Moscow – many thousands of members had left the party after 1977 – yet this was not particularly apparent at the Congress because of the operation of an extremely suppressive form of democratic centralism within the PCF. Nevertheless, the wave of dissidence which occurred within the party from 1984–87 – notably as the *rénovateurs* led by Pierre Juquin and Claude Llabrès – was manifested in a congress speech by Juquin.[12] Juquin called for greater objectivity on eastern Europe and criticized the lack of analysis of the crisis and of the problems in the relationship between the PCF and the PS. Juquin rejected any notion of organizing opposition within the party, however, and expressed his commitment to party unity. At this stage there was no sustained political critique of the party's position – rather a personal 'anti-stalinist' critique by Juquin, who had been an extreme sectarian in the 1960s and 1970s and then turned towards an alliance with ultra-leftists in the 1980s.[13] Clearly, the vast majority of delegates supported the general line of the party, as 65 of the 1700 votes cast on the final resolution were abstentions and the rest were in favour.[14] The Congress ratified the party's strategy since leaving government: an emphasis on campaigning on unemployment and economic hardship; a highly critical approach to the PS; and a call for 'a "New Popular Majority" (*Nouveau rassemblement populaire majoritaire*) to turn back the tide of austerity and free-market capitalism.'[15]

The crisis of identity and direction facing the PCF was further compounded by the crisis of communism in eastern Europe and the Soviet Union. Gorbachev's accession to the Soviet leadership in 1985 and his declared intention to renew and reinvigorate Soviet socialism was greeted with enthusiasm by Marchais and the PCF leadership, who declared that a 'revolution in the revolution' was taking place.[16] It was hoped that Gorbachev's undoubted popularity in the west would have a positive impact on the PCF's electoral support, but this did not prove to be the case. In the 1986 elections, the PCF vote fell to 9.8 per cent, but so did the PS vote as the electorate registered its displeasure over the government's economic austerity programme. The election was a victory for the right and the new government set about redrawing the electoral boundaries in their own favour.

At the party's 26th national congress, held in December 1987, Marchais confirmed the existing anti-PS line of the party and did not comment on the party's severe electoral decline. Marchais warmly commended Gorbachev's policies and concluded 'that "socialism has proved its superiority".'[17] During 1988, however, as Gorbachev moved away from renewal of the existing system to more radical reform that could lead to its destruction, the PCF became increasingly critical of Gorbachev, linking with other more orthodox parties who did not wish to go down a Gorbachevian path. Clearly the PCF leadership had understood the implications of Gorbachev's reforms, and moved to defend the party. In December 1989, Marchais had come to the conclusion that 'It is at the summit in the name of perestroika that these forces [capitalist] are fighting the party'.[18] The definitive break came in 1990 when Marchais refused to endorse Gorbachev's support for the US bombing of Iraq in the Gulf War.

Dissent continued within the party, although the leadership had moved against the *rénovateurs* in 1987, describing them as 'liquidators', leading to a number of key resignations.[19] At the 26th Congress, only two dissenting interventions were made, by Philippe Damette and Martial Bourquin, who criticized the party's 'defeatist strategy' and democratic centralism.[20] Pierre Juquin, the leading dissident at the previous congress was no longer a member of the PCF, and in fact contested the 1988 presidential elections against the PCF candidate, André Lajoinie. The elections were another disaster for the PCF – Lajoinie polled only 6.76 per cent. Juquin, who was attempting to 'create an alternative "red and green" pole between the PCF and the PS',[21] took only 2.01 per cent of the vote.

The political changes taking place in eastern Europe in 1989 did not shake the PCF leadership from its general line on the national and international situation. During 1990, this led to another attempt to bring about reform within the party, this time led by Charles Fiterman, the former transport minister. Fiterman was supported by a number of prominent members, including other former ministers, intellectuals and trade unionists. This move for change emerged clearly at the party's 27th Congress in December 1990. The challenge of Fiterman and the *refondateurs* to the existing line of the party was the first really serious and coherent movement against the continuation of the PCF as a class-based Marxist party. Whilst appearing to articulate and represent the position of the section of the party which supported left unity, they were not actually orientated towards a united front in which the communists would push the socialists to the left. Fiterman's move for a greater orientation towards the PS was to have been based on the discarding of the class positions that defined the PCF's distinctive role. Although Fiterman was not proposing the dissolution of the PCF, the logic of his position ultimately would be the PCF's incorporation into the PS.

Fiterman's challenge to the leadership was not successful and at the 27th Congress in December 1990, the political line of the Marchais leadership was consolidated, although there was both 'a certain relaxation of the strict interpretation of democratic centralist norms' and an announcement by Marchais that the next congress should consider 'a partial rewriting of its statutes'.[22]

The challenge by Fiterman had been widely reported in the French national press, which had strongly supported Fiterman and had urged the members to support him and secure Marchais's replacement. In fact, the predominant attitude of the rank and file of the membership, was that although they were not happy with Marchais, they were certainly not prepared to accept a change of general secretary imposed by the bourgeois press.[23] The congress also elected two new members to the party's political bureau, who were to play a significant role in reform and redeveloping the PCF in the 1990s: Robert Hue, aged 44 from the Val d'Oise, who had joined the Central Committee in 1987 and was to succeed Marchais as general secretary in 1994; and Francis Wurtz, aged 42, an MEP from the Bas-Rhin federation, who had joined the central committee in 1979 and was to become the party's high-profile International Secretary.

In fact, notwithstanding Marchais's political weaknesses such as his clumsy and ambiguous handling of the party's response to the anti-Gorbachev coup of August 1991, his achievement in steering the PCF through the period of the collapse of communism in eastern Europe and the Soviet Union, ensuring its maintenance as a class-based party, and initiating the process of managed structural and leadership change which enabled the PCF to emerge as a significant player in 1997, was remarkable. The only close parallel has been the Portuguese Communist Party, maintaining a unified class-based party whilst engaging in gradual reform and securing increased popular resonance.

In the early 1990s, the PCF continued to stress its communist identity and maintain and develop its international contacts. At its 1991 celebration of the Russian Revolution of 1917, 'the party declared Leninism "un idéal toujours moderne" and added that whereas the collapse of the Soviet system had not discredited Leninism, the evolution of contemporary capitalism showed that Lenin was correct.'[24] It pursued its anti-PS line in the regional elections in March 1992, gaining eight per cent of the vote although its result was adversely affected by the activities of the former party dissident Marcel Rigout, whose Alternative Democratie Socialisme (ADS), achieved better results than the PCF in some areas.[25]

The national referendum on the Maastricht Treaty, held in September 1992, offered a real opportunity for the PCF to clarify its political position in a broad and constructive fashion. Its popular campaigning approach drew on the real strength of the party – a committed and well-organized membership, who were now galvanized into action, exposing the neo-liberal nature of the Maastricht Treaty and opposing the social and economic hardship that would inevitably ensue. The campaign also demonstrated the difference between the PS and the PCF and the continuing relevance of the PCF's class-based politics in the 1990s. Although the referendum was narrowly lost, it was a turning point for the PCF, bringing it back into the mainstream of politics and renewing its militant image as it played a major role in one of the key struggles of the period.

Building on this positive development, the PCF proceeded to organize a series of public debates in November and December of 1992 to draw together and promote dialogue between the party and other progressive forces in French society in the run-up to the legislative elections of 1993. At the time, there was a certain amount of cynicism amongst dissidents in the party about the sincerity of this approach, but the subsequent political development of the PCF has demonstrated that the party was genuinely on a new political course that has proved to be a constructive one. In fact, the increased willingness of the PCF to ally with other political forces to the left of the PS has been noticeable since 1990, when the PCF worked in a committee – Appel des 75 – with Trotskyists, anarchists, ecologists and others, in opposition to the Gulf War. The party had also attempted to initiate more open debate with the left in 1991.

The wisdom of the PCF line has been increasingly demonstrated since the legislative elections of March 1993, which were a massive defeat for the PS. Whereas the PCF showed that it had consolidated its position with over 9 per cent of the vote, the PS slumped from 36 per cent of the vote in 1988 to 19 per cent in 1993. The PS had disappointed millions of those who had transferred their votes to it since 1981, whilst the PCF was busily rebuilding a new left space without its traditional sectarian framework. Its electoral platform included the usual issues, like greater taxation on speculation and capital export, a higher minimum wage, moving towards a 35-hour week and so on, but also rejected any regressive reform of the nationality laws and further urged that the voting rights of immigrants be extended. Most significantly, however, the PCF's approach to the electoral process had changed. Marchais now made a new argument, as Stephen Hopkins has pointed out:

A vote for the PCF should no longer be viewed as an expression of absolute ideological identification; rather, the party should put itself at the service of all those seeking a broad rapprochement of progressive forces, whatever their diverse affiliations.[26]

The leadership also included *refondateurs* on the official party list, underlining the changing attitude towards diverse views within the party.

The overwhelming rejection of the politics of the PS as expressed through their massive electoral defeat created new opportunities for the PCF and their 'strategic aim of "re-balancing" the French left'.[27] Indeed, the election opened a new phase in French politics and returned the PCF to a competitive position that it had not occupied since the breakdown of the Union of the Left.[28]

Changes were also underway within the PCF itself. In June 1993, Marchais proposed that democratic centralism be abandoned as the organizing principle of the party, a change which would give rise to freer debate and discussion within the party. Various commissions were set up to prepare the different aspects of the next congress, a process which itself led to greater decentralization within the party. It was by this point rumoured that Marchais would, in 1994, retire from his post as general secretary and be replaced by Robert Hue. Significant changes were taking place on every front, but in a managed fashion, with the intention of minimizing the damage to the party. In fact, the proposed changes caused confusion in the camp of the dissidents, and further undermined Fiterman's position.

Hue became general secretary in December 1994, and any uncertainty that might have existed about the direction of his leadership was soon resolved – it rapidly became clear that he was going to pursue and strengthen the emerging orientation of the party. Essentially, Hue wanted a more flexible and pragmatic party, but one that certainly remained rooted in the broad labour movement, albeit without its former narrow workerist perspective. His first challenge was the spring 1995 presidential elections, in which he was the party's candidate. The PS eventually put up Lionel Jospin as their candidate, the other major candidates being Chirac and Balladur.

Although the PS had fared disastrously in the legislative elections of 1993, the two subsequent years had begun to turn the tide against right-wing policies under the harsh premiership of Balladur, with the government facing continual popular protests against their harsh economic restructuring. In spite of the PS's recent defeat, therefore, Jospin actually received the highest vote in the first round with just over 20 per cent, Chirac got 18 per cent, Balladur 15 per cent and Hue a respectable 9 per cent of the vote. Chirac cleverly based his campaign on opposition to the ultra-liberal policies of Balladur and spoke about healing the social fractures within France. Chirac went on to win in the second round, although Jospin scored a creditable 47 per cent. Immediately after Chirac's victory, Hue took the position that if Chirac was going to carry out the policies he had proposed during the elections and oppose liberal policies, then the PCF would engage in constructive – rather than blanket – opposition, although there was considerable opposition within the party to this approach. In fact, Chirac immediately did an about-turn and embraced the policies he had so vehemently opposed during the electoral contest.

The PCF then set about rebuilding the left. Hue's first initiative was an appeal to launch a series of forums of the left, with the aim of hammering out a new strategy in the run up to the next legislative elections, which were expected to take place in 1998. The PCF's appeal went out in autumn 1995 and the first forums were held in early 1996, eventually totalling around two hundred in number, nationwide, mostly on a departmental or regional basis. Two were held in Paris, the larger of which was billed as a national event and attracted several thousand people. All the components of the left were invited to these events to discuss the way forward for the left, and they were organized without any preconditions. The most usual line up was PCF, PS, Greens, Radicals, *Mouvement des Citoyens* (a left split from the PS), and one or other trotskyist group, most usually the *Ligue Communiste Revolutionnaire* (LCR), a rather respectable intellectual grouping that constituted the French section of the Fourth International. *Lutte Ouvrière* (LO), the other fairly substantial ultra-left grouping, refused to participate in the forums.

Two factors contributed to the success of the forums. Firstly, it soon became clear that Alain Juppé's government was going to carry out ultra-liberal policies and Chirac had reneged on his electoral pledges. Juppé's plans, for example, for the cost-cutting reform of the social security system, helped to turn public opinion rapidly and strongly against the government and people were actually looking for a framework within which to organize against them. Secondly, a wave of mass demonstrations against the government took off in the autumn and winter of 1995 in almost every town and city. The largest of these, in Paris, was in support of an enormous strike of public sector workers which had huge popular support.

At the peak of the demonstrations, round about two million people were out on the streets against the government. These two factors forced the PS into participating in the forums, thereby guaranteeing that the cooperation forged through them would be a significant factor in the subsequent legislative elections.

The forums took place during the first two-thirds of 1996, following which the PCF launched an initiative for *Rassemblements Populaires* (popular meetings), which would build towards the legislative elections, which were still expected to take place in early 1998. On 21 April 1997, Chirac called the elections for May/June 1997, no doubt expecting to take advantage of a disorganized left, and the left certainly expected to lose.[29] The PS and PCF immediately concluded their discussions on an electoral platform, and on 29 April the *Declaration Commune* was announced. The two parties' positions on Maastricht and the EU were fundamentally different but they agreed that the main issue had to be the fight against both unemployment and ultra-liberal economic policies. These latter two points formed the minimum common position of the agreement, with both parties endorsing a 35-hour week, tax reforms, the creation of 700 000 jobs for young people, a halt to privatizations, and a review of immigration legislation. The election was a victory for the left as a whole, with the PCF increasing its vote slightly to 9.9 per cent and the PS, Radicals and Greens all increasing their vote (see Figure 6.2). The PS did not have an absolute majority, and therefore required the support of the other left parties to form a government.

Considerable discussion took place within the PCF over whether to enter the government or not, with a number of deputies being in favour of staying outside the government and support being granted or not on the basis of each individual measure – similar to the position of the Party of Communist Refoundation *vis-à-vis* the Olive Tree coalition government in Italy.[30] Others, however, including Hue, thought that the PCF should enter the government and after a consultation process with PCF activists, the PCF did so, securing two ministers and one secretary of state. This hesitation was understandable given the negative experience of participation in government in the early 1980s. The balance of forces was different on this occasion, however: the PS did not have an absolute majority – this was a combined left victory; the PCF chose its own ministers whereas previously Mitterrand chose his preferred candidates; the PCF had taken the initiative over the forums which had played a large part in the victory, and the forum participants were basically now the participants in government; the PS had

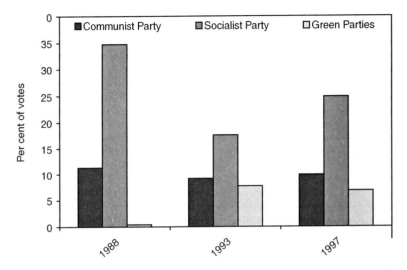

Figure 6.2 Election performance of communist, socialist and green parties in France, 1988–97

agreed the *Déclaration Commune* and the government now had to be constituted on this basis.

The PCF was now in a strong position to put leftwards pressure on the government – a significant victory for the PCF, so few years after most observers had consigned it to the dustbin of history. Hue has proved to be a capable leader and strategist and has been effective in uniting the party around his position, as he still faces criticism from both traditionalists within the party and the remnants of the *refondateurs*, represented by influential figures like the deputies Guy Hermier from Marseilles and François Asensi from Tremblay. Asensi, who is also mayor of Tremblay, publishes his own monthly paper entitled *Futurs*, in which he expounds his views on the obsolescence of political parties and of the state. Since the abandoning of democratic centralism in 1994, it is now legitimate for a party member to publish material that is out of step with the party line.

Following the 1997 legislative elections, the PCF's strategy has emphasized the importance of extra-parliamentary activity to sustain the pressure on the government to stick to the policy approach agreed during the election period – it is considered to be the action of the mass movement that must keep the government on track.

The PCF has also pursued its domestic approach of dialogue with wider left forces on an international level. As well as continuing its traditional relations with other communist parties, offering solidarity to Cuba, and participation, for example, in the World Federation of Democratic Youth, the PCF also participates in the New European Left Forum, the United European Left–Nordic Green Left Group in the European Parliament and has made a number of its own initiatives. In May 1998, the PCF hosted an international symposium in Paris to commemorate the 150th anniversary of the Communist Manifesto. This event was held under the auspices of Espaces Marx, which now goes under the slogan *'Explorer, confronter, innover'*,[31] and was formerly the PCF's Institute de Recherches Marxistes, which has now been opened to wider left forces. The participation of the Trotskyist LCR is notable within Espaces Marx and was also apparent at the Manifesto symposium, where Daniel Bensaïd, a leading LCR member, spoke in the final plenary. The symposium attracted around 700 people from all left perspectives from every continent and another major event is planned for the year 2000, under the title 'Globalization and Human Emancipation'.[32] Working with the LCR – which is a post-1968 new left type organization – on such events, is no doubt intended to draw back a section of the intelligentsia into the orbit of the PCF, having lost much of its support in that sector during the 1980s.

The PCF has also played an increasing role in coordinating the left parties around the question of the direction of Europe. In January 1999, the PCF hosted a press conference in Paris to launch an *appel commun*, signed by 13 European communist and left parties, calling for the construction of Europe to be put onto a new track: social and ecological, democratic, solidaristic and peaceful. Whilst not explicitly a common manifesto for the European parliamentary elections of 1999, the level of agreement reached was the result of numerous high level meeetings over more than a year,[33] and it was, nevertheless, launched to set the common political framework for these parties: 'Our aim is clear: to combine our efforts to contribute to the anchoring of Europe to the left'.[34] The *appel* speaks out against the logic of a Europe united on the neo-liberal terms of Maastricht, with its unemployment and poverty, and, claiming that 'the myth of triumphant capitalism is dispelled', argues for a new orientation, towards the extension of democratic rights, equality of opportunity, an end to racism and prejudice, sustainable development, and against the domination of the United States and the international financial institutions. As the declaration observed: 'The disastrous effects of the global financial crisis on the peoples of the "emerging countries" has revealed the incapacity of the neo-liberal system to respond to the needs of humanity.'[35]

7
Italy

The Party of Communist Refoundation (Partito della Rifondazione Comunista – PRC) is the smaller of the two successor parties to the Italian Communist Party (PCI). Since its foundation in 1991 it has attempted to steer a political course that is anti-capitalist and grounded in working-class militancy, whilst not confining itself to extra-parliamentary activities. Throughout its short existence it has been repeatedly faced – as are the other new European left parties – with the question of whether to compromise its avowed principles to support centre or centre-left governments which are increasingly likely to implement anti-working class policies, or refuse to support such policies and – as the social democrats pose it – risk the election of a right-wing government. The political evolution of PRC has been forced by the pivotal position it has held within the Italian parliament in respect of sustaining centre governments in power.

In fact, PRC has twice split over this question, most recently in October 1998, and it has been possible to see PRC moving to the left, breaking with its previous tradition of the 'Historic Compromise'[1] and resisting the impetus to become just a slightly more militant adjunct of Italian social democracy. PRC has demonstrated a significant capacity for mass mobilization over social issues – for example, 150 000 people turned out onto the streets in Rome in 1995 and 250 000 in Naples in 1996 in response to calls by the party.[2] In its broader political orientation, PRC fits into the international framework of the new European left. It is opposed to both the Maastricht Treaty and NATO, it is a member of the New European Left Forum, and its European Parliamentary deputies belong to the United European Left-Nordic Green Left Group.

In February 1991, the Twentieth Congress of the Italian Communist Party (PCI) relaunched itself as a new party, the Democratic Party of the Left (Partito Democratico della Sinistra – PDS), politically orientated towards the Socialist International. This change, as Newell and Bull point out, was the PCI's 'final renunciation of the desire to achieve any change, however mild, of a structural or irreversible kind, and a removal of any ambiguity surrounding the "anti-system" orientation of the main party of the left.'[3] A minority of the delegates opposed this social democratization of the PCI, and from these opponents – around the orthodox communist Armando Cossutta – came the call to set up the Movement for Communist Refoundation (MRC). This broad grouping, founded with the sole purpose of forming a new communist party, had around 150 000 supporters, including orthodox pro-Soviet communists around Cossutta, militant younger activists who had been supporters of the more radical wing of the PCI under the influence of Pietro Ingrao, and the Magri and Castellini current in the PCI (formerly the new left PDUP).

In May 1991, the MRC held a conference which elected a leadership, with Sergio Garavini as national secretary and Cossutta as president, and embarked on the process of forming a party – the Party of Communist Refoundation, describing itself in its statutes as 'a free political organization of the working class ... of all those inspired by socialist values and marxist thought.'[4] This broad appeal was well-founded, for in June 1991 the PRC was also joined by Proletarian Democracy (Democrazia Proletaria – DP), one of the largest of the Italian extreme left groupings with its origins in the radicalism of the late 1960s and influenced by Maoism and Trotskyism. DP had 9000 members and 1.7 per cent of the vote in the 1987 elections[5] and brought a core of militant activists from a different left tradition to the PRC, including libertarians, ecologists and feminists,[6] ensuring that although initiated by orthodox communists – both Cossutta and Garavini had been supporters of Berlinguer and the 'Historic Compromise' – PRC was to develop as a much more heterogenous and radical party than might have been anticipated. As Newell and Bull point out:

> In effect, the collapse of communism (and the sudden irrelevance of differing interpretations of the nature of the Soviet Union, which had once been the source of implacable hostility between DP and parts of the PCI) brought rapprochement on the left.[7]

PRC also has a strong base in the trade union movement, particularly but not exclusively within the Confederazione Generale Italiana del

Lavoro (CGIL), the trade union confederation traditionally associated with the PCI. General secretary Garavini had himself been deputy leader of the CGIL during the 1970s.

The drawing together of diverse political forces into the PRC was undoubtedly a positive step forward for building a new anti-capitalist left in Italy. Its identity was clear: it was a party for those who, despite the defeats and failures of state socialism, did not accept capitalism as unavoidable and were still advocating communism and a class-struggle orientation. It was, as Livio Maitan observed, 'a party naturally in opposition and from there was drawing an alternative project'.[8] Because of its openness and militancy, PRC did not seem merely like 'a meeting of nostalgics', and in its first two years of existence placed considerable emphasis on building its organization and being present at every level of politics – not only in the towns and cities but also in the villages. PRC appeared, therefore, rather 'as a political formation with a mass audience defending the interests and the demands of the most disadvantaged sectors of Italian society, and which had some electoral significance.'[9]

There were, nevertheless, tensions within PRC about what type of communism was being refounded and how. From the first PRC congress in December 1991, it became apparent that there was a conflict between Cossutta and Garavini over the nature of the refoundation. Cossutta, who had been deputy leader of the PCI in the late 1970s, had combined both an extreme pro-Sovietism – he had been the only member of the PCI central committee who refused to condemn the declaration of martial law in Poland in 1982 – with full support for the cooperation with Christian Democracy in the 1970s. Cossutta did not show any inclination within PRC to analyze the problems and collapse of state socialism. Rather, he appeared to be wedded to the traditional forms of communism and its organizational structures and, as it subsequently became clear, was unable to break from the 'Historic Compromise' framework. Garavini, on the other hand, argued for the PRC to remain an 'area of influence'[10] rather than an organized political party: 'Isn't it true that the cult of organisation has poisoned the lives of generations of communists and blocked open-mindedness, creating armour-plated organisations? We have been fighting for something different.'[11] This perspective was not accepted by the majority of the PRC leadership and so in June 1993, Garavini resigned from his post as national secretary. He was replaced after a period of six months, by Fausto Bertinotti – also a CGIL militant – at PRC's Second Congress in January 1994.

Table 7.1   Results of Italian general elections, 1946–96 (per cent of votes)

	1946	1948	1953	1958	1963	1968	1972
Christian Democratic Party	35.2	48.7	40.1	42.2	38.3	39.1	38.7
Italian Communist Party	18.9	30.7	22.6	22.7	25.3	26.9	27.2
Italian Socialist Party	20.7		12.7	14.2	13.8	14.5	10.7
Italian Democratic Socialist Party		7.1	4.5	4.6	6.1		5.4
Italian Liberal Party	6.8	3.8	3.0	3.5	7.0	5.8	3.9
Italian Republican Party	4.3	2.5	1.6	1.4	1.4	2.0	2.9
Italian Radical Party							
Italian Social Movement		2.1	5.8	4.7	5.1	4.5	9.2
Italian Monarchist Party	2.8	2.8	6.9	4.8	1.7	1.3	
South Tirol People's Party		1.3	0.5	1.0	0.9	1.4	0.5
Val d'Aosta Joint List					0.3	0.3	
Sardinian Action Party		0.4					
Greens							
Proletarian Democracy Party							
Others	11.3	0.4	2.3	0.3		4.5	3.3

	1976	1979	1983	1987	1992	1994	1996
Christian Democratic Party	38.7	38.3	32.9	34.3			
Italian Communist Party	34.4	30.4	29.9	26.6			
Italian Socialist Party	9.6	9.8	11.4	14.3	13.6	2.2	
Italian Democratic Socialist Party	3.4	3.8	4.1	3.0	2.7		
Italian Liberal Party	1.3	1.9	2.9	2.1	2.8		
Italian Republican Party	3.1	3.0	5.1	3.7	4.4		
Italian Radical Party	1.1	3.4	2.2	2.6			
Italian Social Movement	6.1	5.3	6.8	5.9			
Italian Monarchist Party							
South Tirol People's Party	0.5	0.6	0.5	1.4	0.5		
Val d'Aosta Joint List	0.1	0.9	0.4				
Sardinian Action Party		0.1	0.9	0.9			
Greens				2.5	2.8	2.7	2.5
Proletarian Democracy Party		1.4	1.5	1.7			
Democratic Party of the Left					16.1	20.4	21.1
Communist Refoundation Party					5.6	6.0	8.6
Come on Italy (Forza Italia)						21.0	20.6
National alliance						13.5	15.7
Northern League– Federal Italy					8.7	8.4	10.1
Italian Popular Party						11.6	6.8
Segni's Pact						4.6	
Others	1.1	2.0	0.9	0.4	4.6	7.0	2.5

Adapted from: *Elections since 1945: A Worldwide Reference Compendium* (London: Longman, 1989).

At the same time, however, that PRC was attempting to orientate itself politically, establish itself within Italian politics and consolidate what it could of the communist electorate and industrial base, the whole structure of Italian politics, as it had existed since the second world war, was beginning to fall apart (see Table 7.1). Italian political life was riddled with corruption, crime and Mafia connections and the emergence of new parties in the early 1990s, the disappearance of others and a restructuring of the electoral system, was largely a result of the crisis provoked by this untenable situation. Furthermore, structural change was now possible, because the completion of the PCI's transition to social democracy meant that its exclusion from government was no longer a pre-requisite of the functioning of the electoral and political systems.

In the general election of 1992, the PDS took 16.1 per cent of the vote as compared with the PCI's 26.6 per cent of the vote in 1987. PRC took 5.6 per cent of the vote (see Figures 7.1 and 7.2). However, a significant development was the increase in votes for the Northern League (Lega Nord – LN) from 0.5 to 8.7 per cent. LN, a so-called 'movement party' under the leadership of Umberto Bossi, based in northern Italy, argued that corrupt politicians in Rome were using the tax system to bleed the north dry to pay for votes in the south, thus

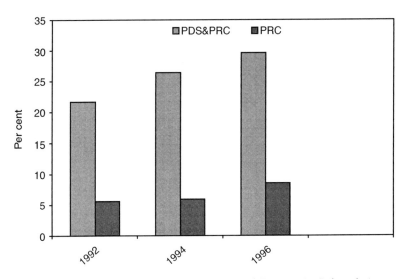

PDS = Democratic Party of the Left; PRC = Party of Communist Refoundation.

Figure 7.1 Election performance of the Italian left, 1992–96

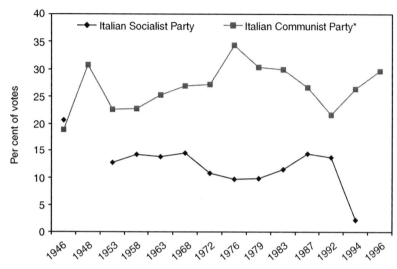

*Votes for the Communist Party from 1992–96 are sums of those won by the Democratic Party of the Left and the Party of Communist Refoundation

Figure 7.2   Election performance of socialist and communist parties in Italy, 1946–96

necessitating a federal system. LN was able to win increasing support basically on an anti-corruption ticket.

Another new political force was La Rete (the Network), whose leaders came from within Christian Democracy, and was a broad range of Catholic left and liberal forces. It saw itself as a 'movement for democracy' and a campaigning force against the influence of organized crime in Italian politics, including the end of parliamentary immunity and a strengthening of the judiciary in the struggle against the Mafia.[12] The following two years, leading up to the general election of 1994, saw the collapse of the existing party system.

In 1992, a series of investigations, known as *Mani Pulite* – 'clean hands' – led to the exposure of huge payments by companies to political parties in exchange for public works contracts. These escalating and constantly unfolding revelations, known as *Tangentopoli* – 'Bribe City' – had a huge impact on Italian politics, not only because of public disgust at these revelations, but also because it financially weakened or in some cases bankrupted parties who had relied on these deals for their funding. By the end of 1993, the former governing parties, Christian Democracy (DC) and the Italian Socialist Party (PSI) were fragmented and destroyed by *Tangentopoli* (see Figure 7.2). At the same time new structures were being created through changes in the electoral laws, brought about by the referendum movement which campaigned for eight referenda on election procedures. These referenda took place in April 1993 and led to the construction of a new electoral system, where three-quarters of both houses of parliament are elected in single-member constituencies on a first-past-the-post basis, and the remaining one-quarter are elected by proportional representation in multi-member constituencies. The electoral threshold for parliamentary representation was 4 per cent. The result of the introduction of such a system was to push parties to cooperate or form electoral alliances to gain sufficient votes to win seats. The new system was in place for the local elections of December 1993, which were a victory for the left, campaigning under the banner of the Progressive Alliance, led by the PDS and including PRC, the Greens, the newly-formed Democratic Alliance and La Rete. The PDS took 103 out of the possible 221 mayoral posts, the DC took only nine and dissolved itself in January 1994.

At its Second Congress in January 1994, the PRC debated its position for the forthcoming general election in March 1994 and decided by a majority of 70 per cent to again participate in the Progressive Alliance. However, the December victory of the left was not to be repeated in the March elections. The rapid emergence of Forza Italia, a new right-wing party created by media mogul Silvio Berlusconi, significantly changed the political dynamic. Berlusconi put together a right-wing alliance with LN in the north of Italy and the neo-fascist National Alliance (AN) in the south, which won 46 per cent of the vote, securing an overall majority in the Chamber of Deputies and constituting the largest block in the Senate. Berlusconi became prime minister.

The result of the election led to a widening gap between the PRC and PDS, as the PDS leaders considered in retrospect that they should have moved further into the centre ground of politics, whereas PRC, under the new leadership of Bertinotti, radicalized its orientation and became a resolutely oppositional party.[13] Indeed, although Berlusconi faced problems concerning the relationship of his business interests to his political position, it was actually a conflict with the organized labour movement that removed Berlusconi from office, and one in which the PRC played a significant role. Berlusconi embarked on a course of reducing public sector spending in order to fulfil the Maastricht criteria for participation in economic and monetary union and in particular, he sought to reduce government spending on pensions which amounted to almost half of social expenditure.

Pension levels, which were amongst the highest in Europe, were index-linked to the cost of living to maintain their real value, and were seen as a real benefit to the working class which had to be defended. Berlusconi's proposals for the 1995 budget included massive cuts in welfare spending, including attacks on the pension system. On 12 October 1994, the month after the announcement of the proposals, ten million workers made a four-hour general strike in protest, and in November over one million demonstrated against the cuts in Rome. Berlusconi was completely opposed to negotiating with the unions, but was eventually forced to do so on the eve of a second planned general strike on 2 December. An agreement was reached and the strike was called off, but Berlusconi now faced opposition within his own coalition and resigned from office.

Berlusconi was succeeded by Lamberto Dini, who had been Berlusconi's finance minister and was a former director of the Bank of Italy. Dini's so-called 'technical' cabinet included no deputies and governed for fifteen months, with the specific aim of introducing pension reform. Dini negotiated a modified version of the pension reform and in this process was supported in parliament by the LN, the Italian Popular Party (PPI) – a successor party to DC, and the PDS, the latter now trying to capture the centre ground that had been disaffected by Berlusconi's extremism. The PRC, however, was generally hostile to the Dini government, recognising that the moderated reform was just a more gradual process towards the same ends as Berlusconi's attacks.

The maintenance of this position, however, caused a split within the PRC. About a quarter of the leadership of the PRC, 16 out of its 57 parliamentarians and two out of its five deputies in the European parliament, including former-secretary Garavini, Lucio Magri, Luciana Castellini, Luciano Pettinari and Famiano Crucianelli, who all had leading positions in the party or in the parliamentary group, broke with the majority position of the PRC and formed the United Communists (Comunisti Unitari – CU).[14] The split had little impact, however, on the party activists, with only around 400 members leaving. The deputies that formed CU supported the vote of confidence for Dini's centre-right government, in spite of its attacks on pensions and social spending, because it was under attack from the more right wing forces of the AN and Forza Italia. CU subsequently moved closer to the PDS, supporting the project of its leader Massimo D'Alema to constitute the PDS as a single federated party of the left. Indeed, in the following elections of 1996, CU ran within the Olive Tree centre-left coalition (Ulivo) led by the PDS, and two of its eight deputies were elected on the PDS-European left list in the proportional representation section.

PRC proceeded in opposition to build its influence and its capacity to mobilize and, indeed, its standing as the only party of the left prepared to defend working class living standards – although its abstention in parliament did on one occasion allow Dini's government to survive a vote of no-confidence.[15] On this basis PRC decided that, for the general election of April 1996, it would campaign on the platform of 'class struggle' under the slogan 'Rinasca la speranza' – 'hope is reborn'. The programme of the PRC was differentiated from the positions of the Olive Tree coalition on all major issues: economic policies, institutional reform, foreign policy, education and so on. Key policies included: full employment based on a 35-hour week with no loss of wages; the linking of wages to a cost of living index; progressive changes to the tax system; the economic development of southern Italy; an end to privatization and a commitment to public ownership; defence of pensions and the health service; defence of state education; public sector dominance of television; defence of the environment; the maintenance and increase of public sector housing; the extension of democracy, including in the workplace; an international policy of peace and coexistence, including the cancellation of third world debt.[16] The strategy of PRC, as it emerged at the general election, was for the PRC to push a government of the 'moderate-left' – that is, one dominated by the PDS – further to the left by the strength of its own position. As PRC's election handbook for party activists pointed out:

> Re-starting from the left also means giving back to the moderate left a space for political and social initiatives linked to the representation of popular demands. But the moderate left will be forced to choose this the stronger Communist Refoundation is. A vote for the communists is therefore doubly useful: it is useful in beating the right and to give direction and spirit to an alternative strategy.[17]

The Olive Tree coalition clearly showed the desire of the PDS to gain the centre ground in Italian politics: although the PDS was by far the largest force within it, it also included the Greens, the PPI (formerly part of Christian Democracy) and Italian Renewal (Rinnovamento Italiano – RI), a new party led by former prime minister Dini. So whilst the PRC scorned the idea of participation within the coalition, the Olive Tree coalition itself certainly did not wish to have PRC within its ranks. However, PRC did engage in a stand-down arrangement with the coalition, which allowed PRC to contest 27 seats in the Chamber of Deputies without competition from the centre-left and 17 in the Senate, in exchange for not contesting against Olive Tree candidates in other constituencies.[18] In this way, it would not allow right-wing candidates to be elected by splitting the left and centre-left vote. Because of this arrangement – and because the LN ran alone and did not participate in the right-wing alliance, the centre-left was able to win the election, even though the parties of the centre-right achieved a greater proportion of the vote than they had in 1994.[19] This arrangement suited PRC because at this point their position was that they did not want to participate in government or a parliamentary majority, but were prepared to see Romano Prodi – the former Christian Democrat leader of the Olive Tree coalition – become prime minister, and they would vote on each individual issue as they saw politically fit.[20]

The election results gave the Olive Tree coalition the largest block of seats in both houses of parliament, although with 284 out of a possible 630 seats in the Chamber of Deputies, the government did indeed have to rely on the votes of PRC, who held 35 seats, or 8.6 per cent of the votes – a million vote increase on its previous general election performance of 5.6 per cent. Thus PRC became decisive in the Chamber of Deputies, and this led to a change in orientation in the leadership of PRC. In June 1996, the PRC declared that it was now part of the parliamentary majority and engaged in a policy of 'critical support' for the government, sustaining it in power, whilst 'slowing down privatization, forcing more taxation and less social spending cuts, protecting pensions and so on.'[21] This position resulted in intense criticism being levelled at the PRC leadership from a small minority within the party, particularly those grouped around the Trotskyist, Livio Maitan, who felt that excessive compromise was being made with the Prodi government.

This issue was debated at the Third Congress of PRC in December 1996. Bertinotti defended the positions both of opposition to the Dini government and of critical support for the Prodi government, describing the general approach as a 'unity-radicality pairing' which has prevented the PRC from being 'either an appendage of the PDS or a ghettoised minority bereft of any political project'.[22] Bertinotti argued that PRC had been able to influence the government over the budget – that it didn't touch health spending or pensions, and that instead of public spending cuts, a progressive income tax had been introduced and measures taken against tax evasion. It was not enough, argued Bertinotti, but these were steps on the path away from neo-liberalism.

The opposition motion argued that 'the Prodi government is committed to completing the process of inserting Italian capitalism into the Europe of Maastricht' and that the forthcoming budget was 'a widespread and well-targeted attack on the working masses',[23] which included privatization, cuts in education, health, local government, employment, public employment and housing. PRC, it argued, should go back into opposition and resistance, representing the interests of the workers, young people, old people and the population of the underdeveloped south of Italy. The Prodi government, it argued, brought together two trends:

1. the strategic choice of the prevailing section of the Italian bourgeoisie which, squeezed by the crisis and international competition, judges that further sacrifices require the cooption of the unions and the PDS; and
2. the governmental ambitions of the PDS, which offers itself as the political guarantor of social consensus.[24]

The Bertinotti/Cossutta position won a majority of 85 per cent support at the Congress, with the opposition motion, associated with Livio Maitan securing 15 per cent. This issue continued to be debated, however, over the following months, until the majority around Bertinotti finally shifted positions in autumn 1998, withdrawing support from the Prodi government over the budget proposals for 1999. Withdrawal of support was first mooted by the leadership majority in early October 1997, however, when PRC stated that it would vote against the 1998 budget proposals, which included massive government spending cuts of around 25 trillion lire (9 billion pounds) – including 5 trillion lire cuts in welfare spending, particularly targeted at the pension system. Amidst widespread speculation that this crisis would derail Italian plans to join EMU and lead to an immediate general election and a new victory for Berlusconi and the right, Bertinotti and Prodi entered protracted talks to try and achieve an acceptable compromise.

After six days of talks, no agreement was reached, so, deprived of a parliamentary majority to pass his 1998 budget, Prodi resigned. PRC was not prepared, however, for the intensive media attacks or hostile criticism that it received from the PDS, or sufficiently politically united over the wisdom of the position, to carry through its withdrawal of support. Shortly afterwards PRC reversed its position, having accepted a government commitment to introduce a 35-hour week in the year 2001 and a modification of the cuts in the pension system, and Prodi was reinstated.

This incident demonstrated the contradiction of PRC's position and led to increased division and eventual polarization of positions within PRC's leadership during 1998, particularly between Cossutta and Bertinotti, with the latter expressing increasing concern over PRC's support of the government. During this period, the PDS had also been undergoing further political change – at its Congress in January 1998 the party was renamed Democratic Left (DS) – part of d'Alema's project to completely distance the PDS from its communist past and create a broader centre-left grouping. The hammer and sickle was also finally removed from the party's symbol.[25] During June and July 1998, Bertinotti launched an offensive within the national political committee of PRC, insisting that PRC demand a turn by the government on socioeconomic issues.[26] If such a turn did not materialize, Bertinotti argued, then PRC should break with the government. Although the committee accepted Bertinotti's formula, an open and sharp debate rapidly ensued in the press between the supporters of Cossutta who did not wish to leave the government majority, and the supporters of Bertinotti who were preparing for a rupture with the Olive Tree government. Cossutta recognised that the kind of concessions made over the budget did not constitute a 'turn' by the government and agreed in principle that with a centre-left government in power, a communist party should be in opposition, but stated that the overwhelming consideration was to avoid the return to power of Berlusconi.[27]

In October 1998, the central committee supported Bertinotti's view that the 1999 budget – and also the government – should be voted down unless Prodi was prepared to make significant concessions – to make a socioeconomic 'turn'. However, Cossutta and the majority of the PRC deputies in the Chamber of Deputies refused to vote against the government – Cossutta himself had resigned as president of the party in order to more easily ignore the discipline of the central committee: 'As a simple deputy who is no longer president of his party, I can now express my total contempt for the decision that has been taken...I will do everything I can to avoid a crisis for this government.'[28] Cossutta and his supporters publicly condemned Bertinotti as 'irresponsible' and 'adventurist'.[29] On 18 October,

Cossutta and around 3000 supporters held the founding meeting of a new communist party, the Party of Italian Communists,[30] but although a significant number of elected representatives supported Cossutta's position, it appears to have won very limited support amongst the rank-and-file – 3000 is a very small proportion of the party's 125 000 membership. Cossutta has declared that the political and ideological basis of the new party is continuity with the approach of Togliatti, and he has reproached Bertinotti, and even more so members like Maitan, for not belonging to the old tradition of the PCI – presumably the historic compromise which brought nothing to the PCI and the Italian working class. Indeed, Cossutta made some play of the increased cooperation and political convergence between Bertinotti and Maitan – from the Italian section of the Trotskyist Fourth International, now inside PRC.

With Cossutta and his supporters voting for the government, the Olive Tree coalition was able to maintain itself in power, although Prodi departed from the premiership and was replaced by DS leader Massimo d'Alema. The impact of these events on PRC's electorate is not yet known, but they will have a significant impact on the party itself. The balance which existed previously between the continuity of the old PCI, those from the extreme and new-left currents, from feminist and environmental backgrounds, and from newly-active youth with no political past, has now been radically changed. Consequently, as Maitan himself observes,

> what Cossutta used to call, quite rightly, the 'Togliatti culture' – the approaches and conceptions inspired by a moderate gradualism of the traditional social democratic type, favouring institutional action and blurring class division – will have lost, following the split, most – if not all – of its supporters.[31]

This 'Togliatti culture' no longer has any supporters in the party's secretariat.

The likely orientation of PRC is towards strengthening its links with grassroots and social movements which have been somewhat neglected since 1996, towards rebuilding the militant left in the CGIL which has suffered through the compromise culture of the Olive Tree period and towards reconsolidating its project to build a new hegemony on the left. The field lies open to PRC, for as d'Alema and DS aim to capture the centre ground, PRC is the only party with a record of attempting – through its defence of pensions, its mass mobilizations against unemployment and its efforts towards a 35-hour working week – to defend and improve the living standards of ordinary Italians. Furthermore, it has been able to argue a coherent political case for the building of a united Europe on a social and equitable basis, rather than on the neo-liberal framework of Maastricht, and through its links and activities with NELF and UEL-NGL has been able to demonstrate that refounded Italian communism is not a 'meeting of nostalgics', but a dynamic political force.

8
Spain

The United Left (Izquierda Unida – IU), was founded in 1986, as a political alliance drawing together a range of forces to the left of the Spanish Socialist Workers' Party (PSOE) which ruled Spain from 1982 to 1996 (see Table 8.1). IU describes itself as 'clearly situated amongst the forces which want to build democratic socialism', and defines itself, ideologically, partly on the basis of its critiques: of so-called 'really existing' socialism which it denies was socialist, of social democracy for its incapacity to transform capitalist society and of capitalism for its reduction of democracy to the ballot box. It stands in favour of a new form of internationalism based on solidarity and wishes to renew the traditional programme of the left incorporating ecological concerns, feminism, pacifism and cultural liberation.[1] Its current programme, agreed in 1994, highlights a 'triple alternative', of government, state and society:

- firstly, political reform, which stresses improved proportional representation systems and greater democratization of the media and the judiciary;
- secondly, the extension of democratic control in the economy and in the work place; and
- thirdly, the reform of the state, with greater citizens' control over the political process.

The IU's support has grown steadily since its foundation in 1986, when it gained 4.7 per cent in the general election of that year, to 10.5 per cent in the general election of 1996 (see Figure 8.1). It shares common positions with other new left forces in western Europe, most notably its opposition to the Maastricht Treaty, and is an active member of both

111

Table 8.1 Results of Spanish general elections, 1977–96 (per cent of votes)

	1977	1979	1982	1986	1989	1993	1996
Union of the Democratic Centre (UCD)	34.3	35.0	7.3				
Spanish Socialist Workers Party (PSOE)	30.5	30.5	46.1	44.3	34.3	33.6	31.8
Socialist Party of Catalonia (PSC) & PSOE					5.5	5.5	6.2
Communist Party of Spain (PCE)	9.3	10.8	4.0				
Popular Alliance (AP)/Popular Democratic Party (PDP)	8.2	5.8	25.4	26.2			
Democratic and Social Centre (CDS)			2.9	9.3	7.9		
Convergence and Union Coalition (CIU)		2.7	3.7	5.0	5.1	5.0	4.6
Basque Nationalist Party (PNV)	1.7	1.5	1.9	1.5	1.2	1.2	1.3
Basque Left (EE)	0.3	0.5	0.5	0.5	0.5		
United People (HB)		1.0	1.0	1.2	1.1	0.9	0.7
Peoples Party (PP)					25.1	34.6	38.9
Izquierda Unida (IU)				4.6	9.1	9.6	10.5

Adapted from: *Elections since 1945: A Worldwide Reference Compendium* (London: Longman, 1989).

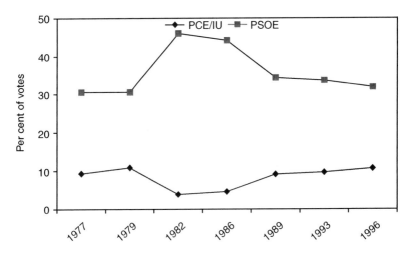

PCE = Communist Party of Spain; IU = United Left; PSOE = Spanish Socialist
Workers Party.

Figure 8.1 Election performance of socialist and communist parties in Spain,
1977–96

the New European Left Forum and the UEL–NGL group in the
European parliament.

The IU was founded towards the end of the first term of office of the
PSOE, Spain's main social democratic party. PSOE had been elected by
a large majority in October 1982 – the first left government in Spain
since the 1930s – but its right-wing political orientation in government
did not live up to its electoral promises. It was this disappointment in
the socialist government which led the Spanish Communist Party
(PCE), with a number of smaller parties, to take the initiative to set up
the IU, despite the parlous state of its own organization in the early
1980s.

In 1977, following the death of General Franco and the end of the
right-wing dictatorship which had been in place in Spain since the
Civil War in the 1930s, the PCE was legalized. Although it had
undoubted prestige for its courageous and clandestine opposition to
the dictatorship, it failed, however, to translate this into electoral
support. Instead of becoming Spain's largest left-wing force, it found
itself trailing behind PSOE in the polls, because in the late 1970s it had
pursued a line of considerable compromise and cooperation with the
conservative government of Adolfo Suárez, and had been outflanked

on the left by the PSOE. Without pressing for concessions to be made to the labour movement – which, arguably it could have won, because of its high standing – the PCE accepted the restoration of the monarchy and supported restrictive trade union legislation. This allowed the PSOE – funded by the Socialist International and the German SPD during the 1970s – to emerge as the more radical of the two forces. The 1982 election – a huge victory for the socialists, under the leadership of Felipe González, was a disaster for the PCE – it polled only 4 per cent of the vote, down from 9.3 per cent in 1977.

This electoral catastrophe led to a crisis within the PCE which forced significant political divisions within the party out into the open, for many within the PCE opposed what they considered to be the rightist line pursued during the late 1970s. The PCE's leader was Santiago Carrillo, one of the chief proponents of Eurocommunism and the architect of the line of rapprochement and cooperation with the right. His leadership and political orientation had created significant problems within the PCE and there were two main groupings within the party which opposed him. The first was a straightforward right–left split over the political direction of the party – over Eurocommunism and attitudes towards the Soviet Union. The second was based on a repudiation of Carrillo's authoritarian style of leadership within the party, and a group of *renovadores* (renovators) who agreed with his political line but wished to democratize the party also sought his replacement.

Thus Carrillo, held responsible for the catastrophic decline of the party, and opposed from all sides, stood down from office after the 1982 election disaster, in favour of his protégé, Gerardo Iglesias, whom he hoped to be able to manipulate or perhaps use as a stop-gap leader before his own eventual restoration. Iglesias, in fact, refused to play this role and began to work closely with the *renovadores*. Carrillo subsequently left to form his own group, the 'Mesa para la Unidad de los Comunistas'. This, transformed into the Spanish Labour Party, received virtually no popular support – 0.4 per cent of the general election vote in 1989 – and subsequently joined the PSOE in October 1991. Carrillo moved to the right through Eurocommunism to social democracy, like the majority of the Italian Communist movement with which he had close links in the 1970s, and he made his position completely clear in September 1991: 'the Communist movement as such has completed its historical cycle and it makes no sense trying to prolong it'.[2]

The crisis of the PCE in the early 1980s gave rise to two other new organizations: on the left, there was a pro-Soviet split, the Communist

Party of the Peoples of Spain (PCPE) led by Ignacio Gallego, who definitively rejected the PCE's Eurocommunist course; and on the right, the Progressive Federation (FP) was founded, under the leadership of Ramón Tamames, by *renovadores* who had resigned from the PCE or had been expelled by Carrillo. The PCE emerged from the crisis as somewhat more politically homogeneous than before, but in urgent need of reestablishing its political role in Spanish society.

From 1984, the PCE began to advocate a process of convergence with other left forces, but the real opportunity for the PCE to overcome its isolation and develop this approach came in 1985 as a result of a *volte face* by the PSOE government. When in opposition, PSOE had promised that if elected, it would hold a referendum on Spain's membership of NATO, a controversial decision which had been made by the PSOE's right-wing predecessors in government. Rapidly moving to the right once in government, PSOE now favoured Spain's membership of NATO and tried to renege on its electoral promise of a referendum. A huge anti-NATO movement rapidly developed, which was given leadership by 'La Plataforma Cívica para la Salida de la OTAN',[3] which included the PCE and its trade union allies, the PCPE, the FP and various other smaller groups, with the exception of Carrillo's group which refused to associate with the campaign.

Whilst the referendum was lost in March 1986, the campaign had won nearly seven million 'no' votes, and had galvanized the left into united action. This led many of the forces in the coalition to attempt to prolong this unity and try and convert some of the referendum 'no' votes into anti-PSOE votes in the imminent general election. To this end, the IU was created in April 1986, less than two months before the June 1986 general election, 'embracing the principal groupings associated with the Plataforma Cívica'.[4] The main components of the IU in 1986 were: the PCE; the PCPE; the Socialist Action Party (PASOC) – primarily formed from left dissidents from the PSOE and led by Alonso Puerta; the Progressive Federation (FP) – the small grouping comprised of former members of the PCE led by Ramón Tamames; the Republican Left (IR) – the much reduced remnants of the movement from the 1930s; and the small and inconsequential Carlist and Humanist parties. The election results were not promising – the IU took 4.6 per cent of the vote but, nevertheless, the PCE remained committed to the IU and the following three years saw the consolidation of its membership and its emergence as a serious force on the left. The Carlists and Humanists left in November 1986, the FP left in 1988 and joined Adolfo Suárez' Social and Democratic Centre (CDS) party, and in 1989 a substantial part of the PCPE rejoined the PCE. By the end of the decade, the main component organizations of the IU were the PCE and PASOC.

By the late 1980s, the PSOE's neo-liberal economic policies were giving rise to massive popular dissatisfaction and creating the conditions which would increase the support for a political force to its left advocating the defence of workers' living standards. In February 1988 the two major trade union confederations, the socialist General Workers' Union (UGT) and the communist-led Workers' Commissions under the leadership of Antonio Gutiérrez, signed an eleven point 'united action' agreement and 'embarked upon a series of strikes and protests designed to bring about a "social shift" in government policy'.[5] A huge general strike in December 1988, backed by the IU, indicated that trade union votes for PSOE might not be so secure.

This proved to be correct, for in the general elections of 1989, IU almost doubled its support to 9.1 per cent, becoming Spain's third largest national political force, displacing the CDS from that position. Furthermore, as Gillespie points out:

> IU's additional 920 000 votes were obtained chiefly in industrial and working-class areas where the Socialist Party lost support heavily, although to a limited extent the PSOE compensated for these losses by winning new seats in more conservative parts of Spain.[6]

The political map was now becoming clearer: the PSOE had taken up the centre ground in Spanish politics, and the IU was increasingly occupying the space to its left.

Through this process of campaigning and mass activism and a reorientation away from Eurocommunist compromises with the centre parties, the PCE was clearly moving to the left and was able to consolidate itself in a more left position during the late 1980s, particularly after the election of a new leader in February 1988, when Julio Anguita succeeded Iglesias as general secretary of the PCE. Anguita came from Andalucía, the Spanish region where the IU was strongest – it took 18 per cent of the vote there in the regional elections in June 1986 – and had been mayor of Córdoba, where the communists received 58 per cent of the vote in the municipal elections of 1983. Anguita took a clear and non-sectarian view that the IU was 'a popular and not overwhelmingly communist project,' and that it constituted a strategy for the left rather than merely being of tactical benefit to the PCE.[7] This position indicated Anguita's commitment to the IU project as the way forward for the Spanish left, and was to direct his approach after he succeeded Iglesias as president of the IU in October 1989.

Anguita was not unconcerned about the development of the PCE, however, rather taking the view that a strong PCE was needed within a strong and united IU. Most significantly, Anguita gave the PCE a much stronger left profile, reversing the image of the party which continued from the Carrillo years and attempting to reinvigorate the PCE as a Marxist party which would be a stable force within the IU. He had supported Gorbachev in his early period when he appeared to be attempting to renew Marxism and the soviet system, but subsequently took a position closer to those of Cunhal of Portugal and Marchais of France when the likely outcome of the Gorbachev reforms became clear. He also favoured the encouragement of militancy and political strikes, and rejected collaboration with the PSOE.[8]

This turn to the left had an important impact on communist unity as well as for the strategic development of the IU. In 1989, the majority of the left-wing PCPE and its leadership, including Ignacio Gallego, reunited with the PCE, now considering it to have returned to its course as a Marxist party. This orientation of the PCE and its concurrent impact on the IU was to secure its political relevance and growth in the 1990s and its position as the major political force to the left of social democracy. This trajectory was confirmed in 1991 when the IU opposed Spanish involvement in the Gulf War, decisively breaking with Gorbachev, and has remained the majority position subsequently. Anguita has maintained both the PCE and the IU on a left course, despite the attempts by minorities both within the PCE to dissolve the party, and within the IU to support the Maastricht Treaty, and take the IU unambiguously into the orbit of the PSOE.

In fact, the history of the IU in the 1990s has been dominated by the attempts of various minorities to drive the PCE – still the fundamental core of the IU – off its Marxist course, and to push the IU away from its distinctive democratic socialist perspective.

The first challenge to this perspective came at the Thirteenth Congress of the PCE in December 1991 where an attempt by the *renovadores* to dissolve the PCE was defeated by 75 per cent to 25 per cent of the delegates. Their intention was to reconstitute the IU as a broader left party rather than as an umbrella organization with a Marxist party at its core; it could then more easily be drawn into a social democratic framework. In fact, the Congress adopted a position to maintain the PCE but as a party which would conduct its political work only through the IU and would forsake an independent role in

Spanish politics. The dissolutionists, gathered around Francisco Palero and Juan Berga, then proceeded to continue this struggle within IU, which they also lost. They were to become the most numerous forces in Nueva Izquierda (NI), the right-wing current in IU formed from its Third Federal Assembly.[9] Whilst the question of the status of the IU continued to be debated, the crucial division that emerged at the Third Federal Assembly of the IU in May 1992 was over the Maastricht Treaty. The right-wing forces within IU, under the leadership of Nicolás Sartorius, attempted to push IU onto a line of support for the Maastricht Treaty – a position that was defeated by 60 to 40 per cent of delegates. The majority, under the leadership of Anguita, were intensely hostile to the Treaty – objecting to its neoliberal orientation and what they described as its democratic deficit. Other disagreements between the two groups, such as differing analyses of the collapse of communism in eastern Europe were permitted to coexist, but nevertheless shed light on the nature of the divide between the groupings: the majority termed it 'a historic frustration', whilst the minority described it as 'a relief'.[10] Although having been defeated, the pro-Maastricht minority decided to form a current within the IU called New Left (Nueva Izquierda – NI), to continue to fight for their position within the organization.

1992 saw the peak of the influence of the NI current within IU, particularly because it was overly represented amongst the IU's elected public representatives. Around half of the IU's parliamentary group were supporters of NI, which was clearly demonstrated in the October 1992 vote on the Maastricht Treaty: eight of the 17 IU deputies went against the IU line of abstention and voted 'yes', of which three were from the IU's sister organization, Initiative for Catalonia (Iniciativa per Catalunya – IC). The NI held its first congress, shortly after the crucial Maastricht vote, in November 1992, but internal divisions emerged almost immediately. The NI was comprised of two major groupings as well as a number of independents: the PCE *renovadores*, and PASOC, the Party of Socialist Action, the second largest grouping within the IU. PASOC was formed in 1982 by the fusion of a section of the historic PSOE which had refused to accept González' leadership in 1972, with a left current from the PSOE led by Alonso Puerta, a leading figure in the PSOE who was expelled for opposing corruption.[11]

In 1990, PASOC was further reinforced by a small group of PSOE members, including two notable figures from the party's left wing, Francisco Bustelo and Pablo Castellano. In fact, PASOC has continued to attract left-wing members of PSOE who have become disillusioned with its policies. In 1992, PASOC participated in the creation of NI, along with independents and currents from the PCE favourable to its dissolution. With the latter, which it described as 'socialists of the PCE', PASOC at first attempted to constitute a socialist counterbalance to the influence of the PCE inside the IU,[12] but by 1994 the PASOC leaders broke with the PCE grouping in the NI, and moved back into Anguita's political framework, explaining that they refused to be a staging post for a fraction of the PCE on its way to the PSOE.[13]

This move towards greater support for Anguita's leadership was also partly the result of favourable election results: in the legislative elections of June 1993, the IU polled 9.6 per cent of the vote and in the Euroelections of June 1994, achieved 13.6 per cent, which led the IU leadership, in July 1994, to express the idea of 'il sorpasso' – the electoral overtaking of the PSOE.[14] The move towards greater unity was also, however, the result of a systematic attempt by Anguita to reintegrate the minority forces and win them for the majority position, most notably the heads of regional parties and federations who were often members of the PCE and of PASOC. Anguita succeeded almost entirely in winning them back. Thus by 1994, the core leadership of the NI was reduced to a handful of historical figures from within the PCE and a number of independents who had previously been in the PCE.

At the Fourth Federal Assembly of the IU in December 1994, therefore, Anguita's position was considerably strengthened. The NI, although significantly weakened, did maintain a profile, constituting the majority of delegates from the Valencia region, from Galicia, and Castilla-La Mancha, with seven per cent of delegates from Madrid and ten per cent in Andalucía.

A significant political force, sharing common positions with the right wing of IU, and in sympathy with the NI forces, was Initiative for Catalonia, the associated organization of the IU in Catalonia, whose deputies voted for the Maastricht Treaty. IC was founded in 1987 and had some close parallels to the development of the IU, particularly in relation to the communist forces. In the same way that the left-wing PCPE split from the Eurocommunist PCE, so the left-wing Catalan Communist Party (PCC) split from the Eurocommunist PSUC in 1982, associating itself closely with the PCPE. The PSUC was the initiator of the IC and was initially joined by the PCC, left Catalan nationalists and various independents. By the mid 1990s, the IC was also politically divided along similar lines to the divisions in the IU, although their numerical positions were reversed.

At the 1993 IC congress, approximately 65 per cent of delegates supported the positions of Rafael Ribó, an old Eurocommunist close to the NI. They took a pro-Maastricht position, favouring privileged relations with PSOE and making electoral pacts with PSOE contrary to the position of the IU in the rest of Spain. The remaining 35 per cent of IC was on the left, the most significant part being the Left Platform, with a political position equivalent to that of Anguita in the IU. Its main leaders came from the Workers' Commissions, and it had the support of around 20 per cent of delegates. IC obviously looked favourably upon the founding of the NI, as they had common political positions, but, as IC was an associated organization and not a full member, it was not entitled to join an internal current.

Although the division in the IU emerged initially over the Maastricht Treaty, the underlying issue was clearly whether they should exist as a force to the left of the PSOE or not and what relations they should have with the PSOE. Indeed, the Spanish press openly discussed the issue, describing the NI as 'submarines' for PSOE within the IU, with particular reference to Nicolás Sartorius, who was known to have very close relations with PSOE. This issue was the crucial debate at the IU Fourth Assembly in December 1994. As the official report to the Assembly stated, when discussing the disputes within IU, 'the formal reason for the division was the Maastricht Treaty. Nevertheless, it was nothing else than the concretisation, by reduction, of a more important divergence: our policy towards alliances'.[15] Whilst taking a moderate position on this issue in his formal speech, Anguita subsequently asserted in the debate that for him there was no difference between the right and those who practised the policy of the right – a clear reference to the PSOE.[16] Although the minority positions were again defeated, a further crisis was to erupt within the IU over relations with PSOE, leading to an internal struggle to finally clarify the left positions of the IU.

The catalyst for the crisis was the defeat of PSOE in the general elections of May 1996 by the Popular Party (Partido Popular – PP) led by José Maria Aznar, which then, in coalition with right-wing nationalists, formed Spain's first conservative government since the PSOE victory in 1982. The IU again increased its vote, to 10.5 per cent (see Figure 8.2), but nevertheless, this ended the IU's 'sorpasso' policy of overtaking the PSOE, and generated a debate, followed by real decisions posed by regional elections, about how to relate to the PSOE in opposition. The position of the IU leadership was that they are not opposed in principle to forging an alliance with the PSOE to

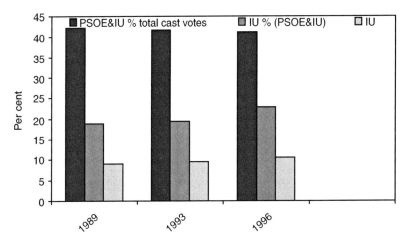

PSOE = Spanish Socialist Workers Party   IU = United Left

Figure 8.2   Election performance of the Spanish left, 1989–96

form a new left majority – but the alliance has to be on the right political terms. The IU wishes to use an alliance to push PSOE to the left.

A minority within the IU, however, wished to pursue, and indeed actively pursued, alliances with the PSOE without pressing for any political change from PSOE – in spite of the fact that PSOE was facing investigation for corruption and the abduction, torture and murder of suspected ETA supporters[17] – basically because they agreed with PSOE politics. This minority within the IU was the Democratic Party of the New Left (Partido Democratico de la Nueva Izquierda – PDNI), the former NI minority current, defeated at the Fourth Congress, reincarnated as a party within IU and pursuing the same right-wing politics as in the early 1990s – supporting Maastricht, opposing union actions in defence of working conditions and so on.[18]

This approach was also shared by some of the regional leaderships of IU, and events came to a head around the regional elections in Galicia where the regional IU leadership formed a coalition with PSOE but failed to follow the IU line on Maastricht, NATO and so on. This resulted in an 'official' candidate being fielded by the IU national leadership, in competition with the regional IU–PSOE–Green coalition, and the expulsion of the Galician IU leadership. The IU leadership's strong response was an attempt to stop the break down of the progressive anti-capitalist position of IU and take a firm stand for left unity on a principled basis.

The issue of the Galician election, however, also provoked a rupture with IC, IU's Catalan sister party, which refused to support IU's position. IC's preference was for a Spanish parallel to the Italian Olive Tree coalition, where the IU/IC would presumably play the role of the PRC as Cossutta – rather than Bertinotti – wished to play it, hence their support for the Galician IU/PSOE electoral alliance.

Essentially what happened during 1997 was a definitive break between the majority left-wing politics of the IU, centred on Anguita, and the increasingly right-wing politics of the PDNI, some of the regional IU leaderships, and of the majority of IC which had been moving to the right for some time. As IU member Diosdado Toledano observed in 1997:

> The recent declarations of Initiativa leader Rafael Ribó in favour of Spanish compliance with the Maastricht Treaty are the latest step in what has been a long evolution towards the right. Initiativa is now even to the right of classic social democratic positions. Not as a result of 'tactical' or superficial adaptations to deal with the neoliberal offensive, but as the result of a shift in the convictions of Initiativa's leadership.[19]

In addition to its support for Maastricht, the IC leadership had consistently opposed social or trade union militancy, including a broad movement of community and neighbourhood groups – largely led by its own rank and file militants – against an increase in water prices in preparation for privatization, and the industrial action of Barcelona metro workers in defence of their early retirement agreement. Indeed, IC's deputies in the Spanish parliament, unlike those of IU, supported attacks on pension rights and cuts in redundancy payments.[20]

By the autumn of 1997 it was clear that there was no fundamental common ground between the IU and IC leaderships and the link was therefore broken. Pro-IU sections of IC subsequently broke away from IC and have formed a new organization on anti-capitalist lines, along with various other parties and groups, including the PCC and a section of the Trotskyist Fourth International in Catalonia. This new Catalan organization participated in the Fifth Federal Assembly of the IU and joined the IU's federal leadership.

The Fifth Federal Assembly of IU was held in December 1997, in the wake of these events, and election results indicated that the overwhelming majority of the organization backed Anguita's stand. In the composition of the new Federal Political Council, 82 per cent came from the Anguita's majority slate, and 9 per cent went to each of two minority slates – Alternative Space and the Third Way. Alternative Space is a small diverse grouping which includes a number of supporters of the Trotskyist Fourth International, most notably Jaime Pastor, who has served on IU's federal leadership. Alternative Space were critical of Anguita's treatment of the PDNI and IC, failing to take a position on the fundamental political issue, and raising instead questions of centralization and democracy within the IU, posing the treatment of IC and the Galician leadership as an infringement of pluralism and regional autonomy.[21] Third Way is probably the most right-wing current within IU – being politically very similar to the PDNI, and has considerable support from the majority sector of the Workers' Commissions – Spain's largest trade union federation, under Antonio Gutiérrez. According to Montes and Albarracín, '[Gutiérrez] denounces imaginary interventions by IU and the Spanish Communist Party (PCE) in CCOO but has openly put "his" union confederation at the service of the PDNI or the Third Way'.[22]

However, the Fifth Assembly adopted Manifesto and Programmatic Fundamentals documents, which expressed a strengthened left position: including clear anti-capitalist objectives, anti-neoliberalism, autonomy from the PSOE, proposals for unity in action of the left, the 35-hour week, a strategy of popular mobilization, and a federative Spanish state.[23]

The IU emerged politically strengthened from its Fifth Assembly, having inflicted major defeats on the right, but still facing a war of attrition from the remaining right-wing forces. Its left position was further consolidated in December 1998 at the 15th Congress of the PCE. Anguita – who remains leader of the IU – was replaced as general secretary by Francisco Frutos, who has been a close collaborator of Anguita's since 1988. Frutos comes from a trade union movement background, having been one of the leaders of the Catalan Workers Commissions during the 1960s. At the 9th Congress of the PCE in 1978, he opposed Carrillo, and in the divisions within the Catalan Communist Party of the early 1980s, led a centre tendency between the Eurocommunists and the orthodox pro-Soviets. Having supported the Eurocommunists to exclude the latter, he was subsequently himself excluded by the Eurocommunist Catalan leadership, and went instead to Madrid, to work with the PCE.[24] There is every indication that he will pursue a similar position to that of Anguita.

Despite its internal problems, the IU has continued to project itself actively in the European arena, and its international orientation shows it to be clearly within the framework of the new European left. In the 1980s, the PCE identified quite strongly with the Italian Communist Party (PCI), having shared its Eurocommunist trajectory. However, with the social democratization of the PCI's right-wing successor, the Italian PDS, and its membership of the Socialist International, which the IU rejects, the PCE and also the IU, have transferred their sympathies and support to the Italian Party of Communist Refoundation (PRC) – to the left of the PDS. This was clearly demonstrated at the IU's Fourth Federal Assembly in 1994, when 'the applause for the PDS was polite and short and noticeably very much warmer for the PRC'.[25]

At its Fourth Federal Assembly, the IU stated that it had relations with all communist, left socialist, green and alternative parties in western Europe, as well as participating in multilateral structures like the green federation of Europe. It also pointed out that the IU had participated in the setting up of two important new initiatives: the New European Left Forum (NELF) and the United European Left (UEL) group in the European Parliament, indeed, NELF was founded in Madrid in November 1991. From its founding in 1986 to 1989, the IU delegation – including one non-PCE Member – was included within the communist group within the European parliament, led by the PCI. In 1989, the PCI announced its intention to leave the group and constitute a new group with close links to the socialist group. The PCE persuaded the PCI to found a new group, the UEL, but not to have privileged links with the socialists, which was effected in 1994. Rapidly, however, the transformation of the PCI into the PDS led the Italians to leave the UEL altogether and join the socialists.

The new phase of European left unity became most noticeable from 1996, with an international meeting held in Paris in May 1996, entitled 'For employment and social progress in Europe'. Its timing in the wake of France's massive social protests helped to reinforce the significance of the renewed coordination of the anti-capitalist left in Europe around campaigning for a different type of Europe – not for withdrawal from the EU, but for the social, economic and democratic transformation of a united Europe. As Julio Anguita has observed, IU presents:

credible alternatives to ensure that the development of a united Europe turns in favour of democratic and social progress in our countries, changing the Union into a factor of peace and stability on the level of international relations. This implies a profound turn in the dynamic opened by Maastricht – which IU considers to be inadequate on the political plane and incorrect on the economic plane, because it is dominated by essentially neoliberal conceptions.[26]

The IU has played a significant role in the development of this left unity around the struggle for a socially progressive Europe, not only helping to initiate the two key organizations, but also hosting a number of significant meetings. In July 1996, 18 organizations from 14 countries met in Madrid for a summit meeting called 'Madrid I', the most extensive and high level meeting of the European left for many years. All the members of both NELF and UEL-NGL were invited, and in addition the newly-formed Socialist Labour Party from Great Britain was invited.[27] The meeting stressed demands for a social Europe – against racism and xenophobia, for employment, for labour's share – as opposed to the type of economic and monetary union envisaged by the Maastricht Treaty. The IU also hosted a second Madrid conference, Madrid II, in July 1997. In January 1999, the IU participated in the meeting for the European left hosted in Paris by the PCF, launching a joint declaration calling for a progressive way forward for Europe, as a preparatory step for campaigning in the European parliamentary elections in 1999.

The IU places considerable emphasis on UEL–NGL and NELF and it is in the framework of these developments that IU poses itself as a model for the left in Europe: anti-capitalist but also green and socially progressive; united yet pluralistic in character; realistic yet principled, ensuring real electoral success. The political space has certainly been defined, and is shared on a pan-European basis by NELF members.

The key question facing the IU, however, remains what relations it should have with PSOE – under its new leader Joaquin Almunia, elected in June 1997, after PSOE's election defeat under the leadership of González. Almunia was a close collaborator and supporter of González and his election to the leadership was opposed by left-wingers within PSOE.[28] Whilst IU remains, in principle, open to cooperation with PSOE – on the right political terms – there will have to be a significant shift to the left within PSOE to make that possible prior to the next general election. It is always possible, however, that a close result at the next election could put IU, as Spain's third largest electoral force, into the position of holding the balance of power. That might push PSOE to negotiate, as such results have pushed other social democratic parties, elsewhere in Europe, to negotiate with smaller parties to their left.

9
Germany

Despite predictions in the early 1990s that the German Party of Democratic Socialism (PDS) would not remain in the Bundestag beyond 1994,[1] the German parliamentary election results of September 1998 have shown that the PDS's brand of democratic socialism has increased in popularity sufficiently for the PDS to win over 5 per cent of the vote in the federal republic as a whole, adding half a million new votes to its previous score (see Table 9.1). Although the PDS was the direct successor to a former ruling party, the Socialist Unity Party (SED) of the German Democratic Republic (GDR), its experience since 1989 has been different to those of the other former ruling parties of eastern Europe. As the GDR was absorbed into the Federal Republic of Germany in 1990, so the party system also absorbed the new Länder. It was not open to the PDS to try and fill the social democratic space in German politics – as did the former Polish or Hungarian ruling parties with some success – for the German Social Democratic Party (SPD) already existed and, indeed, was extremely hostile to the emergence and continuation of the PDS.

The example of the Communist Party of Bohemia and Moravia (CPBM) might suggest a closer parallel, as it gains in the Czech Republic the same levels of votes as the PDS does in the eastern Länder, but the parallel is not borne out by the political profile of the two parties. Whereas the CPBM is undoubtedly a reformed party, it is nevertheless specifically 'communist' in its identification, and the PDS is explicitly not so. Since the PDS emerged from an emergency Congress of the SED in December 1989,[2] it has clearly undergone a considerable political transformation. As its chairman, Gregor Gysi, has observed: 'We are not a communist party, but a party which includes communists', drawing together different anti-capitalist left traditions. Its

Table 9.1   Results of German general elections, 1949–98 (per cent of votes)

	1949	1953	1957	1961	1965	1969	1972
Communist Party (DKP)	5.7	2.2					
Christian Democratic Union (CDU)							
Social Democratic Party (SPD)	29.2	28.2	31.8	36.2	39.3	42.7	45.8
Free Democratic Party (FDP)	11.9	9.5	7.7	12.8	9.5	5.8	8.4
Christian Social Union (CSU)							
Green Party-West (GP-W)							
Party of Democratic Socialism (PDS)							
Republican Party (RP)							
Alliance 90/Green Party-East (AGP-E)							
National Democratic Party (NPD)					2.0	4.3	0.6
CDU/CSU		31.0	45.2	50.2	45.3	47.6	46.1	44.9
Others		22.2	14.3	10.3	5.7	1.6	1.1	0.3

	1976	1980	1983	1987	1990	1994	1998
DKP	0.3	0.2	0.2				
CDU					36.7	34.2	28.4
SPD	42.6	42.9	38.2	37.0	33.5	36.4	40.9
FDP	7.9	10.6	6.9	9.1	11.0	6.9	6.2
CSU					7.1	7.3	6.7
GP-W		1.5	5.6	8.3	3.85		6.7
PDS					2.4	4.4	5.1
RP					2.1	1.9	1.8
AGP-E					1.2	7.3	
NPD	0.3	0.2	0.2	0.6			
CDU/CSU	48.6	44.5	48.8	44.3			
Others	0.3	0.1	0.1	0.7	2.1	1.7	1.2

Adapted from: *Elections since 1945: A Worldwide Reference Compendium* (London: Longman, 1989).

founding Congress defined the new party as 'a modern socialist party in the tradition of the German and international labour movement. It proclaims itself to be part of the tradition of Marx, Engels, Lenin and of the democratic, socialist and pacifist movement.'[3] In this sense, the PDS shares more political common ground with the new left political formations of western Europe which situate themselves to the left of social democracy but do not confine themselves to the communist tradition.

The PDS has also recognized the responsibility of the former SED for crimes committed during the period of state socialism in the former GDR – and therefore by implication accepts some responsibility itself as the successor organization – but sees itself as the activist section of the SED 'which broke with stalinism'.[4] The membership, stabilized by the early 1990s at around 115 000 is a mere fraction of the former SED membership – round about 2.4 million members. The main losses were in the nomenklatura category – around a third of SED membership, which do not have membership in the PDS – and the orthodox communists, who 'defend the tradition of Stalin, Thaelmann, Brezhnev and Honecker'.[5] The latter category founded a new Communist Party of Germany (KPD) in 1989 and is ideologically closer to the west German DKP, the small orthodox communist party founded in 1968 – the original KPD was banned in the Federal Republic in 1956.

The PDS has also undergone profound changes in its internal structures and democratic procedures. Breaking with the rigid organizational structures of the traditional communist parties, the PDS now permits the organization of political platforms within the party. Whilst a number of these were established initially, throughout the course of the 1990s it was the Communist Platform, led by Sarah Wagenknecht, that effectively acted as an internal opposition to the majority left-socialist current – also described as the Gysi–Bisky majority, after party chair, Gregor Gysi and party president, Lothar Bisky. There is also a small Social Democratic Platform, a Marxist Forum and an Ecological Platform, founded in June 1994 and affiliated to the PDS.

The international orientation of the PDS was indicated early in 1991 at the PDS's 2nd Party Congress, which was dominated by the Gulf War. Like the other parties that were eventually to form the new European left, breaking with Gorbachev's pro-imperialist position, the PDS opposed the war, condemning both Saddam Hussein's occupation of Kuwait, and the UN intervention, which it described as 'American aggression'.[6] In fact, the PDS is strongly anti-militarist, supporting a demilitarized Europe, the dissolution of NATO, the transformation of the Eurocorps into a civil aid corps and the halting of the construction of the Eurofighter.[7] The PDS has also been an active participant in the New European Left Forum (NELF), valuing the open discussion, equal cooperation and possibilities for common action that the Forum affords – for example against unemployment – without any of the centralized constraints of previous international communist organizations. The PDS hosted the Twelfth NELF conference in Berlin in April 1997 with the theme: 'For a Social and Democratic Europe', to which, in addition to 16 parties from western Europe, the Bulgarian Socialist Party, the Social Democracy of the Republic of Poland and, from

Russia, the Socialist Party of the Working People and the Committee of the Soldiers' Mothers were invited.[8] In June 1998, the PDS hosted a meeting of 20 left European parties including the left in the European parliament. An exchange of views took place including on common campaigning for a 35-hour week and a proposed common platform for the 1999 European parliamentary elections.[9] Although it is not yet represented in the European parliament, the PDS has cooperation agreements with the UEL–NGL group in Strasbourg.

The PDS won 16.4 per cent in the last GDR elections to the People's Chamber, in March 1990, where they argued for a more democratic independent GDR, and strongly opposed German unification.[10] However, the grand coalition of the Social Democratic Party (SPD) and Christian Democratic Union (CDU) that emerged from these elections, rapidly negotiated unification with the Kohl government in Bonn, which was declared on 3 October 1990. The PDS vote subsequently declined in the first elections to the Bundestag in the unified Germany in December 1990. Campaigning on a Left List/PDS alliance in the western Länder, featuring non-PDS members on the electoral list, the PDS won only 0.3 per cent of votes in the west. In the eastern Länder it won around 11 per cent of votes, totalling 2.43 per cent overall and entitling the PDS to 17 deputies, as the 5 per cent threshold was applied on a one-off basis separately to either western or eastern Germany.[11]

This decline of the PDS vote was to be dramatically reversed, however, in the Bundestag and Länder elections in 1994, as the real social and economic impact of the unification was felt. As the PDS pointed out in their assessment of five years of unification, by 1995, 3.4 million of the 9.6 million jobs that existed at the time of union had been made redundant: two million in manufacturing and more than 600 000 in agriculture and 75 per cent of East Germans had lost the job they had before unification. Older members of the workforce were particularly badly hit, for of those who were between 52 and 63 in 1990, only one in ten were in employment by 1995. The PDS also argued that official unemployment figures concealed the scale of the problem: 'the number of people registered as unemployed is put at 1.2 million although another 2 million people are looking for jobs whilst receiving money from the state, either as participants in temporary job-creation schemes or retraining courses, or as people receiving transitional benefits until they reach retirement age and can claim their old age pensions'.[12] Women have also suffered particularly badly in the jobs market – of the 4.9 million women working in East Germany in 1989, by 1995 more than two million had lost their jobs, with women constituting over 50 per cent of the unemployed.[13]

In the PDS's view, these disastrous developments were not a 'direct and logical result of the errors and omissions of the GDR and its "moribund economy"',[14] they occurred because Kohl's government was unwilling to integrate the GDR into the Federal Republic – they wished rather to force the new states into the mould of the old, leaving no differences between the two, with nothing learned from the positive experiences of the GDR, and certainly with no room for economic competition. The GDR used to be a major exporter of industrial products, notably tools and machines, but by 1995 the new Länder contributed only 2 per cent of Germany's total exports of manufactured goods.

Whilst in the short term after unification, the population of eastern Germany benefited from increased purchasing power due to the favourable conditions of economic union and the increase in domestic demand within the new Länder, by 1992 the serious nature of the economic problems in the former GDR were recognized and the PDS, which spoke out nationally about the social and economic crisis in the new Länder, began to receive increased popular support. Many people within the former GDR felt that the culture of solidarity and communal support that had existed under state socialism had been positive, as had the many welfare and social benefits that had existed at an advanced level of provision. Indeed, as Betz and Welsh point out, a 1993 survey showed:

> that large numbers of eastern Germans believed that compared to West Germany, the GDR had been more advanced with respect to employment security, child care, social security and social justice, protection from crime, human relations, education, and gender equality.[15]

Germany, in common with the other EU nations, also entered the process after 1991, instigated by the Maastricht Treaty, of major public spending cuts, which resulted in the reduction of social benefits, attacks on free collective bargaining, the acceptance of mass unemployment and an increase in racism. These problems particularly affected eastern Germany.

In this framework, it was not surprising that the results of the PDS in the so-called 'super-election year' of 1994 constituted a significant overall advance on those of the federal elections in 1990. 1994 saw European, local, regional and federal elections within Germany. In the June 1994 European elections, the PDS campaigned on the basis of 'Europe sure, but not with the Maastricht Treaty', arguing the case for left representation: 'a consistent representation of Left policy is indispensable for effective resistance to the democratic and social decline, militarism, the destruction of the environment, racism and Euro-chauvinism.'[16] The PDS won 4.7 per cent of the vote, a significant increase on the 2.9 per cent of 1990, but observers pointed out that as the turn-out was low (63 per cent) this only represented a slight increase in votes – 1 459 261 as opposed to 1 129 290 in 1990 on a 77.8 per cent turn out. The PDS observed that it was difficult to mobilize its supporters in eastern Germany because of their lack of experience with European integration and its institutions.[17]

However, the Bundestag elections of October 1994 really did represent what Angela Klein described as 'a great leap forward for the party'.[18] (see Figure 9.1) The PDS won 2 067 387 votes, an increase of half a million over the European results and taking 4.4 per cent in a turnout of 79.1 per cent.[19] In the former GDR the PDS vote was between 16 and 20 per cent in the different Länder. The main demands in the general election programme were for:

a halt to the social decline, the implementation of the right to work by means of an active employment policy, affordable housing and the elimination of paragraph 218 ([the Constitution's] ban on abortion).[20]

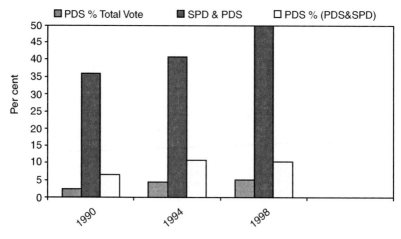

PDS = Party of Democratic Socialism; SPD = Social Democratic Party.

Figure 9.1   Election performance of the German left, 1990–98

Although its overall result did not cross the electoral threshold of 5 per cent, the PDS was still eligible to take up seats in the Bundestag because electoral law specifies that parties may do so if they win three or more of the directly-elected seats. The PDS won four of the five seats in East Berlin and narrowly missed further direct victories in Berlin-Köpenick and Rostock.[21]

PDS support had also increased in the west to 369 038 votes, reaching 5.4 per cent in the west Berlin constituency of Kreuzberg-Schöneberg, 3.4 per cent in Hamburg-Centre and 2 to 2.6 per cent in constituencies in Cologne and Frankfurt.[22] Although small in overall terms, these results indicated that the PDS was not only a regional protest party, but had distinct politics – a new left agenda to the left of the SPD – that could attract votes throughout Germany as social and economic conditions deteriorated. This was reflected in the open attitude that the PDS took towards its electoral list – its 'open list' policy – including many non-PDS members. Furthermore, the idea that the PDS was supported only by former bureaucrats and SED members was finally proven to be wrong. As Klein observes: 'Around 20 per cent of young first-time voters in the east voted PDS. Those over 60 in the east voted overwhelmingly for the conservatives, the CDU'.[23]

A notable feature of the campaign had been the hostility expressed towards the PDS by both the CDU and the SPD, which the PDS described as revealing 'a new degree of aggressiveness and destruction of political culture.'[24] Chancellor Kohl described PDS members and candidates as 'red painted fascists', an attitude which no doubt contributed to a political climate where the party and its representatives received threats of violence and anti-semitic slogans were painted on PDS posters, particularly on those of Gregor Gysi, who is himself Jewish. The CDU's most famous anti-PDS campaign took place in the run up to the general election of 1994. On 26 June 1994, the CDU/FDP coalition was voted out of government in the regional elections in Saxony-Anhalt – with the Free Democrats (FDP) losing all its seats – and a minority government of the SPD and Alliance 90/The Greens was tolerated by the PDS. This was the first minority regional government dependent on PDS support, and led the CDU to launch their 'Rote Socken' (red socks) campaign poster, with the slogan 'Into the future ... but not in red socks', which Laurence McFalls aptly observes, 'attempted in the most primitive anti-Communist manner to mobilize opinion against the threat of a social-democratic–Communist "Volksfront".'[25] The campaign backfired, as even non-PDS voters in the east felt that this was an attack on a specifically east German political force, and the PDS humorously co-opted the red socks symbol during its campaign for the federal elections.

Despite their crude response, however, the CDU had realised the significance of the PDS toleration in the Saxony-Anhalt regional parliament, for the SPD state prime minister Hoeppner could instead have chosen to form a 'grand coalition' with the CDU, but rejected this option in favour of PDS toleration. A continued pattern of such cooperation could lead to massively reduced possibilities for the CDU in forming governments in the eastern Länder. The attitude of the SPD federal leadership, however, at that time under Rudolf Scharping, was hostile towards cooperation with the PDS in eastern Germany, favouring a strategy of 'intensive competition' for the votes in the new Länder.[26] In the two other states where informal coalitions between the SPD and the PDS were a possibility, in Thuringia and Mecklenburg-West Pomerania, the choice was again between a grand SPD/CDU coalition or an SPD minority government with PDS support and in both cases the CDU became the leading force in a coalition government with the PDS as the only parliamentary opposition.[27]

These developments forced the PDS to think about its role in the state parliaments in a different way – rather than being simply a party of militant opposition. As Lothar Bisky, the PDS chairman pointed out:

> The east German electorate has cast its vote for a new responsibility on our part ... Those who really want democracy can't just take a stance for the rights of minorities in society and parliament, but must exercise these rights as a minority. At any rate, we have never understood opposition as merely turning things down.[28]

However, this question of the PDS's relationship with the SPD has been a controversial one within both parties, and has raised similar issues to those faced by other new European left parties.

The SPD has been divided over the issue – as indeed German social democracy has been for decades – of its relationship with communism, and now its successor party. Whereas, for example, in the 1970s, the SPD leadership maintained its attitude of an unbridgeable divide between communism and social democracy, the left within the SPD occasionally formed alliances with communists in the peace movement, against *Berufsverbote* (exclusion from public service) towards the left and in anti-fascist campaigns.[29] After unification in 1990, the SPD leadership maintained its hostility to the PDS, declaring prior to both 1990 and 1994 elections that there would be no cooperation between the two parties. In fact, as Eckhard Jesse points out, in August 1994 the SPD party chairman and those of the new Länder pledged that there would be no cooperation, and after the federal elections, in October 1994, Scharping firmly restated the position:

> Coalitions with the PDS at regional or federal level are out of the question. Where the SPD is in government, the PDS is in opposition, where the SPD is in opposition there can be no coalition within the opposition.[30]

Nevertheless, the SPD leaders in the eastern Länder were faced with different considerations to those that faced the SPD leaders in Bonn. The SPD minority government in Saxony-Anhalt continued to maintain itself with PDS support, but attempts by the SPD leadership in Mecklenburg-West Pomerania to initiate an arrangement of support with the PDS were prevented by the Bonn leadership. The replacement of Scharping, in 1995, with Oskar Lafontaine, who spoke openly of a 'majority of the left', led to hopes that the situation might change, and although there was still the absence of a coherent policy it appeared that there would be some regional flexibility allowed. During 1996, the SPD chairmen in both Thuringia and Mecklenburg-West Pomerania requested that they be able to choose appropriate coalition partners after the elections of 1998 and that a coalition with the PDS should not be ruled out. This was agreed to by the SPD leaders at the end of 1996.[31]

The PDS has also been divided over the issue. Whilst the party's attitude in the early 1990s was categorically opposed to cooperation with other parties, the position in the majority section of the PDS began to change after 1994, accelerated by the situation in Saxony-Anhalt. A minority within the PDS, primarily around the Communist Platform maintained opposition to such arrangements but eventually at the 1997 PDS conference took the position that 'the question whether a PDS parliamentary party can take on a coalition role in a parliament will be decided by the PDS by analyzing the power constellation at the time.'[32] The Gysi/Bisky position reaffirmed that the aim of the PDS was to break the conservative hegemony in Germany and that its decisions on toleration or coalition would be made 'according to the circumstances at the time in order to best achieve its overriding political aim of effecting maximum change of the social order.'[33] Gysi also made it completely clear that decisions on collaboration would be made on a political basis and no support would be given for measures that would attack the living standards of the working class, for example, cuts in the welfare state. Furthermore, the PDS continued to support extra-parliamentary struggle as crucial in bringing about social change. The question of PDS/SPD coalition/toleration has been the main focus for the ideological division within the PDS but other areas of disagreement also exist. A number of these issues were sharply drawn out at the PDS's Fourth Congress in January 1995 which was perhaps the most marked point of internal conflict in the PDS and politically very significant, for it was this congress which restrained the leadership from drawing the PDS too close to social democracy. The party leadership submitted a 'ten theses' resolution to the Congress, which was received with considerable criticism for its advocacy of greater cooperation with the SDP and Greens and its acceptance of 'anti-communist socialist factions' within the PDS.[34] The criticism did not only originate with the more orthodox communist groups, like the Communist Platform and the Marxist Forum, however, it was also opposed by the Young Comrades, an anti-traditionalist, new left grouping, led by Angela Marquardt from Berlin. Their concern was that 'PDS leaders were taking the party too much in the direction of social democracy, leading to the "embourgeoisement" of the party'.[35] The document was withdrawn in order to prevent a split in the party, and a compromise position was put entitled 'Concerning the five most important points of discussion in the current debate in the PDS'. These affirmed:

- firstly, the socialist character of the PDS, absolutely anti-capitalist, but equally pro-democracy and human rights and against a 'stalinist or post-stalinist model of socialism';
- secondly, the PDS as a party in opposition to the dominant social conditions, seeing as its main priority its engagement with extra-parliamentary movements, and 'its comprehension of social opposition remains untouched by the role it would assume in any given parliament';
- thirdly, whilst the pluralism of the PDS not only excludes nationalist, chauvinist, racist and anti-semitic views, but also stalinist views, the PDS also rejects anti-communism and 'does not intend to renounce on democratic communist positions within its ranks';
- fourthly, the commitment to a real socialist evaluation of the GDR, recognizing responsibility for errors and crimes but also acknowledging the positive results; and
- finally, that the PDS does not see the SPD and Alliance 90/The Greens as enemies and recognizes that the necessary social transformation

cannot take place without the SPD: 'They are political competitors, with whom we may have hard disputes, but with whom we will remain ready to cooperate'.[36]

Subsequent party congresses in 1996 and 1997 also debated the role of the PDS in German politics, and as Olsen observes, 'the overriding issue was whether the PDS should continue its fundamental "system opposition" or seek to govern at all levels: communal, state, even national.'[37] By 1997 the overwhelming majority had come round to support for the position of cooperation and possible coalition with the SPD and the Greens, put forward by party chairman Lothar Bisky, and this general orientation was consolidated at the PDS congress in 1998. In fact, the results of the 1998 Bundestag elections and the regional elections in the state of Mecklenburg/West Pomerania, were to provide the circumstances for testing PDS policy on these issues.

The elections of 27 September 1998 brought 16 years of conservative government – the Kohl era – to an end, and saw the SPD emerge as the largest single party in the Bundestag and an overall majority – including the PDS and Alliance 90/The Greens – for a change of policy away from Kohl's neo-liberal policies, the dismantling of the welfare state and mass unemployment. With a high turn-out of 82.3 per cent, the SPD took 40.9 per cent of the vote, the CDU/CSU with their worst vote ever took 35.2 per cent, Alliance 90/The Greens 6.7 per cent, the FDP 6.2 per cent and the PDS, with half a million more votes than its previous best, won 5.1 per cent. This latter score was the great achievement that the PDS had fought for – to pass the 5 per cent threshold throughout Germany, entitling it to normal participatory rights in the Bundestag with 35 seats, parliamentary fraction rights and so on.

A number of other positive achievements could also be accredited to the PDS: firstly, in east Berlin it again directly won four constituencies – in one of them Petra Pau, the young chairperson of the PDS in Berlin, defeated Wolfgang Thierse, the SPD vice-chair; secondly, 6 per cent of first time voters throughout Germany supported the PDS – a fact that the PDS understood as a confirmation of its consistent work for a solution to Germany's many social problems, for its specific support for east Germans and for its attention to the concerns of young people.[38] In particular, the PDS assessed that the other political parties had to recognize that the PDS was not just a temporary aberration resulting from German unification, but a distinctive part of German domestic politics with increasingly popular positions.[39]

Particular areas of growth for the PDS were the east German states of Thuringia, Saxony and Saxony-Anhalt and the west German states of Schleswig-Holstein and Hesse, with six deputies entering the Bundestag from west German PDS lists. Once again the PDS operated its open-list system, with 28 of its 35 deputies being party members and seven being 'non-party personalities'.[40] A high representation of women was achieved – indeed this was a significant feature in the election campaign – with 21 out of the 35 deputies being women. Attempts by the SPD to defeat the PDS in their direct mandate constituencies failed, despite their using high profile candidates, and CDU attempts to win support through 'conjuring the ghost of a "popular front" of SPD, Greens and PDS'[41] were equally unsuccessful.

The regional elections, also conducted on 27 September 1998, in the east German state of Mecklenburg-West Pomerania, also saw an increase in support for the PDS. The SPD emerged as the largest single party, rising by 4.8 per cent to 34.3 per cent of the vote, the CDU dropped 7.5 per cent to 30.2 per cent, and the PDS rose 1.7 per cent to 24.4 per cent. The FDP and the Greens did not gain sufficient support to enter the regional parliament and the extreme right parties were also below the electoral threshold.

The same situation presented itself in Mecklenburg-West Pomerania as in Germany nationally – the results clearly required the SPD to enter into coalition government, but the issue was whether the SPD would opt for a CDU/SPD 'grand coalition' or turn to the smaller parties. In both instances the grand coalition option was rejected, although prior to the election it was suggested by commentators that Schröder – the SPD chancellor candidate – favoured such a move. The PDS made it clear that whilst they opposed a grand coalition solution, which would be 'tantamount to twisting the voters' will',[42] they would support an SPD/Green coalition – whilst putting pressure on the government from the left – and promised to: 'support any real step towards fighting unemployment, overcoming the social division in society and ushering in a sustainable development'. They also made clear their position on participation at any level, stating that: 'We are not available for forming majorities without standing up for our own opinion.'[43]

Whilst the SPD at national level entered a coalition with Alliance 90/The Greens, in Mecklenburg-West Pomerania the outcome was different. The PDS was prepared to join the Land government with the SPD and, as PDS vice-chair Sylvia-Yvonne Kaufmann has described it, 'put pressure on from the left for real change'.[44] Significantly, however, the final decision on the coalition was not made by the PDS leadership, but by the regional party organization. Three extra-ordinary regional party congresseses were held in Mecklenburg-West Pomerania to discuss this issue and at the final congress the great majority – with only six votes against – agreed to go into a coalition with the SDP.[45] So, for the first time the PDS entered a state government with three ministers, one of which, Helmut Holter, became deputy Land prime minister. Very hard negotiations were pursued in drawing up the coalition treaty, an agreement which specifies and agrees in advance the policies that the government will undertake. This safeguards the position of the PDS to a great extent because it has already ensured the inclusion of a number of key issues including education policy, measures to combat unemployment and fiscal policy.[46] These agreements amount to a shift to the left in Mecklenburg-West Pomerania.

Towards the end of 1998 the PDS held its first national conference, drawing together over 400 members from all over Germany. The conference discussed the new government's policies, being particularly critical of its foreign and security policy – most notably participation in the threatened NATO intervention in Kosovo without a UN mandate, which the PDS described as 'a grotesque travesty of international law'.[47] The unemployment problem was discussed and five steps proposed to curtail it:

- firstly, the regulation of financial markets and taxation of profits from capital and currency markets, in cooperation with other left governments in Europe;
- secondly, the strengthening of domestic economies through investment in the third sector and stabilization of minimum incomes;
- thirdly, a 35-hour week with economic and tax compensation for companies with less than 15 employees;
- fourthly, the lowering of the retirement age to 55 and improved regulations for early retirement; and
- fifthly, a public employment sector providing 350 000 training spots and jobs, particularly aimed at youth.[48]

It was noticeable, however, that the conference did not discuss the question of government participation, or the balance between radical opposition and government responsibility, in spite of it being a crucial issue that will surface again during the Länder elections of 1999.

The key focus for 1999 was instead placed on the elections for the European Parliament held on 13 June 1999, suggesting the consolidation of a more electoral approach within the party. At the national conference, PDS vice-chair Sylvia-Yvonne Kaufmann specified the four fundamental positions that the PDS would hold in the campaign – its main aim being to pass the 5 per cent threshold and enter the European parliament:

- firstly, to put a strong left socialist pressure on the governments of Europe to change the politics of the Union away from being profit-oriented to being socially-just, democratic, peaceful, environmentally sound and solidaristic towards the South.
- secondly, that the union be a social and employment union where workers of different nationalities are not played off against each other and nationalist and xenophobic sentiments can be countered.
- thirdly, for a civilian government and against Bundeswehr (the army) operations abroad and for the scrapping of the Eurofighter.
- fourthly, that the European Central Bank be reorientated away from the neo-liberal role ascribed to it in the Maastricht Treaty and towards the objectives of a sustainable economy and full employment.[49] This is one of the key areas of difference with the SPD which has given full support to the Maastricht Treaty, the Amsterdam Treaty and the Euro without any conditions or doubt, and has followed the same line as the Kohl government.

The PDS also participated in an event hosted by the French Communist Party (PCF) on 15 January 1999, which under the banner 'Forum progressistes européennes', launched a common appeal entitled 'For a new direction in the construction of Europe' which was signed by 13 European left parties. Whilst not directly a joint manifesto for the European elections, this was clearly the common launch of their campaigning work with a strong profile for the UEL/NGL European parliamentary group. The framework of the appeal was a condemnation of neoliberalism, and a call for a progressive reorientation of the European project – not to oppose European integration – but to fight for a Europe that is social, ecological and democratic, a Europe of peace and solidarity.[50]

With the PDS as with the other west European left parties, the current project is clear – to be an anti-capitalist left party with a strategy to push both national and European politics to the left through a combination of parliamentary and extra-parliamentary struggle, and in unity with other like-minded European parties through a high level of discussion and interaction between the new left forces. Yet as Kaufmann observed at the beginning of 1999: 'The left is consolidating itself as shown by the election results in the countries of Europe. The tide has turned for the left in the last two or three years, but the left pressure must be continued and increased.'[51] The main danger is that rightwards tendencies will be strengthened within these parties as they cooperate more closely with mass social democratic parties to their right.

Whilst the right was defeated within the PCF and IU in Spain and separated itself from PRC in Italy, the situation evolved differently in the PDS, where at the 1995 Congress a coalition of diverse forces forced the leadership off an apparently rightwards track. Increased governmental responsibility in the eastern Länder, however, and absorption into the state institutions, may well strengthen the tendency within the PDS that favours evolution into a regional social democratic party. This has been mooted in the past and would mean abandoning the current official line of establishing an all-Germany democratic socialist party.

In Germany, as in all these countries, pressures to move to the right will constantly reassert themselves, particularly amongst those directly involved in public office-holding, and events of the next few years will show how successful these parties are in maintaining their left positions.

Part III

Postcommunists in Power in Central and Eastern Europe

144

10
Introduction

By the mid-1990s, former communist parties had been returned to power in most of the countries of central and eastern Europe – to the consternation of many western observers. In 1993, the Polish successor party – the Social Democracy of the Republic of Poland (SdRP) had been elected to government, followed in 1994 by the Hungarian Socialist Party (HSP). In 1996, Václav Klaus in the Czech Republic lost his parliamentary majority in a leftward shift by the voters and lost the government to the Social Democrats in 1998, and in the mid years of the decade, the successor parties in Romania and Bulgaria also held governmental office. Whilst this might, superficially, appear to be a surprising development, the social and economic costs of the transition meant that the electorate turned against those parties most associated with the hardships of free-market economic reform. Most of the citizens of eastern Europe entered the post-communist period with expectations of higher living standards and a consumer society, for the pledge implied in the much-vaunted 'return to Europe' was that eastern living standards would be raised towards west European levels. They were rapidly – and brutally – disabused of this notion, however, and used their votes to register their disapproval. As Heinrich Machowski pointed out, '... So far there have been a few winners but many, many losers in the transition. And it's the many losers who are deciding the election outcomes.'[1]

Far from improving the living conditions of the populations in the 'transition' economies, the attempts to restore capitalism in the region resulted in a severe economic downturn from which it has not yet recovered. Of the 25 transition economies of eastern Europe and the former Soviet Union, by 1997 only Poland had finally surpassed the level of GDP that they had in 1989, with Slovenia and Slovakia projected to do so during 1998.[2] In Russia, GDP dropped almost 50 per cent between 1990 and 1997.[3] As Anthony Browne commented in *The Observer* at the end of 1998:

> Between 1989 and 1997, far from growing overall, the Czech economy has shrunk by 2 per cent ... Hungary has shrunk by 10 per cent in the past decade, and Bulgaria by 37 per cent. The further East you go, the worse it is. The Russian economy grew last year – by only 0.8 per cent. But that was the *only* year the economy hasn't shrunk since Russia embraced the free market.[4]

In fact, the fall in output in the former Soviet Union has been the largest anywhere in peacetime in modern history – even larger than that of the Great Depression in the 1930s.

The region's economic crisis, exacerbated by the break up of the CMEA trading bloc, gave the western powers huge leverage over it and enabled the US and the main western European states – through avenues such as IMF conditionality on loans – to impose a new, less socially and economically protected model of capitalism on these countries. The long-anticipated achievement of the Open Door policy meant that eastern Europe could be a marketplace for western goods and a source of cheap, skilled labour, but the west, with its own economic problems, had no intention either of helping these countries to become industrial competitors or of opening the EU to cheap imports. As Peter Gowan pointed out: 'These regime goals were given the label "market economy" but were in reality geared towards ensuring that these economies occupied subordinate places in the projected new European division of labour.'[5]

The concept of the 'return to Europe', which fed people's illusions that the end of communism would raise the east to the levels of the west, was historically inaccurate, for the division of Europe had far deeper roots than merely the post-1945 period, as outlined in Chapter three. Whilst there were a number of religious, cultural and institutional differences that derived from events such as the division in the christian church in 1054 and the extension of Ottoman rule into central Europe in the sixteenth and seventeenth centuries, the fundamental difference between east and west was the difference in the rate of economic development. Prior to the communist period, eastern Europe was enormously economically backward – a fact to some extent offset by the 'catching-up modernization' of communist economic development, which far from creating the economic backwardness of the region, helped to bring it into the modern age.

In Romania, for example, during the 1920s approximately 80 per cent of the population lived in small villages engaging in low productivity agriculture, with a per capita production of 48 per cent of the European average. Literacy levels were only 57 per cent, and Romania had the highest general death rate and highest infant mortality rate in Europe. Similar patterns existed throughout many of the eastern Europe states at a time when the western part of the continent had achieved high levels of industrial development. Indeed, by the end of the 1930s, eastern Europe – with the exception of the Soviet Union – still only produced 8 per cent of Europe's industrial capital. Of this amount, one third was produced in Czechoslovakia, the western part of which was the region's most industrialized area.

Whatever the long and short-term factors in the region's economic difficulties, however, the severe crisis of the early post-1989 years had a profound impact on the political choices made by the electorate. Electoral support given to former communist parties was from voters, 'seeking to shift the region's politics away from the bare-knuckled freemarket capitalism of early reformers toward the kind of socialised market economy on which Western Europe built its postwar prosperity.'[6]

It would be wrong, however, to see the former communist parties in eastern Europe as a uniform political category, even if their increased electoral support stems from similar reasons across the region – and notwithstanding their common political origins. Three basic patterns can be identified, which are largely the result of their political evolution prior to 1989, and determine the types of programmes and policies that they have embraced during the 1990s.

1. In Poland and Hungary, the regime changes were the result of managed transitions where reform communists – favourable to the reintroduction of capitalism – attempted, through playing a major role in roundtable negotiations, to strengthen their popular support and emerge as newly viable leaders for the postcommunist period. The successors to the ruling parties in Hungary and Poland rapidly transformed themselves into west-European-style Social Democratic parties and sought membership of the Socialist International. The social-democratic space on the political spectrum was, on the whole, vacant, for apart from the example of the Czech Social Democrats, attempts to reestablish former social democratic parties had little success, despite considerable support from the Socialist

International. Social democracy had received most support in eastern Europe in the inter-war period in Czechoslovakia, with some support also in Hungary and Poland, but there was not an extensive tradition to revive on a region-wide basis. Indeed, the fact that the social democratic parties in Hungary and Poland had merged with the ruling communist parties in the late 1940s meant that in 1989, they were not seen as an untainted left alternative. In fact, they did not pose themselves in that light – most of the social democratic parties in eastern Europe merely stressed the anti-communist, pro-free market line of their west European sister parties and this did not appeal to the socialist-oriented section of the electorate.[7]

2. In contrast, in Czechoslovakia and the German Democratic Republic, the ruling parties were not, in the late 1980s, evolving towards social democracy, and the successor parties – the Communist Party of Bohemia and Moravia (CPBM) and the German Party of Democratic Socialism (PDS) – maintained an anti-capitalist position, whilst undergoing considerable political renewal. Both have mass social democratic parties to their right, and have consolidated a respectable share of the vote – for the PDS between 10 and 20 per cent in the east German Länder, and for the CPBM between 10 and 15 per cent in the Czech lands. Whilst the CPBM has retained its communist label, it has some shared political features with the new left parties in western Europe. It has embraced a more radical social agenda, including ecology, anti-racism and gender issues and has adopted a more open attitude to other left forces and the inclusion of non-party members on its electoral lists. The CPBM formed the largest opposition party to Klaus's coalition in the first half of the 1990s and, although it has maintained a stable level of electoral support of 10.3 per cent in 1996 and 11 per cent in 1998, it was overtaken by the re-established pre-war social democrats in 1996, whose share of the vote increased from 6.5 per cent to 26.4 per cent, and then further in 1998, when it increased to 32.3 per cent.[8]

3. In Bulgaria and Romania, the removal of the pre-1989 communist leaderships were largely the result of the actions of sections of the communist leaderships, who, whilst desiring reform of the political status quo, were not in favour of the introduction of capitalism. There were no significant opposition movements, and the successor parties, the Bulgarian Socialist Party, and, effectively, the National Salvation Front and subsequently the Social Democratic Party of Romania, maintained positions in favour of a significant state sector and against the full introduction of a free-market economy.

In 1989/90, these successor parties faced multi-party competition in what are often described as the 'founding' elections of 1989/90 and in central Europe saw crushing electoral defeat at the hands of the new, violently anti-communist – often dissident movement-based – electoral forces. The shock that was expressed by many western observers in the mid-1990s, after the rapid electoral recovery of the SdRP in Poland in 1993 and the HSP in Hungary in 1994 was based on the assumption that these first elections established a pattern for the future – that communism and socialism had been so discredited by the period of communist party monopoly rule that they would never constitute an electoral force again. It was assumed, quite wrongly, that everything associated with those regimes would be abhorrent to the electorates. It is more accurate, however, to see the first round of elections as a plebiscite against the regimes as they had existed, rather than a rejection of all of the values of socialism – many of which, through redistributive economic and social policies, had improved people's lives.

In fact, large parts of civil society remained attached to the values of socialism, both in the 1980s, and evidently in the 1990s, and this has been widely underrated. The notion expressed in 1989 that the communist period had somehow been an aberrant blip in the history of eastern Europe and that this could now be washed away through democratization and restitution is clearly inaccurate. Election results indicate that there were aspects of the state socialist regimes which are viewed favourably by large sections of the populations. Peter Gowan cites opinion polls from Eurobarometer Surveys and elsewhere to support this argument:

> From 1985, competitive elections were taking place in Hungary, and these demonstrate that as late as 1989, the Hungarian Communists were gaining 30% or more of the vote and such votes were indicative of support for left-wing political and social values.[9]

The pattern in the GDR was similar, with polls conducted in November 1989 giving the ruling SED 31 per cent – ahead of any other party. A poll taken in Czechoslovakia in December 1989 showed majority support for both socialized property and central planning. Clearly a substantial political constituency remained for the left in these countries. Indeed, in Romania and Bulgaria, both former ruling parties received popular majorities in the first free elections.

As the right-wing coalitions in central Europe fragmented through their internal contradictions, and lost mass popular support in the early 1990s as a result of harsh economic and social conditions, the second wave of post-1989 elections saw electoral victories for former communist parties in Poland in 1993 and Hungary in 1994, as voters hoped to alleviate the suffering of the transition period. As Frances Millard observes on Poland:

> A general pessimism about the economy was accompanied by a growth of negative attitudes to the private sector, and especially privatization … From August, 1991, onwards there was a systematic fall in the numbers regarding privatization as beneficial to the Polish economy, with the exception of small firms and retail establishments. In mid-1992, 60 per cent again believed that large industrial enterprises should be exclusively state-owned.[10]

The Hungarian Socialist Party, which had secured only 32 seats in 1990, surged ahead in the general elections of 1994 with a total of 209 out of a possible 386 seats, giving them an overall majority of 16 seats. Whilst the scale of the victory was surprising even to the socialists themselves, the move to the left was already an established feature of political life in central and eastern Europe, which László Andor observes in Hungary was largely provoked by discontent arising from an increase in poverty and unemployment and a decline in living standards.[11]

The Polish and Hungarian general election victories were followed in November 1995 by the election of SdRP leader Alexander Kwaśniewski as President of Poland. Kwaśniewski's opponent, former Solidarity leader and Polish President Lech Wałęsa, tried hard to mobilize support for his campaign by referring to the injustices and oppressions of the communist regime with which Kwaśniewski was associated, but clearly, this was not a convincing enough argument for the majority of voters.[12] Anti-communism did not prove to be a sufficient force to maintain support for parties and leaders who had overseen what was by 1994 being described as an 'economic disaster'.[13]

However, if the electorates in central Europe were expecting significantly different policies from the former communist parties in government, they were sadly disappointed. In both Poland and Hungary, the new governments showed serious commitment to privatization, huge public spending cuts, sweeping reforms of the welfare system and an eagerness to join the EU and NATO, justifying the description often used of 'nomenklatura capitalism'. If anything, the former communists were more effective in implementing

IMF-endorsed policies than their formally more right-wing predecessors, because they did not have to contend with a nationalist lobby within their ranks. The conservative coalition government in Hungary from 1990–94 had actually intended to retain long term majority state ownership of many strategic companies which the HSP subsequently proceeded to privatize.

The commitment to economic transition by all parties of government in central Europe since 1989 has not, however, been paralleled by all ruling parties throughout eastern Europe. It became clear by the early 1990s that the region was undergoing a kind of two-speed transformation, where central Europe – Poland, Hungary, the Czech Republic and Slovakia – was more advanced in most areas of economic reform than the countries further east – Romania and Bulgaria – particularly in relation to the privatization process. Romania and Bulgaria were much slower in establishing the institutional framework for capitalism as well as being the most reluctant privatizers.

This latter point can be shown through gross domestic product figures.[14] In 1995, private sector shares of GDP in percentages were as follows: Czech Republic 70 per cent; Hungary 60 per cent; Poland 60 per cent; Slovakia 60 per cent; Bulgaria 45 per cent; Romania 40 per cent. Private sector shares also include new start up, however, so they are not an accurate indication of levels of privatization. The figures for privatization of large-scale state-owned enterprises, therefore, are the most revealing. In the Czech Republic and Hungary, by 1995 over 50 per cent of large state-owned enterprises had been privatized, in Poland and Slovakia over 25 per cent, and in Bulgaria and Romania the figure had been minimal.

The slower development of privatization in Romania and Bulgaria has been the direct result of the political situation in those countries since 1989 and the unfavourable attitude of the former ruling parties to full-scale transition. In Romania the political dominance of Ion Iliescu and his Social Democratic Party of Romania until 1995, prevented both a rapid transition to capitalism and the witch-hunting of people associated with the former regime. In Bulgaria, the dominance for most of the post-1989 period of the Bulgarian Socialist Party until 1996, similarly prevented rapid structural change. Peter Gowan argues that geo-political factors have also been significant in the slow pace of change in Bulgaria – the west European states did not seek to rapidly draw Bulgaria into their sphere of influence, whilst preoccupation with Yugoslavia led the US to be more concerned with political stability than economic reform. This situation eventually changed, as Gowan observes:

> With the Dayton Accords and manoeuvring between the USA and Russia over NATO enlargement, however, Bulgaria became a target of intense Western interest and its financial difficulties were used by the IMF powers to destabilise the BSP government, leading to a continuing grave crisis within the party itself.[15]

In Romania, Iliescu's orientation in the immediate post-Ceauşescu period, was towards the Gorbachevite Soviet Union, but after 1991, under western pressure, Iliescu moved more towards market reform, although retaining a traditional somewhat autarchic approach to the Romanian economy. In the early 1990s, the IMF had little leverage with the Romanian government to alter this approach because Romania had no foreign debt at the beginning of the transition period.

By the mid-1990s, however, both the BSP and the SDPR were under enormous pressure from western financial institutions, and began to implement liberal economic policies, which greatly reduced their popularity at the polls and led the way for more pro-liberal coalitions to be elected. The ousting of these former communist parties from government has led in both cases, through splits, to their greater political homogeneity and they have both consolidated as more left parties. Their replacement in power, by pro-western liberal coalitions committed to increased structural reform will no doubt lead to an increase in their support at the next round of general elections, as both countries are likely to face increased economic and social problems.

The pattern in the region can therefore be summarized in the following way: in central Europe, the reforming communists were overwhelmingly defeated in elections, usually by coalitions of oppositional forces. During the period of the first governments, the former communist parties – with the exception of the Czechs – underwent profound changes, establishing themselves as centre-left, nomenklatura capitalist parties, claiming the social-democratic space – whilst the governing coalitions fragmented. In eastern Europe, where dissident movements were not widespread, the less-reformed communists were elected with mass popular support and attempted to follow an economic course short of full-scale transition.

The second wave of developments led, under increasing economic crisis, to a shift to the centre-left in central Europe – to the former communist parties in Poland in 1993, Hungary in 1994 and a significant swing to the left-leaning trade union-oriented Social Democrats in the Czech Republic in 1996.

A reverse process occurred in eastern Europe, as the opposition forces consolidated themselves as parties with significant western backing and came to power in 1995 and 1996. The third round of general elections in central Europe, in Poland in 1997 and Hungary in 1998, saw the defeat of the former communist parties and the election of right-wing coalitions. These electoral defeats did not – in terms of numbers of votes cast – constitute huge swings to the right, for the HSP percentage of the vote remained stable and the SdRP's alliance increased its share of the vote, but they certainly indicated a level of dissatisfaction with the economic policies of these governments and an increasing level of cohesion and organization amongst the right-wing forces. The results further suggest that there is a left constituency – attached to socialist values – of roughly a third of the electorate in these two countries that have continued to support former communist parties, in the absence of a left alternative, even if the parties' policies do not necessarily coincide with the electors' social and economic needs. The strategic requirement of these parties, therefore, has been to extend their electoral base beyond the 'left' sector, and this has led both the HSP and the SdRP to seek support in the centre ground – from people who might otherwise support liberal parties.[16]

Under the circumstances of the impact of their economic policies – combined with the considerable anti-communism which remained in certain sections of these societies, and was obviously directed at the successor parties – it was difficult for these parties to make significant advances. In Hungary, for example, there had been a 15 per cent cut in real incomes between 1995 and 1997; at the time of the election, 40 per cent of children were living in poverty; unemployment was around half a million in a country of just over ten million; tuition fees had been introduced in universities; mass privatizations had weakened the trade union movement; and homelessness had become a significant social problem. The main victor party, FIDESZ, was founded in 1988 as an autonomous youth movement, playing a significant part in the opposition round-table which negotiated the system change in 1989. Since then it has moved steadily to the right, occupying the ground vacated by the fragmenting conservative forces like the Hungarian Democratic Forum which led the coalition government from 1990–94, and has now emerged as the major conservative force in

Hungary. FIDESZ campaigned on a 40-point programme which attacked the HSP-led government from both left and right, pledging, for example, to restore free higher education.

In all countries of central and eastern Europe, former communist parties or successors to them, are major players in the mainstream of political life in central and eastern Europe. They have been electorally successful during the 1990s where they have been seen as a defense against the erosion of living standards and particularly as a defender of the welfare state. In their reformed condition, embracing multiparty democracy and liberal democratic freedoms, they were perceived by the electorate to occupy the political space traditionally held by social democracy in the west – redistributive and interventionist – which they had themselves claimed.

Whilst that description may still be appropriate for the Bulgarian and Romanian postcommunist parties, it is now clear that the postcommunist parties in Hungary and Poland, when in power, became more like the new-style western social democratic parties, in the tradition of Gonzàlez and Blair. They pursued neoliberal economic policies, arguing that their economies could not sustain the welfare policies that the electorates had put them in place to provide. Indeed, that is a very real issue – whether there is, in fact, a material base for social democracy in these countries.

The Hungarian prime minister, Gyula Horn's own assessment of the record of his government since election in 1994 was the following: 'To appreciate what we have done you must realise that we have abolished what Hungarians grew up to accept as sacred rights'.[17] Lajos Bokros, Horn's finance minister who gave his name to the controversial austerity programme on March 1995, was also clear about the HSP's purpose: 'The historic task of the Socialist government is to roll back the frontiers of the welfare state.'[18]

Bokros' austerity programme was designed to cut government spending and lower interest rates in an attempt to reverse the widening of the trade and current account deficits and reduce the cost of financing enormous levels of domestic and foreign debt. The impact of Bokros' programme on the average Hungarian, earning about $300 a month, was an 11 per cent cut in real wages in 1995 with a planned further 3 to 4 per cent decline in 1996. This cut in living standards was further compounded by reforms of the whole social security and health systems to reduce, amongst other things, spending on an old age and disability pension system which accounted for 11 per cent of GDP in 1993. The 1996 budget, conforming to IMF targets, included a budget deficit set to fall below 4 per cent of GDP, in contrast with 9.5 per cent in 1994.[19] As Bill Lomax has correctly observed, 'Fears that a socialist victory would mark a communist restoration, or that a landslide would bring into parliament a band of old Stalinist functionaries, can largely be discounted'.[20]

Daniel Ziblatt describes the HSP as having three different content themes within their strategic vision:

- firstly, a currently marginal theme of a vaguely defined 'democratic socialist' party with links to a Marxist past, which was only really significant in the HSP until the first elections of March 1990;
- secondly, dominant in the period of opposition from 1990–94, the theme of the HSP as a traditional social democratic party representing those harmed by the economic transition; and
- thirdly, emerging during the period in government from 1994–98, the HSP as a party of technocrats, experts and professionals, committed to pragmatic leadership.

As Ziblatt observes:

Taken together, [these] constitute a strategic vision for HSP party and government leaders that allows the party, as a governing party, to walk on a narrow tightrope between being the social democratic 'protector' of the social welfare state as well as being its 'technocratic' and 'pragmatic' dismantler.[21]

This analysis clearly charts the development of the HSP from reform communism through to a social democratic party of the new type found in western Europe and discussed in Chapter one. Whilst the HSP is a successor party of the former ruling Hungarian Socialist Workers' Party, it is more specifically the successor of the reformist factions within it which brought about its dissolution.[22]

In Poland in 1993, the SdRP campaigned on the basis that its government would 'alleviate all the socio-economic hardships that the Solidarity-led transition had imposed on society',[23] but also committed itself to following the basic direction of the reform, and stressed its professionalism, experience and merit. The SLD (the Democratic Left Alliance led by the SdRP) also committed itself to following the established direction of Polish foreign policy, towards rapid membership of the EU and NATO.

It is apparent, then, that the pattern described previously in the west European communist parties is also apparent in eastern Europe. The western parties included trends towards dissolution, towards social democracy, towards socialist renewal, and towards old-style dogmatism. In the same way that this has led to the DS in Italy becoming Italian social democracy, so the HSP or the SdRP have become the main western new-style social democratic forces in Hungary and Poland. However, in other cases Marxist parties or parties to the left of social democracy have been consolidated, like the German PDS and the CPBM.

Whilst it is harder to define the successor parties of Bulgaria and Romania, both of these parties are significantly to the left of the HSP and the SdRP on economic questions. The BSP includes a significant marxist platform and the SDPR has a statist and interventionist approach.

There are also what could be described as new left forces, both in Hungary and Poland. In Hungary, these forces coalesce around both the Left Platform within the HSP and the Hungarian Left Alternative – an umbrella organization drawing together a number of left groupings and individuals. This trend takes its political framework from the traditions of the workers' councils movement dating from 1956 and defined itself in 1988 not as a party but as 'a social organization building a democratic society based on workers' property, self-management and self-governmental organizations'.[24] In Poland, the left opposition which emerged out of Solidarity as the Union of Labour polled 7.3 per cent in the 1993 elections, but was subsequently split over their attitude towards supporting Kwaśniewski's presidential candidacy and lost further support in the general election of 1997 and the local elections of 1998.

For the forseeable future it would appear that the former communist parties will be the electoral choice of most left-oriented voters throughout central and eastern Europe, notwithstanding their implementation – to a greater or lesser extent – of neo-liberal economic policies, including privatization and cuts in the welfare systems. As the party systems have stabilized during the 1990s, it has become clear that the successor parties face two main political challenges – from liberal 'bourgeois' and from conservative traditionalist forces. The challenge facing the successor parties is how to enlarge their electoral support and avoid being excluded from government in the future.

11
Bulgaria

In April 1990, during the process of change towards a multi-party system, the Bulgarian Communist Party (BCP) changed its name to the Bulgarian Socialist Party (BSP). The BCP/BSP did not undergo any significant splits at the point of system change and retained more or less its pre-1989 composition until a split occurred in 1996. It has, since 1989, been a major force in Bulgarian politics, either as the party of government or as the leading opposition force (see Figure 11.1). During that period, however, the BSP has not been a homogeneous party. Different political currents, which in Hungary, for example, formed the basis for, or participated in, different parties from the late

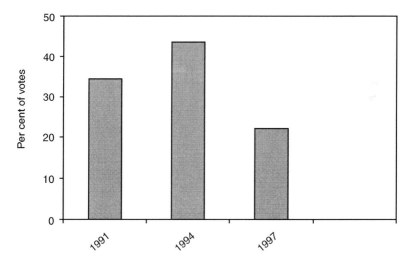

Figure 11.1   Bulgarian Socialist Party election performance, 1991–97

1980s, remained within the BSP. However, whilst this allowed the largest sections of the left to remain unified (only small far-left parties existed outside it), the diversity of positions did, despite very real attempts at compromise, often politically incapacitate the BSP and render it incapable of effective action, particularly in the face of severe economic crisis. Bulgaria was particularly hard hit in the early 1990s by the ending of the CMEA system and the break up of the Soviet Union with which it had strong economic relations.[1] The fall in Bulgarian GNP in the years 1990–92 was in the region of 40 per cent[2] and the devastating impact of this economic collapse on the population can be indicated by the death rate: between 1989–93, the death rate rose by 12 per cent.[3]

Although internally divided over its attitude towards free market policies, the BSP in government did not fully comply with the conditions of the international financial institutions on the pace of economic reform, and financial support from the west was withdrawn. Seeking a way out of the crisis, the BSP government finally embarked on a number of neo-liberal economic reforms which led to an electoral defeat for the BSP, accused of reneging on their electoral pledges, and a victory for the liberal UDF coalition. The BSP, having split prior to the 1997 election, is now a more homogeneous party, which defines itself as democratic socialist.

By the 1980s, the BCP had 'gradually changed from a working-class party into a national party representing a specific section of several social groups and strata',[4] including sections of the bureaucracy who desired the 'transformation of acquired privileges into real economic use.'[5] On the whole these groupings remained together within the BSP as, from the mid-1980s, reform communists in the leadership endeavoured to inaugurate a Bulgarian 'perestroika' to deal with Bulgaria's worsening economic problems and to introduce political reforms to end the inertia of the Zhivkov years. These actions by the reform communists ensured that the BCP was itself the major actor in the process of systemic change. Political forces both inside and outside the BCP emerged in the late 1980s to form a small opposition movement, but this was not a feature of political life in Bulgaria prior to the reform communist initiatives. In this sense it is accurate to describe the changes in Bulgarian political and economic life as initiated from above,[6] and the reform process was embarked upon in a peaceful fashion. There was very little dissent within the party about the need for some reform, both politically and economically, at the time of the ousting of Zhivkov.

The contradiction which existed in the BSP from the very start, however, was how far the reforms should go, and exactly what political space the BSP should occupy. As the differences emerged, it became clear that within the BSP there were supporters for a renewed Marxist politics, for traditional social democracy and for the new neoliberal socialism of the changing west European social democratic parties. There was no clear majority for any of these positions and so a workable consensus was constantly sought. The BSP's search for a viable political identity was, however, further complicated by external factors: the country's profound and worsening economic crisis; the region's economic transition and the interests of the western powers as mediated by the international financial institutions; and the geo-political location of the country between east and west with its orientation towards Russia and the Black Sea region and its strategic position in relation to the crises in Yugoslavia and its potential for escalation into a regional crisis involving Turkey.

Economic stagnation in the second half of the 1980s had led the government to engage in heavy borrowing to 'compensate for the loss of competitiveness, chronic current account deficits, and shortages on the domestic market'.[7] Similar indebtedness had been incurred during the late 1970s, but, as Pishev observes, this had been paid off by re-exporting Soviet oil and petrochemicals and through arms exports during the Iran-Iraq war. No such solutions manifested themselves during the late 1980s and net interest payments on foreign debts grew from US$98 million in 1984 to US$425 million in 1989.[8]

This extreme economic crisis led to the first open manifestation of the division within the Bulgarian communist leadership at the July 1987 Plenum of the Central Committee. The reformists, whose leading figure was Andrei Lukanov, were attempting to push party leader, Todor Zhivkov, towards economic reform. They succeeded in getting the Central Committee to take decisions on the decentralization and liberalization of economic management – the so-called 'July Concepts' – but most of these were subsequently overturned by the more orthodox section of the leadership at the Central Committee plenum of December 1987, and Zhivkov remained completely opposed to any fundamental change, instead attempting to deflect attention from the regime's problems by pressing assimilation policies upon the Turkish minority.

During 1988, opposition forces began to emerge within Bulgaria, primarily around the issues of environmentalism and human rights, such as the Independent Association for Human Rights, the Movement for

Civil Initiative and the Club for the Ecological Defense of Ruse. Ecoglasnost, founded in April 1989, emerged from the latter, and became the first officially registered opposition organization in December 1989.[9] There was considerable support within the BCP itself for change from the kind of Brezhnevite political and economic stagnation which existed. In November 1988, eighty prominent intellectuals, mostly members of the BCP, established the Club for the Support of Glasnost and Perestroika, and once it became clear in December that Zhivkov was attempting to turn back the reforms, Reform Clubs were set up within the BCP to pursue the reform course. In January 1989, Decree 56 was introduced, which basically rehabilitated private initiative within the economy, allowing a variety of types of firm ownership, including private, and relaxing restrictions on foreign investment. The position of the reformists was strengthened during the spring of 1989, when Gorbachev visited Bulgaria, and on 10 November 1989, Zhivkov was forced to resign, after the suppression of human rights and environmental demonstrations, as a result of collective pressure brought to bear by both reformers and orthodox members of the leadership. Zhivkov had appealed to Gorbachev for help, but Gorbachev also told him to resign, so he reluctantly did so.[10]

Zhivkov was replaced as both party leader and head of state by Petur Mladenov, who had been foreign minister since 1971. Mladenov and Prime Minister Georgi Atanasov represented a transitional phase in the reform process, much as Grósz did in Hungary, helping to oust Zhivkov, but preferring 'socialist pluralism' or reform within the framework of the one party state. Mladenov rapidly moved to grant an amnesty to political prisoners and end the policy of assimilation or expulsion of the country's large ethnic Turkish minority. He also met with members of the leading pressure groups like Ecoglasnost, indicating 'that his own criticisms of the Zhivkov regime would be even more damning than theirs.'[11]

On 7 December 1989, ten independent political organizations, including the Club for Glasnost and Perestroika, Ecoglasnost, and a new oppositional trade union federation, the Independent Federation of Labour (Podkrepa), formed the Union of Democratic Forces which was to become Bulgaria's other party of government, alternating in power with the BSP throughout the 1990s. The UDF was also joined by a number of left forces, including the Bulgarian Social Democratic Party, a historic party reformed in 1989 and subsequently a member of the Socialist International; the New Social Democratic Party; and in November 1990 the Alternative Socialist Party founded by reformist defectors from the BCP. The UDF is a coalition of diverse forces but it is united by 'several basic parameters: unyielding anti-communism, commitment to speedy market reforms, pro-western orientation, and a focus on the democratic rights and liberties of the citizen.'[12]

On 22 January 1990, round-table talks commenced between the BCP, the UDF and the Bulgarian Agrarian National Union (BANU). The BANU had been, along with the BCP, one of the leading political forces in the inter-war period, and had been part of the government throughout the communist period. In February, on the formation of a new government, the BANU refused to join, presumably now wanting to develop an independent political role for itself, but this did not actually materialize. The round-table talks effectively laid the basis for a bipolar political system – the red–blue *'chervenite/sinite'* divide, which Daskalov describes as the 'inelastic concentration of the electorate around the two poles of the BSP and UDF'[13] – within which the BANU was marginalized. The BANU fragmented, part of it subsequently joining the UDF, and has been unable to play any serious political role.

A further indication of the shift within the BCP leadership towards reform, occurred at the extraordinary party congress in January/February 1990, which took place during the course of the round-table talks. Mladenov was replaced as party leader by Aleksandur Lilov, who had been demoted from the politburo in 1983 for criticizing Zhivkov and proposing system reform. Atanasov was replaced as prime minister by Andrei Lukanov, who had been minister of foreign trade since 1987. Mladenov remained head of state until his resignation in July, after it was revealed that he had advocated the use of tanks against an opposition demonstration the previous year.[14] He was succeeded as President by Zhelyu Zhelev, the UDF candidate – elected by parliament with the support of the BSP, who still hoped at this point that the UDF could be a 'controlled' opposition.

A number of fundamental changes ensued from the round-table talks in March 1990, which coincided with an intensification of the country's economic crisis and the government's suspension of foreign debt repayments: all communist party cells were closed in state enterprises and other work places; social organizations like the Fatherland Front and the Komsomol (the communist youth movement) were divorced from BCP control; the official trade union organization officially detached itself from the BCP and reorganized as the Confederation of Independent Trade Unions in Bulgaria; and the BCP newspaper, *Rabotnichesko delo*, became *Duma*, a more accessible publication aimed at improving the image of the BCP for the forth-coming free elections.[15]

In January 1990, legislation had been enacted to remove Article 1 from the constitution, which had given the BCP the right to the 'leading role' – political and social predominance – in Bulgaria. In April the BCP changed its name to the Bulgarian Socialist Party and abandoned the ideological label of Marxism-Leninism, confirming itself as a Marxist and 'modern left-wing socialist party'. It also announced a commitment to multi-party elections, which were to be held in June. The BSP emerged as the largest party from the June elections for the National Assembly (see Table 11.1), with 211 out of 400 seats. The UDF took 144, the Movement for Rights and Freedoms (MRF) which was the party of the Turkish minority, took 23, and the BANU 16. The BSP's strength was in the small towns and rural areas while the UDF polled well in the larger cities such as Sofia, Plovdiv and Varna.[16] The former communists had also had an electoral victory in Romania in the previous month and this established a different pattern in south-eastern Europe from that in central Europe where all former communists were defeated in the first free elections. The main reason for the socialist victory in Bulgaria was that there was considerable support for the continuation, albeit reformed, of socialist governance. Bulgaria had a strong socialist tradition throughout the twentieth century, and the BCP was a genuinely popular political current in the inter-war period. This, combined with the traditional pro-Russian sentiments within Bulgaria had meant that communism in Bulgaria had never suffered from the taint of being a foreign import, imposed by a traditional enemy, as it had in Poland, against which a kind of quasi-national liberation struggle could be waged.

Following the BSP's victory, Lukanov did not form a government for three months, as he sought a coalition with the UDF – on the basis that his reforms would need a government of national unity to implement – which he failed to achieve. Lukanov's new programme of economic reforms, outlined in September, was never implemented and thus the type of economic transition which was being undertaken in the central European countries did not get underway in Bulgaria. As Michael L. Wyzan observes, 'One cannot escape the impression that there was a greater continuity between the Zhivkov era and the immediate post-Zhivkov era in Bulgaria than with transitions elsewhere in Eastern Europe.'[17] Whilst the formal aspects of a market economy had been adopted under Decree 56 in 1989, there were few substantive structural changes of the type undertaken elsewhere, and the Lukanov

Table 11.1 Results of Bulgarian general elections, 1990–97

	Grand National Assembly *Election (per cent votes) June 1990		General elections October 1991		December 1994		April 1997	
	% votes	seats	% votes	seats	% votes	seats	% votes	seats
BSP	47.1	211	34.3**	106	43.5***	125	22.1***	58
UDF	38	144	33.1	110	24.2	69	52.3	137
UDF-Centre			3.2					
UDF-Liberals			2.8					
Peoples Union****					6.5	18		
MRF	5.7	23	7.5	24	5.4	15		
BBB					4.7	13	4.9	12
DAR					3.8			
BANU-United	8.3	16	3.8					
BANU-N. Petkov			3.4					
BEL *****							5.6	14
ANS ******							7.6	19
Independents					0.2			
Others	1.0	6	11.6		10.4		7.6	n/a
Total	100	400	100	240	100	240	100	240

* The Grand National Assembly was elected to draft and ratify a new Constitution and work as an assembly until a National Assembly was elected based on the new Constitution.
** BSP (Bulgarian Socialist Party) contested in coalition with Bulgarian Liberal Party, Fatherland Party of Labour, Christian Women's Movement, Christian Republican Party and many minor parties.
*** BSP contested as 'Democratic Left' in alliance with BANU-Stambolski and Ecoglasnost Political Club.
**** An electoral alliance between the right-wing BANU and the Democratic Party; in the 1997 election BANU contested along with UDF and the Union was not operational.
***** BEL (Bulgarian Euro-Left), a centre-left defector from the BSP
****** ANS (Alliance for National Salvation), a centre-right grouping formed in the run-up to the 1997 election by MRF, monarchist formations, splinter group of Ecoglasnost and members of the Peoples Union not wanting alliance with the UDF.
Compiled from internet election sites

government maintained a commitment to maintaining 'controlling participation' by the state in a number of sectors.[18] In September 1990, the BSP held its 39th Congress which indicated that further reform was not a popular option. Not one of the 151 members elected to the party's Supreme Council were reformers. The crisis in the economy continued to worsen, for in addition to the disruption in economic relations with the Soviet Union,

the economy suffered further from the knock-on effect of international sanctions on its former major trading partners Serbia-Montenegro and Iraq, the costs of which were estimated by finance officials at $11 billion.[19]

In September 1990, food rationing was introduced into Sofia, leading to considerable social and industrial unrest, and following a general strike organized by the opposition trade union movement Podkrepa, Lukanov was forced to resign on 21 November 1990, despite his parliamentary majority. He did not take the course chosen by Iliescu, who, when opposition demonstrators attempted to disrupt his government – in spite of his overwhelming electoral majority – called on the miners to clear them from the streets.

An agreement had been reached with the opposition for a multiparty government led by non-party prime minister, D. Popov. In December 1990, the BSP, BANU, UDF and MRF signed the 'Agreement Guaranteeing the Peaceful Transition to a Democratic Society', thus committing themselves to support the Popov cabinet, the drafting of a new constitution, the introduction of a market economy and new general elections to be held during 1991. In January 1991, in an attempt to stabilize the country and end the political and social turmoil, a tripartite agreement was signed between the government, representatives of the major trade unions and employers' associations, followed by the establishing of a Tripartite Commission as a mechanism for dialogue between the three signatories, with the intention of containing social unrest. In October 1991, the BSP lost the general election. The UDF emerged as the largest party, although being short of an overall majority it formed a minority government with the support of the ethnic Turkish MRF.

It had become clear during the course of 1990 that the BSP was politically split, and a number of platforms emerged, particularly during 1990–1. The most significant of these, which continued to play a role within the BSP, were the Union of Social Democracy (USD), the

Marxist Platform (MP) and the Technocratic group. The USD contained a number of the reform communist leadership, most notably Lukanov, and was a significant force within the BSP, organizing affiliated political clubs throughout the country and effectively being a party within a party. In June 1992, the USD held its first Congress, which was attended by representatives of the German SDP, a number of other social democratic parties, and the embassies of the USA, Russia and Hungary. The USD 'embraced the principles of democratic socialism and a social market economy', and stood for the legitimacy of both state and private ownership – within the framework of traditional west European social democracy. This grouping has earned the nickname '*cherveni mobifoni*' – red mobile-phoners, from *Duma* editor Stefan Predev, to denote its socioeconomic base – the new business class,[20] and can be described as for 'nomenklatura capitalism plus efficient social policy'.[21]

The MP is the largest grouping and is closely linked to Aleksandur Lilov, former ideology chief of the BCP until 1983, and now the BSP's political strategist. The Platform is comprised of a number of fractions including more orthodox Marxists, organized in the Marxist Alternative. Its main commitments are to a social market economy, selective renationalization, and the furthering of national interests in relation to the international financial institutions. The Platform also, in the interests of marxist renewal, advocates the consideration of development alternatives like the Chinese economic reform. Predev describes this grouping as '*cherveni babichki*' – or red grannies, describing its resilience for socialism.[22]

The Technocratic group was founded by young reforming 'modernizers' with a background in the Komsomol, or communist youth movement. With its origins in the bureaucracy, it has become the most pro-market reform group within the BSP and through playing the role of power-broker between the USD and the MP it has assumed dominance in the BSP. Its leader Zhan Videnov became party leader in December 1991 and prime minister in the BSP-led Democratic Left coalition government in 1994.

During the BSP's period in opposition from 1991, the UDF government, under Filip Dimitrov, embarked upon a Bulgarian version of shock therapy, including land reform, the dissolution of agricultural cooperatives, price liberalization and privatization legislation.[23] Price liberalization led to the rapid erosion of savings and spending power as inflation reached 338 per cent in 1991 and industrial restructuring led to a rapid increase in unemployment. In September 1992, the MRF withdrew its support from the UDF government, in opposition to the drastic changes in the economy and with accusations of discrimination against the Bulgarian Turks in land privatization measures. This brought down the Dimitrov government, and during the following two years, the BSP backed two 'governments of experts', under Berov and Indzhova. Neither government introduced any significant reform, indeed Berov reinstated some price controls[24] and there were minimal privatization sales.

The BSP went into the 1994 election with a new party programme which attempted to unite the differing perspectives within the Party and outlined a traditional social democratic vision of a 'social market economy' based on a mixed economy where private and state forms of ownership are treated equally: 'they are to interact in a market environment of competition and state regulation, linked together to facilitate nationally strategic and socially coherent development.'[25] The programme emphasises the importance of transformation being a gradual process and explicitly rejects neo-liberal economic policies. Whilst criticizing Bulgaria's communist past, the programme regards the failure of 'real socialism' as the failure of a particular type of socialism and that a new democratic socialism can be developed in Bulgaria rather than embracing free-market capitalism: 'We dissociate [ourselves] from the first [real socialism] not to identify with the injustice and social tyranny of the second [capitalism].'[26] A major role in the transformation is identified for workers' shareholding schemes, participatory democracy and the welfare system.

The specific strategy for economic reform focuses on production-led economic stabilization, where the controlling of inflation and the correction of other economic imbalances are secondary to investment-led recovery.[27] A balance between direct sale and voucher privatizations is advocated to meet concerns of both social fairness and government revenue requirements. In relation to foreign investment and membership of international financial institutions, these are seen as essential for the economic development of the country, but the programme advocates relations on the basis of mutual benefit. For example, receiving credits on the condition of financial-led stabilization, is seen as detrimental to the national interest, and within the BSP there are those that see the IMF and the World Bank as institutions that 'serve us today in order to use us tomorrow'.[28]

The foreign policy orientation is towards achieving a balance between further integration into European political economic structures, maintaining good relations with Russia, and developing

Bulgaria's economic relationship with the middle east and Black Sea regional cooperation. Membership of NATO is seen as desirable only if Russia were to be included within it as an all-European security system. The programme, unanimously accepted by the BSP's 40th congress, was co-authored by M. Minchev and G. Pirinski, leading members, respectively, of the MP and the USD. Thus a political compromise between the two main groupings was effected on paper but was not so easily translatable into actual policies when in government. In the parliamentary elections of December 1994, the BSP won an overall majority forming a Democratic Left coalition government in January 1995 with Zhan Videnov as prime minister. Progress on reform remained slow, because as Videnov himself observed, 'within the party and its coalition partners there is no unanimous political conviction to start implementing [reforms].'[29] In May 1995, the BSP set out its 'Action Programme' of policies for the period 1995–98, including the development of democracy, constitutionality and civil society, the introduction of market reforms and the reduction of inflation and unemployment. In foreign policy, the intention was to further integrate Bulgaria into west European institutions. Yet, as East and Pontin observe, 'the BSP's likely ideological direction was not clear after one year in office'.[30] The 1995 budget both increased state subsidies to industry and cut social spending.

Peter Gowan considers this contradiction to be intentional: 'The BSP sought to maintain some element of ambiguity, favouring privatization and 'market reform' in general public statements, but remaining unenthusiastic in practice'.[31] The divisions within the party, however, make it more likely that the contradictory messages were the result of conflicting approaches within the BSP and the increasing significance of the different economic lobbies with which the USD and the Technocratic group were associated.

Although the economy had made a small upturn in 1995, by early 1996 the government was unable to keep up its interest payments on its foreign debts. Disagreements between the IMF and the Bulgarian government led to a mounting crisis in the banking and enterprise sector and a crash of the Bulgarian currency, fuelling considerable domestic inflation. The IMF wished to use this opportunity to extract specific policy concessions from the Bulgarian government, which the BSP had been unwilling to undertake, in exchange for economic assistance. In the summer of 1996, the government acceded to the IMF requirements, which included asset sales to foreign investors and the closure of unprofitable state enterprises, which resulted in over 40 000 redundancies.[32] As well as leading to public outcry, this compliance provoked increased tensions amongst the three main factions. The MP and the USD were united in their criticisms of Videnov's handling of the crisis with the IMF. Lukanov, of the USD, accused Videnov's cabinet 'of capitulating to IMF pressure and preparing a structural reform programme effectively bordering on treason.'[33] Some observers considered that Videnov had consciously undertaken negotiations with the IMF when the economy was in a weak condition so that harsher IMF conditions could be justified; the economic interests associated with the Videnov group would then benefit from the structural reforms initiated by the IMF terms. Videnov was able to resist any attempts to oust him from government, however, and he avoided any significant cabinet reshuffle.

The agreement with the IMF led to a wave of shock therapy economic policies which resulted in popular dissatisfaction with the BSP government who were perceived to have reneged on their election promises. Lukanov, the leading figure in the USD, was assassinated in October 1996, and in November 1996 the BSP's candidate in the presidential elections was overwhelmingly defeated by the opposition candidate P. Stoyanov. Following this defeat, a group of leading members of the MP and USD formed 'Group 19', which demanded an extraordinary party congress with the intention of forcing a change of government. The 42nd congress, which took place on 21–23 December 1996, resulted in Videnov's resignation as both party leader and prime minister. He was succeeded as party leader by G. Pervanov, a compromise candidate agreed upon by the main party factions. N. Dobrev was elected to succeed Videnov as prime minister, but continued daily strikes and demonstrations by the opposition and further internal disagreements within the BSP prevented him forming a new government. A caretaker government was formed in early 1997, with President Stoyanov nominating Stefan Sofianski, UDF mayor of Sofia since 1995, to lead the government.

A general election was called in April 1997. The BSP contested as the Democratic Left coalition again, in alliance with BANU–Stamboliski – the more left-wing agrarian party, and Ecoglasnost. The BSP had now suffered its first serious split since the system change. Prior to the election, a section of the USD grouping broke away from the BSP to form the Bulgarian Euro-Left party, under the leadership of Alexander Tomov – a likelihood noted in 1993 by Georgi Karasimeonov: 'Two trends exist within the [USD] itself – one upholding the line of greater

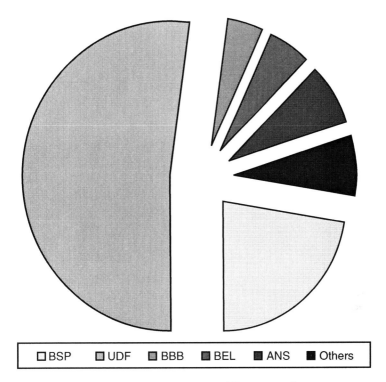

□ BSP   ▨ UDF   ▨ BBB   ▨ BEL   ▨ ANS   ■ Others

BSP = Bulgarian Socialist Party; UDF = Union of Democratic Forces;
BBB = Bulgarian Business Block; BEL = Bulgarian Euro-Left; ANS = Alliance for
National Salvation.

Figure 11.2   Bulgarian general election, 1997 (% votes)

independence and even for separation from the BSP (Tomov), the
other hoping to win positions inside the party (Kyuranov, Pirinski)'.[34]
The Euro-Left contested the elections as an independent force. The
elections were an overwhelming victory for the UDF (see Figure 11.2),
who contested in alliance with the right-wing agrarian BANU. The UDF
polled 52.3 per cent of the votes cast, the Democratic Left polled
22.1 per cent and the Euro-Left 5.6 per cent.

During the course of 1998, the difference in political position
between the BSP and the Euro-Left was clarified, but positive steps were
also taken towards forming a new left coalition to structure opposition
to the UDF both inside and outside parliament. In May 1998 the BSP
held its 43rd Congress and confirmed itself as a left-of-centre party. In

June 1998, both the Euro-Left and the Bulgarian Social Democratic Party (BSDP) – but not the BSP – were invited to participate in the Berlin Conference of European Social Democracy. From the summer of 1998, however, various political initiatives have been undertaken to bring some measure of unity of action to the Bulgarian left. In July 1998, representatives of the BSP, the Euro-Left and other smaller left parties attended a conference entitled 'New-left Social Democracy 2001' organized by the Euro-Left. Agreement was reached to establish a joint working group, and at the same time all left-wing parties and the two labour unions for the first time took a united stand against the UDF government's three-year programme of stabilization and adjustment.

In August 1998, the Party of European Socialists hosted a conference in Thessaloniki in Greece to attempt to unite the Euro-Left, the BSP and other social democratic forces. However, the parties decided to maintain their political independence, but to work together to oppose the UDF.

Although tensions had existed within the BSP about the extent of economic reform and the balance between state and market, they were uneasily reconciled until forced to a decisive point by the conflict with the IMF over the implementation of reforms and structural adjustment. The eventual split of the Euro-Left from the BSP removed that section of the party which either saw no alternative to accepting the wishes of west European capitalism and the neo-liberal requirements of the international financial institutions, or wished to benefit from embracing them. The BSP remains a party troubled by internal political differences, but it has now clarified its political identity as a socialist party, to the left of European social democracy. The orientation of the Euro-Left is as a social democratic party of the new type.

12
Romania

The experience of Romania since 1989 is quite different from that of the other central and east European countries. In 1989 the despotic Ceauşescu was removed from power by a combination of forces, effectively led by high-ranking communists in opposition to Ceauşescu. The National Salvation Front, under the leadership of Ion Iliescu, replaced the Romanian Communist Party as the state party, and its intention to continue to pursue a predominantly state-controlled economy was overwhelmingly endorsed by the electorate in free parliamentary elections in 1990 (see Figure 12.1). Iliescu's expectation was that Gorbachev's reforms of the Soviet Union would be successful and that a socialist Romania would reorientate towards the Soviet Union. Indeed, in 1987, Iliescu had advocated a transition in Romania towards 'Soviet-style perestroika'.[1]

It was in this context that Iliescu 'embraced "market socialism" defined as the continuation of a non-capitalist economy, thus rejecting the regime programme set out by the West.'[2] The ruling group was not intending to initiate a transition to capitalism, although it did introduce economic reforms allowing small-scale private enterprises to operate. This perspective foundered with the demise of the Soviet Union at the end of 1991, leading to the eventual reorientation of Iliescu's party, renamed in 1994 the Social Democratic Party of Romania (PDSR), towards the introduction of capitalism, albeit 'a strongly national one rather than the "globalized" variety.'[3] Romania has a strong tradition of economic autarchy, both before and during the communist period and the desire to maintain national control over the national economy has been a popular one. Economic problems in the mid-1990s, however, led Iliescu to adopt a number of IMF-inspired reforms which were unpopular, which resulted in victory by the liberal Democratic Convention in the elections of 1996

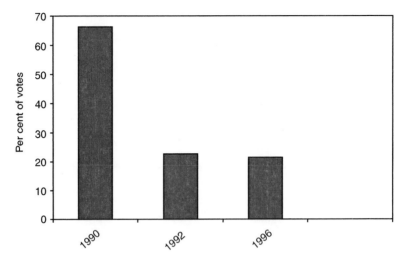

Figure 12.1 Election performance of the Social Democratic Party of Romania, PDSR,* 1990–96

* The Social Democratic Party of Romania (PDSR) is effectively the main successor party of the Romanian Communist Party. It began life in the 1990 elections as the National Salvation Front (FSN), was renamed in 1992 as the Democratic National Salvation Front (FSND), and in 1996 as the PDSR.

(see Table 12.1). This led observers to anticipate an acceleration in the reform process but this has not been forthcoming, obstructed by the bureaucracy and the labour movement.

National autonomy was indeed a significant and popular thread during the period of Ceauşescu's leadership of the Romanian Communist Party (RCP). The break with the Soviet Union during the 1960s was primarily the result of Khrushchev's attempts to institute a socialist division of labour through CMEA to introduce bloc-wide economies of scale. Romania was designated to be an agricultural producer, which Ceauşescu rejected. He wanted the modernization and prosperity which would be brought by industrial development and so broke with the Soviet leadership.

Highly successful during the 1960s, the economy began to decline in the 1970s, and Romania began to borrow from the west. By 1981, Romania had foreign debts of US$10 000 million, which Ceauşescu decided he was going to repay, 'convinced that the debt that Romania had amassed was a threat to Romanian economic autonomy and ultimately to political autonomy.'[4] Indeed, by April 1989 Romania had

Table 12.1   Results of Romanian general elections, 1990–96

	1990		1992		1996	
	% votes*	seats	% votes	seats	% votes	seats
FSND			22.7	117		
PDSR					21.5	91
USD					12.9	53
CDR			20.0	82	30.2	122
FSN	66.3	263	10.8	43		
PUNR			7.7	30	4.4	18
UDMR	7.2	29	7.5	27	6.6	25
PRM			3.9	16	4.5	19
PSM			3.0	13	2.2	
PDAR	1.6	9				
NLP	6.4	29				
PNT–CD	2.6	12				
EM	2.6	12				
EP	1.4	8				
RUA	2.2	9				
Reserved**				13		15
Others	9.7	5	20.0		9.2	
Total	100		100	328	100	328

* Percentage of votes cast for party lists.
** Fixed minority representation
FSND = Democratic National Salvation Front;
PDSR = Social Democratic Party of Romania; USD = Union of Social Democracy;
CDR = Democratic Convention of Romania; FSN = National Salvation Front;
PUNR = Romanian National Unity Party; UDMR = Hungarian Democratic Union
of Romania; PRM = Greater Romanian Party; PSM = Socialist Party of Labour;
PDAR = Democratic Agrarian Party of Romania, NLP = National Liberal Party;
PNT-CD = National Peasant Party – Christian Democratic; EM = Ecological Movement;
EP = Ecological Party; RUA = Romanian Unity Alliance.
Compiled from internet election sites

completely repaid its foreign debt through surpluses achieved by increasing exports and decreasing imports. As Teodorescu observes:

> The official figures seem to indicate that between 1981 and 1989 Romania paid US$10 000 million on its loans, plus US$6000 million in interest, that is US$16 000 million over eight years, an average of about $2000 million each year.[5]

Whilst this was an extraordinary feat, it was achieved at huge cost to the ordinary Romanian citizen, so that on Ceaușescu's fall Romania had the lowest standard of living in eastern Europe, with the exception of Albania.

This policy of repayment shifted the attitude towards Ceauşescu away from the popularity he had achieved in the 1960s. Greater and greater sacrifices were extracted from the population through slashing their living standards on all fronts – including domestic fuel and energy supplies which caused considerable hardship. As Ceauşescu resorted to increasingly brutal and repressive policies, so overt signs of resistance began to appear at different levels within society. On the one hand, there were alleged attempts at coups by senior army officials and party members in 1983 and 1984, and in 1987 Sylviu Brucan, former ambassador to the US, and Ion Iliescu, openly aired their criticisms;[6] and on the other, there were the beginnings of popular demonstrations, in particular strikes.

In 1977, the first real act of dissent against Ceauşescu's policies of any mass significance occurred in the form of the Jiu Valley miners' strike. Ceauşescu, facing economic problems, was beginning to implement austerity measures, and attempted to end disability pensions for miners and raise the retirement age from 50 to 55. The government was forced into a humiliating set of concessions and Ceauşescu himself had to meet the miners and hear their demands. The government subsequently reneged on the deal, but the power of the regime had been challenged in a way that was personally threatening to Ceauşescu. From this point, the state security force, the securitate, was strengthened and its remit was extended to include propagating the personality cult of Ceauşescu and silencing the regime's critics abroad, for example, the dissident emigre writer, Paul Goma, who received a parcel bomb, addressed from Madrid in February 1981.[7]

In November 1987, thousands of workers at the Red Flag Truck Enterprise in the city of Braşov protested against reductions in heating quotas for domestic consumption. These were in addition to wage cuts for the second consecutive month for failure to meet production targets. The protest was joined by many onlookers, as the factory workers marched on the city's party headquarters, 'who proceeded to destroy records and equipment'.[8] Troops were required to restore order. Again, Ceauşescu ordered a further improvement in the effectiveness of the security forces and new special security units were set up in the major provincial cities. Clearly Ceauşescu's approach was to pursue an increasingly coercive and repressive policy while the austerity programme was being implemented.

Intellectual opposition came out in the open in the late 1980s, encouraged by international concern about Romania's human rights record, particularly around Doina Cornea and the writer Mircea Dinescu. This opposition was also ruthlessly suppressed by Ceauşescu, although working-class opposition to the regime was always of greater concern to Ceauşescu because it struck at the foundations of the regime's claim to be a socialist state. The major challenge from within the party occurred in March 1989 when six of its most distinguished members – including two former general secretaries of the RCP, Gheorghe Apostol and Constantin Pârvulescu[9] – wrote an open letter to Ceauşescu complaining of the systematization policy, appealing for the restoration of the rule of law, and human and constitutional rights. The protestors were placed under house arrest.

The systematization policy was a brutal and far-reaching plan for rural redevelopment which constituted one of the last straws before the back of toleration of the Ceauşescu regime was broken. In March 1988, Ceauşescu announced the reduction of the number of villages from around 13 000 to around 5000 to 6000. The surplus villages were to be destroyed and the land given over to agricultural use. The 11 million displaced villagers were to be concentrated into new 'agro-industrial complexes'. This process of 'systematization' was to be completed by the year 2000. Given Ceauşescu's record in achieving his 'redevelopment' aims – most notably the destruction of vast and beautiful parts of old Bucharest – there can be little doubt that he would have pushed this plan to completion. The systematization of the countryside was justified on both economic and ideological grounds. Additional agricultural land could be handed over for collectivization and superior economies of scale. It would have the ideological advantage of stamping out smallholding, as *Scînteia* observed: 'The "autarchic cultural existence" of villagers stood in the way, so it was explained, of the socialist homogenization of Romanian society'.[10]

This approach to total and compulsory socialization caused considerable alarm throughout the countryside, meeting with resistance, and rebellions were reported in several areas. In some areas officials concealed villages by merging them administratively into larger units. Even so the programme went ahead, with villagers receiving little notice of eviction – in one instance only 48 hours and having to demolish their own homes before leaving. These events were widely publicized and criticized in the west and finally shifted western support away from Ceauşescu, whom many governments – including the British – had been keen to support in the light of his anti-Soviet stance.

This was now, of course, irrelevant anyway, because of the changes in Soviet policy since the arrival in power of Gorbachev.

Ceauşescu's systematization policy was probably based on the fact that the collectivization campaigns in the late 1950s and early 1960s led to the most successful period of rapid economic development in Romanian history. In the mid-1950s, two-thirds of the labour force were still in the primary sector.[11] The collectivization of agriculture, which was accompanied by an increase in the mechanization of agriculture, released labour from the land and its traditional unproductive methods. It was also accompanied by the development of manufacturing industry, which meant that there was a big shift from under-utilized rural labour to employment in the industrial and manufacturing sector. As Ronnas observes: 'The share of the non-agricultural population in the total labour force increased from 30.3 per cent in 1956 to 42.9 per cent in 1966, and to 63.5 per cent in 1977'.[12] This process led to huge gains in productivity and the high overall growth rates in the 1960s and early 1970s 'were largely a result of these transfer gains'.[13] Ceauşescu's crude response to the need for further economic development in the 1980s, which should have been orientated towards light industry and consumer goods manufacturing for export and domestic consumption, was, rather, an attempt to emulate the successes of the 1960s through creating surplus agricultural labour and further developing large scale heavy industry. The programme was terminated by the National Salvation Front (NSF).

The immediate event which triggered the overthrow was a popular demonstration in the western town of Timişoara, over the forcible removal of the local pastor, László Tökés. Violent suppression of this peaceful demonstration led to a wave of demonstrations – also no doubt encouraged by news of the popular protests and changes of regime in a number of the other east European countries – which Ceauşescu dismissed as the work of foreign agents and terrorists. This wave of popular anger and resentment against the government was accompanied by a movement amongst reform-minded communists, which was critical in gaining the support of the generals for a change of leadership and therefore securing the ultimate defeat of Ceauşescu's forces. As Martin Rady observes:

> By the swift measures that they put in train on the day of Ceauşescu's flight, Iliescu and his supporters did not so much hijack the revolution as ensure its ultimate triumph over the remnants of the Ceauşescu government.[14]

The exact balance of forces in the overthrow of Ceauşescu, between the extremes of 'palace coup' and 'popular revolution' has been much debated.

Iliescu was the leading figure in the NSF and had been a critic of Ceauşescu during the 1980s, orientating towards Gorbachev and perestroika-style reforms whilst maintaining a state socialist system. He was closely supported in the leadership by Silviu Brucan who had also maintained a critical stance towards Ceauşescu in the 1980s. In fact, in 1987 he had criticized the suppression of the workers' protests in Braşov 'predicting with great accuracy that, "repression will generate a rupture between the party and the working class".'[15] A number of prominent intellectuals were appointed to the Council of the NSF, including László Tökés, Doina Cornea and Mircea Dinescu, but real control lay with communist party, army and securitate leaders.

The main activity of the NSF between Ceauşescu's fall in December 1989 and the general election in May 1990 was the allocation of resources to the population, including food, energy and other basic necessities. This was fairly effectively achieved and food supplies increased dramatically. Restrictions on the supply of domestic energy were also removed. Many of the more repressive laws were repealed, including those on systematization, worker contribution to social funds, territorial self-sufficiency and anti-birth control and anti-abortion measures.[16] In February, agricultural reform was undertaken, allowing long-term leases on collective farm land and increased size personal plots and state procurement prices for both agricultural and animal products were increased which provided, as Ronnas observed, 'a sorely needed stimulus to agricultural production.'[17]

Legislation was passed in March 1990 allowing the operation of private enterprises, although in the first instance the number of employees permitted was restricted to ten. There was very little change, however, in the centrally-planned state sector. The NSF's economic reform programme in 1990 was based on the implementation of gradual changes in the economy, with the retention of state ownership in key sectors, the development of a private sector and the maintenance of Romanian control over its own national economy. The programme specified that: 'the fundamental aim of the FSN economic policy is to ensure the welfare of the entire people and the quality of life in all respects.'[18] With a turnout of 86 per cent, the elections resulted in an overwhelming victory for Iliescu and the NSF. In the presidential election, Iliescu won 85 per cent of the vote and the NSF

66 and 67 per cent of seats in the Chamber of Deputies and Senate respectively.

Many western observers expressed surprise at the widespread support which the NSF received amongst the Romanian population, given its high level of correspondence to the former Romanian Communist Party. This sentiment increased after the party again performed well in the elections in 1992 and exasperated the political opposition in Romania. Younger, more western-oriented oppositionists were frustrated by what they perceived as the inertia, or even stupidity, of the mass of the population. But in fact, continued voting for the NSF and for Iliescu, constituted a vote for stability.

For a population where an estimated one-third of adults had been party members and much of the rest drawn into some form of collaboration, whether willing or unwilling, the approach of the NSF, that simply declared the system finished and the past dispensed with, was bound to be hugely popular. The enormous level of suffering that had been endured, particularly during the 1980s was something that people generally wanted to set behind them. Thus:

> the appeals from young people to expose and punish collaborators seemed not only a measure of their own previous insulation from the responsibilities of adulthood but also the prelude to a potentially limitless witch-hunt.[19]

A huge majority of the population voted against the introduction of a new punitive regime.

However, there was undoubtedly a level of extreme hostility towards former communists among some sections of the population. In the run up to the general election, the two anti-NSF daily newspapers, *Romania Libera* and *Dreptatea*, launched a campaign to cancel the new electoral law and introduce another, whereby, irrespective of what they had actually done, no one who had ever been an RCP activist would be allowed to stand for parliament in the three subsequent general elections. As Patrick Camiller observed in 1990:

> This anti-democratic demand, without parallel elsewhere in Eastern Europe, was widely seen as a crude and desperate manoeuvre to revive the fortunes of the two 'historic' right-wing parties – the National Peasants and the National Liberals – which in their heyday in the thirties had vied with each other in electoral fraud and manipulation.[20]

During the election campaign, several hundred protestors occupied the centrally-located University Square – mostly youth and students – also making the demand for the exclusion of former communists from the electoral process. For two months the NSF leadership allowed this demonstration to continue, but a hard core remained – even after the overwhelming popular mandate for Iliescu's policies – demanding the resignation of the government and a 'second revolution'. In June, an attack by demonstrators on the police–army cordon around the government building where negotiations on government concessions to the demonstrators were taking place, led to the clearing of the square by riot police. This was followed by an arson attack on the police headquarters and the interior ministry by demonstrators, a number of whom carried fire-arms. There was also a Molotov-cocktail attack by around 5000 demonstrators on the Romanian television centre.

Iliescu was clearly not going to be bullied out of government when he had such widespread popular support and proceeded to mobilize some of that support in defense of the government. Workers from Bucharest's IMGB industrial complex were called upon to help recapture the television centre, which was successfully achieved. Miners from the Jiu Valley and other pits arrived in Bucharest the following day and the demonstrators disappeared. This was, unfortunately, followed by some acts of violence by the miners, but this was, as Camiller points out 'a response to the savage actions of a tiny minority', who were attempting to overturn a democratically-elected government. Expectations, from some anti-NSF observers, that these events would lead to an authoritarian turn in Romania were shown to be incorrect as the opposition press immediately reappeared after the crisis without any restrictions.

During 1990, different attitudes began to emerge within the NSF towards the nature and pace of the transition process. Whilst Iliescu and other leading figures remained opposed to any radical reform on the lines of those undertaken in the central European countries and maintained a national economic plan, other leaders indicated that they were in favour of more substantial change. As Martin Rady points out, 'A radical group gathered around Adrian Severin, the Minister for Privatization, advocated the shock treatment of the economy'.[21] In 1990, Prime Minister Petre Roman also stated that he favoured privatization, the reduction of the bureaucracy and the market economy. He distanced himself from a more radical economic approach, however, in favour of championing a more gradualist social democracy. He was, presumably, aiming to occupy the centre-left political ground at a time when it was becoming increasingly evident that socialism was not going to survive in the Soviet Union and that Romania would find it increasingly difficult to resist economic transition. Thus there was a division within the NSF between pro and anti- capitalist restoration groupings. In April 1991, the Roman government introduced price liberalization. This was its first major economic reform, enacted with the intention of attracting western financial assistance which had largely been withheld, pending reform measures acceptable to the west. The liberalization doubled the prices of many basic necessities, and led to a high level of industrial unrest throughout 1991 as workers' real wages fell. In September 1991 the Jiu Valley miners returned to Bucharest to make violent protest against Roman's austerity policies and their declining standards of living. Roman resigned, 'describing himself as the victim "of those who want to maintain the old system".'[22] Roman's successor, Theodor Stolojan, improved Romania's relations with western institutions, and particularly NATO and the EU, but the general pace of economic reform was slow.

The political division within the NSF became an organizational one in the run up to the September 1992 general elections. Iliescu's wing of the party formed the Democratic National Salvation Front, whilst Roman's reformist section retained the name NSF. (In 1993, Iliescu's DNSF was renamed the Social Democratic Party of Romania (PDSR), and Roman's NSF, the Democratic Party-NSF.) Following this separation, Roman made clear his views about Iliescu, attacking him 'for neo-communism, for obstructing democratic and economic reforms, and for protecting former Securitate agents'.[23] Nevertheless, Iliescu's party emerged from the 1992 parliamentary elections as the largest single party, whereas Roman's party polled only ten per cent of votes, indicating again that his austerity measures had been deeply unpopular.

The results also pointed to the consolidation of opposition forces: the DNSF polled 27.7 per cent in the House of Deputies and 28.2 per cent in the Senate; the Democratic Convention of Romania (CDR), a coalition of opposition parties, polled 20 per cent and 20.1 per cent respectively; and the NSF polled 10.1 per cent and 10.3 per cent respectively. In the presidential elections, Iliescu defeated the DCR candidate, Emil Constantinescu, with 61.6 per cent. The DNSF formed a minority government under non-party Prime Minister Nicolae Vacaroiu, which from August 1994 was joined in a coalition by the small nationalist party, the Romanian National Unity Party (PUNR), led by Gheorghe Funar and from January 1995 by the Greater Romania Party (PRM), led by Corneliu Vadim Tudor, and the orthodox communist Socialist Labour Party (PSM), under former communist-period Prime Minister,

Ilie Verdet. Clearly, the PDSR had decided to make a tactical alliance with the small nationalist and communist parties, who favoured economic autarchy, to avoid the type of western open-door economic policy which was favoured by the opposition.

The record of the government was a mixed one. By 1993, economic decline had halted, although there was increasing unemployment, a decline in real wages and increasing industrial unrest. Further price liberalization took place, value-added tax was introduced and a four-year economic reform programme, including privatization, was announced; but in fact the reform process advanced very slowly, with no restructuring of large-scale state-owned enterprises. In 1993, the IMF withheld funding because of the slow reform progress, particularly with regard to the privatizing of state-owned enterprises.

From 1994, the situation began to change. Under severe pressure from the IMF, and unable to see any forthcoming change in the international balance of forces which would make any other option possible, the PDSR government began to shift its economic policy. In February 1994, the Romanian parliament passed an IMF-approved austerity programme in exchange for credits of around $450 million. The programme included restructuring and privatization of state-owned companies; currency convertibility; and the reduction of inflation to under 100 per cent by the end of 1994.[24] Inflation was actually reduced from 256 per cent in 1993 to 62 per cent in 1994.[25] By 1995, the economy had emerged from the disastrous decline of the early 1990s and was in growth of around 5 per cent. Even the industrial sector, which had contracted by 54 per cent between 1990 and 1992 was beginning to grow, by just over 2 per cent in 1994. Agriculture, banking and financial services and construction were all major positive growth areas.

By 1995 a concurrent political shift had also taken place within the leadership of the PDSR. By the end of 1995, the PDSR was attempting to distance itself from its more extreme coalition partners and the PRM was expelled from the governing coalition. The PDSR ran a minority government whilst making attempts to form a new coalition with some of the opposition parties in a 'government of national unity'.[26] The PDSR, with an eye to the forthcoming elections of 1996, were now trying to establish themselves as a reforming centre-ground party, seeking western economic support and inclusion in western institutions. They now undertook further steps in the reform process which had long been demanded by the western financial institutions. In August 1995, the mass privatization scheme was launched, which aimed to privatize 3904 enterprises by the spring of 1996. All

Romanian citizens received $500 worth of vouchers. In November 1995, restitution legislation compensated around 200 000 former owners or their descendants whose property had been nationalized.

A shift in the economy had begun to take place but, nevertheless, Iliescu still attempted to keep it within certain limits, balancing the relationship between what was necessary to secure western support and what could be maintained of the state control of the economy. According to government estimates, private sector share of GDP rose from 35 per cent in 1994 to around 55 per cent in 1997. However, as the EBRD pointed out, these estimates included firms with a state-owned minority stake. Whilst the private sector constituted around 23 per cent of employment in 1995 and 47 per cent in 1996,[27] the most significant part of the private sector was still in new start-ups, however, rather than the privatization of state-owned enterprises. Between 1992 and October 1996 the number of state-owned enterprises was reduced slightly, from around 8000 to 6000, whilst the number of private companies rose from 200 000 to 500 000.[28]

In October 1995, whilst waiting for another delayed round of IMF/World Bank stand-by financing, Iliescu visited the United States to secure international respectability for his leadership. Indeed, James Wolfensohn, the President of the World Bank, congratulated him on Romania's economic development. As the *Eastern Europe Newsletter* commented at the time, 'After over two years of "social market economy" policies (i.e. delays in the implementation of key reforms) the government is in a panic to get things done quickly to ensure international financial support and to win the 1996 elections.'[29]

Iliescu had finally decided that there was no alternative to participation and cooperation with the international financial institutions, although he continued to maintain a position for strong national control of the economy which differentiated the PDSR from the more western-oriented opposition. This approach is apparent from the figures for the privatization of enterprises scheduled to be sold off. By the end of 1996, '70% of small enterprises had been sold, but only 24% of medium-sized and 13% of large enterprises'.[30] Iliescu hoped to maintain national control over the 'commanding heights' of the economy, attempting to keep state control of large enterprises rather than either opening them to foreign ownership – as insufficient private capital existed within Romania – or closing loss-making enterprises with the concurrent problems of unemployment that such a step would produce.

During the course of 1996, however, the PDSR's popularity declined, with banking and agricultural crises having a negative impact on large sections of the population. The problems in agriculture, partly caused by drought, were a particular blow for the PDSR, which had previously relied heavily on rural votes. Local elections in June gave the PDSR 24 per cent of local council seats; the CDR took 16.5 per cent and the Union of Social Democracy (USD) – an alliance led by Roman's Democratic Party-NSF – took 15 per cent. It was now clear that an opposition alliance of the CDR and USD could defeat the PDSR.

This indeed turned out to be the case, for in November 1996 the CDR–USD alliance secured victory in the parliamentary elections, although the PDSR remained the largest single party (see Figure 12.2). The CDR took 30 per cent of the vote in the Chamber of Deputies, the

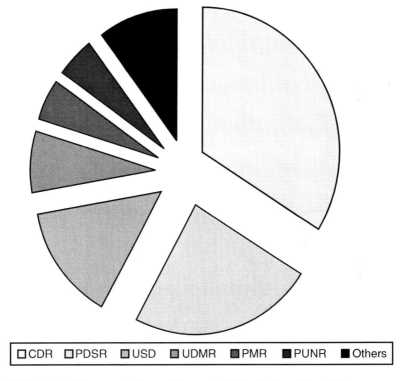

□ CDR □ PDSR ▨ USD ▨ UDMR ▨ PMR ■ PUNR ■ Others

PDSR = Social Democratic Party of Romania; USD = Union of Social Democracy; CDR = Democratic Convention of Romania; PUNR = Romanian National Unity Party; UDMR = Hungarian Democratic Union of Romania; PMR = Greater Romanian Party.

Figure 12.2   Romanian general election, 1996 (per cent of votes)

PDSR took 22 per cent and the USD took 13 per cent. Of more surprise to observers was the fact that Iliescu was beaten in the presidential elections by Emil Constantinescu, the candidate of the CDR, by 54.1 per cent to 45.7 per cent on a 72 per cent turn out.[31] The two small left parties, the Socialist Labour Party and the more reformist Socialist Party, polled less than 3 per cent each.

A new coalition government was formed under the leadership of Victor Ciorbea, including the CDR, the USD and the Democratic Union of Hungarians in Romania (UDMR), now participating in government for the first time. At the end of January 1997, Ciorbea announced the introduction of a programme of shock therapy policies, worked out in consultation with the IMF and the World Bank. The programme was intended to reduce inflation, halt the depreciation of the currency and reduce the substantial budget deficit. Key policies were to be a 'renewed privatisation initiative'[32] and a drive to increase foreign investment. The conditions required by the IMF and World Bank for their one-year standby agreement and structural adjustment loan resulted in a harsh attack on the standards of living of the Romanian population. As Tom Gallagher observed:

> Between February and May prices for energy and fuel were completely liberalized and, during the first quarter of the year, prices in the shops for a wide range of commodities doubled. Business suffered greatly from the slump in domestic demand and average living standards were expected to drop by around 20% in 1997 in a country where the average wage was only $80 a month.[33]

Ciorbea's government received high ratings in opinion polls throughout 1997, and the anti-corruption drive proved a popular initiative, yet the promised economic take-off did not come about – not least because the expected foreign investment did not materialize. Despite the widespread assumptions that the long-delayed economic reforms would now take place and Romania would take its place among the advanced transition economies of central Europe, the reform process was actually hesitant and ineffectual, ending the modest growth of the period since 1993 and leading Romania into negative GDP growth.

The government was not, however, confronted by an effective opposition, either within parliament or, initially, from the labour movement. Whilst the governing coalition faced a lack of internal cohesion, the PDSR was facing grave internal divisions, which materialized in June 1997 with the founding of the Alliance for Romania (ApR) – a party of moderate reformers split from the PDSR. The ApR breakaway was led by Teodor Melescanu, PDSR foreign minister from 1992–96, who was responsible for improving Romania's relations with Hungary and strengthening the country's western orientation. Its declared principles included:

> morality in political life; a responsible attitude towards electoral campaign promises; realism and pragmatism in economic and social problems; a new relationship between government and opposition to ensure governments exercise power for the benefit of the people; and consistent upholding of social democratic principles, especially the redistribution of wealth.[34]

This move of a section of the PDSR towards the political centre left a smaller PDSR, still under Iliescu's leadership, maintaining its support for national economic development through direct state intervention. Melescanu and the ApR were also perceived as a challenge to Roman and the USD, whose political space they were clearly threatening. In fact, there seemed to be an increasing movement towards the centre ground of politics, as the extreme nationalist PUNR, formerly led by Gheorghe Funar, mayor of Cluj, was now under the leadership of the more moderate Valeriu Tabara. This apparent trend led *Eastern Europe Newsletter* to observe in August 1997, that:

> Party politics are settling down into a conventional pattern in which a liberal, social democratic majority dominates the expanded centre ground at the expense of the neo-communists and national-ists on the fringes.[35]

By December, however, there was still no sight of economic improve-ment – indeed conditions were worsening, and industrial unrest was again occurring as the government declared its intention to close down loss-making state-enterprises. Support was increasing for the extreme right-wing PRM under the leadership of Corneliu Vadim Tudor whose Congress in November 1997 was attended by the French National Front leader, Jean-Marie Le Pen.

By January 1998, Ciorbea's leadership was coming under sustained attack from within the governing coalition, particularly from Roman, who was demanding his resignation over the country's poor economic performance. Total 1997 inflation was calculated to be around 150 per cent, and the EBRD's estimated decline in GDP for 1997 was –6.6 per cent – a disaster, having been in growth since 1993, and forecast to continue in severe decline.[36] Its GDP in 1998 was forecast by the EBRD to be 78 if its GDP in 1989 was taken to be 100.[37]

In April, Ciorbea was replaced as prime minister by Radu Vasile, who also entered office with the intention of forming a new and effective privatization plan and thus securing IMF support and foreign investment. But no progress was made by Vasile either, partly because of differences within the governing coalition and opposition from the trade unions, but the most widely-blamed culprit was the bureaucracy, which appeared to be obstructing the implementation of reforms. By the end of 1998, Romania was facing a current account deficit approaching $2 billion for 1998, inflation of around 250 per cent and GDP down by at least 10 per cent in 1998.[38] The IMF was still withholding further loans pending the closure of loss-making state companies and a loan of $500m from the World Bank depended on the closure of a number of state farms.[39]

However, as the government attempted to implement a number of cuts and closures, it was faced in January 1999 with a strike and demonstration by 10 000 miners under the leadership of Miron Cozma, who began the march on Bucharest demanding negotiations with Prime Minister Vasile. The march was ended on agreement by the government to increase wages and reopen a number of closed mines. Cozma is reported to be close to Vadim Tudor's Greater Romania Party, supporting its protectionist and anti-western economic policies. Tudor's party increased rapidly in the opinion polls during the last few months of 1998 from 4 per cent to over 16 per cent.[40]

In the event of an early general election being held, the PDSR could be expected to perform well, if it distanced itself from its mid-90s policies of compromise with the international financial institutions. With the departure of Roman's wing in the early 1990s and Melescanu's grouping in 1997, the PDSR is politically far more homogeneous than previously and can be expected to maintain a position for greater economic autarchy and support of the state sector – a popular choice for many faced with unemployment under IMF-backed austerity programmes.

13
Hungary

There can be no doubt that the Hungarian Socialist Party (HSP) had an enormously swift and successful metamorphosis on its journey from the reform wing of the former ruling Hungarian Socialist Workers' Party (HSWP) to its destination as a socialist party of the new type (see Figure 13.1). As outlined in Chapter 10, the HSP enthusiastically embraced neo-liberal economic policies during its period of government from 1994–98 and fell in behind the new model of social democracy, pioneered by Gonzàlez in Spain in the 1980s and reinforced by Blair in Britain in the 1990s. Yet, in many respects, the HSP had a headstart in their own transition from socialism to capitalism, for social and economic reform were not a new phenomenon in Hungary even prior to 1989. From 1980–1 the formation of small-scale semi-private businesses

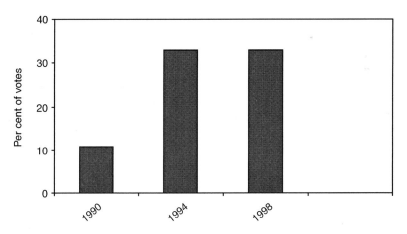

Figure 13.1   Hungarian Socialist Party election performance, 1990–98

was stimulated; in 1982, Hungary joined the IMF and the World Bank and a small capital market began to emerge as enterprises were allowed to offer interest-bearing bonds; in 1988, the HSWP government introduced a Law on Foreign Investment allowing 100 hundred per cent foreign ownership and favourable rates for repatriation of profits; stock exchange operations were introduced in January 1989 and, from the beginning of the same year, the government began to implement legislation to transform state enterprises into joint stock companies.

In other words, even before the Hungarian communists had reformed away their leading constitutional role, they had introduced a considerable amount of the legal and institutional framework necessary for the full introduction of capitalism and western-style parliamentary democracy. The establishment of free civil associations was permitted, and from 1987 organizations that were really emergent *de facto* opposition parties began to appear, including the Hungarian Democratic Forum, the Alliance of Young Democrats and the Alliance of Free Democrats. From November 1988, former parties from the pre-communist period reconstituted themselves, like the Smallholders Party, the Social Democratic Party and the Christian Democratic People's Party and in February 1989 multi-party democracy was formally accepted. As Attila Àgh observed:

> The 'old' parliament [1985–90] played a very important role in preparing and managing political change ... [it] certainly prepared the way for the new parliament in many ways, and thus continuity in parliamentary affairs in Hungary has been much stronger than in any other ECE country.[1]

After the suppression of the Hungarian Uprising in 1956, Janos Kádár instituted a comparatively liberal regime, which whilst still repressive, nevertheless made significant improvements in the material quality of people's lives and also relaxed constraints on intellectual and academic freedom, bringing about a reasonable level of satisfaction with the regime amongst both the workers and intellectuals. In particular, the populist intelligentsia, figures like Németh and Illyes who had opposed the regime in 1956 and whose constituency was really the rural poor and the provincial lower middle classes, had by the early 1960s decided to support Kádár's new course. Culturally nationalist, the populists were opposed to commercialized mass culture and stood for the eradication of social backwardness and economic injustice. They accepted Kádár's approach as a 'viable national "Third Road" between the equally unpalatable alternatives of Soviet Stalinism and Western capitalism',[2] and proved to be 'indispensable allies' for Kádár's regime. In fact, as Rudolf Tökés points out, it was this informal alliance between the communists and the populists which was, in the late 1980s, to form the basis of the political partnership between the populists and the reform communist Pozsgay which gave rise to the founding of the Hungarian Democratic Forum in 1987.[3]

During the 1980s, Hungary entered a profound economic crisis. Amongst many other economic problems, Hungary had a huge and increasing national debt and by 1986, 60 per cent of hard currency exports went on debt-servicing. By 1982, Hungary had joined the IMF and subsequently undertook a series of austerity measures which further undermined the living standards of the population and eroded their support for the regime. The overall economic and social crisis which Hungary was undergoing led to a breakdown in the relationship between the regime and the intelligentsia. In addition, much of the party's own intellectual strata and a number of leading members of the HSWP were now looking to more radical economic and political solutions.

In 1986 a large number of economists, encouraged by reformer Imre Pozsgay, produced what proved to be the key economic reform document of the period, entitled 'Turn and Reform'.[4] The article argued for 'a radical turnabout in economic policy and in the direction of the economy'. Previous reforms, the article argued, had been ineffective because, 'the rise and fall of firms was based on bureaucratic selection rather than market selection, governmental direction was substituted for the selection of the market'. The article recommended marketization, private property ownership and radical political reforms incorporating decentralization and democratization – although multi-party democracy was not mentioned at this point. The original document was suppressed for some months by the Central Committee, but was eventually published in June 1987. In fact, there were no economic alternatives put forward for the solution of Hungary's problems and there was no real conflict in the top leadership about Hungary's economic path towards the free market. There was, however, a political conflict between the party reformers and the party establishment. Kádár, refusing to recognise there was a crisis, remained in office until May 1988 when his position was taken by Károly Grósz. The two leading reformers, Pozsgay, who tended towards the populist and Rezső Nyers who had originally been a social democrat, became members of the politburo and pushed the more orthodox Grósz down a more reformist and ultimately social democratic path. Pozsgay continued to help promote the populist Hungarian Democratic Forum as an opposition movement presumably with the intention of power-sharing. At the same time, the urban-based dissident intellectuals formed the Network of Free Initiatives, which was later to become the Alliance of Free Democrats, the most openly pro-western, pro-bourgeois party in Hungary, encouraged into existence by the US Ambassador.[5] Grósz tried to preserve the political status quo, stalling on discussions with the Opposition Round Table and attempting to maintain the one party framework, but was unable to do so. In November 1988, Grósz resigned as prime minister whilst retaining the position of party general secretary, and was succeeded by the reformer Miklos Németh; but, shortly after, Grósz stated that the reform process had gone too far, and warned of a 'white terror'. Grósz later admitted that he had prepared a stand-by plan for the imposition of martial law,[6] but that it went no further than that because he could secure the support of neither the Ministry of the Interior nor the army. Clearly, in this regard, the impact of the changes in the Soviet Union strengthened the hand of the reformers, as did a number of historically-related events which further undermined the HSWP. In January 1989, Pozsgay declared that the events of 1956 had been a 'national uprising' rather than a counter-revolution, and public opinion pulled behind him over the following weeks. The rehabilitation and reburial of Imre Nagy turned into a huge demonstration against the regime, even though Nagy himself had been a communist.

The left within the leadership was also for reform – and indeed, under Kádár, had pioneered it for decades – and it was now identified only really by its desire to maintain the one-party system, and once that was lost to maintain the strength of the party, including workplace branches and the Workers' Militia. After Kádár's resignation, the leading left figures were Grósz, Janos Berecz and the more extreme-left Robert Ribanszki, all of which had significant bases in the county and local party apparatus. A number of platforms or groupings of more orthodox members had also been set up since the autumn of 1988: for example, the Ferenc Munnich Society, the Marxist-Leninist Unity Platform under the leadership of Ribanszki and the Union for Renewal of the HSWP under Berecz.[7] The most significant of these organizations was the Ferenc Munnich Society, named after a leader of the state security services in 1956 and after, which had 10–12 000 members and was closely linked to the 60 000-member Workers' Militia, set up in 1957 to defend the party and its role in society. The Workers' Militia and workplace party organizations were abolished following a referendum on their continued existence in November 1989. Less than a quarter of a million votes were polled for their continued existence with over four million votes cast for their abolition.[8] At the party congress in October 1989, there was effectively a split in the HSWP. The reformers launched the Hungarian Socialist Party, whilst the HSWP maintained Kádárist positions. Of the 800 000 members of the ruling HSWP in the summer of 1989, some 100 000, including Károly Grósz, rejoined the orthodox HSWP and around 30 000 had joined the HSP by the beginning of 1990. The HSP membership remained stable around this number, being around 34 000 in June 1997.[9]

The HSP has, since its inception, combined different political groupings into one organization, including what can be described as the 'pragmatic technocrats'[10] or apparatus members who were prepared to shift their political positions to go along with the pro-capitalist reformers, and also democratic socialists, who were initially organized within the HSWP as the People's Democracy Platform. This grouping sought a non-statist democratic socialist alternative, in the tradition of the workers' councils and rejected both the previous state socialist system and the restoration of capitalism. At the HSWP's final congress, the People's Democracy spokesman, historian Tamás Krausz, attacked the HSWP as a party of 'cadres and careerists', and condemned both the 'liberal extremists' and conservatives in the party. He called for 'the formation of a true party of the peoples that would lay the foundation for a political and economic "third road" based on the experiences neither of the East nor of the West'.[11] This grouping has maintained a home within the HSP as the Left Platform. These two somewhat incompatible groupings formed the basis for the HSP. As László Andor has observed: 'In effect, the right and the left opposition of the Kádárists formed a new party together.'[12]

It is basically these three trends which have constituted the left in Hungary since 1989: firstly, the dominant trend within the HSP – the group which reformed away the state socialist system and sought to replace it with the political structures of liberal parliamentary democracy and the economic structures of free-market capitalism. The second trend is the grouping which coalesces around both the Left Platform within the HSP and the Association of the Left Alternative – an umbrella organization drawing together a number of groupings and individuals, which defined itself on foundation in 1988 not as a party but as 'a social organization building a democratic society based on workers' property, self-management and self-governmental organizations'.[13] The third trend is the other successor party to the HSWP, at first retaining the same name but subsequently renaming itself as the

Hungarian Workers' Party. This party does not manage to translate its numerical largeness – probably the largest party in Hungary – into popular support. It regularly secures around 4 per cent of the vote and is therefore excluded from parliament by the 5 per cent threshold. Faced now with charting an anti-capitalist path without its previous material and ideological moorings, the Workers' Party is politically more akin to the Communist Party of Bohemia and Moravia than it is to the HSP or to the main successor party in Poland.

The historic Hungarian Social Democratic Party (HSDP) had merged with the Hungarian Communist Party in 1948, made a brief re-emergence in 1956 and was then reformed as a separate party in 1988 under the leadership of the veteran social democrat, András Révész. It did not recapture its popular working-class support from former times, however, and has not broken through the 5 per cent barrier to achieve representation in parliament. In its early refoundation phase it suffered a split, where Révész led an Independent Social Democratic Party to the polls against the 'official' HSDP. It was divided between the 'historic platform' which wished to redevelop its traditional role as a Marxist class-based party, and the younger 'renewal platform' which thought that the party should be bourgeois democratic, based on justice and equality within the framework of capitalism, but with no reference to Marxism.[14]

However, the HSDP's earlier absorption into the ruling party and the active participation of many of its members within the system during the communist period meant that it was not identified as an oppositional force. Few of its members participated in the democratic opposition which arose from the late 1970s, and the orientation of the intelligentsia was towards either the bourgeois opposition forces in the form of the Alliance of Free Democrats or the populist opposition forces in the form of the Hungarian Democratic Forum. In a sense, the HSDP fell between two stools. It is also the case, as the historian György Földes, elected chair of the national council of the HSP after the election defeat in 1998, has observed that:

> this period was also characterized by the conservative wave, the strengthening of the monetarist economic philosophy and the disappearance of the Keynesian ideas. The Hungarian opposition did not think about revival in the framework of Social Democratic ideas and values.[15]

Nevertheless, the HSDP was welcomed as a member of the Socialist International in 1990 – although this was later adjusted to observer status – and it was assumed for a brief period that it would be the vehicle for the reemergence of social democracy in Hungary. This assumption was rapidly overturned, and in 1996, the HSP was welcomed as a full member of the Socialist International. Led since 1994 by László Kapolyi, who was minister of industry in the 1980s, the position of the HSDP remains a traditional social democratic one, and is situated politically between the HSP and the Workers' Party. The main support of both of these parties is drawn from elderly left-wingers.[16]

The development of the HSP during the 1990s and its future development following its electoral defeat in 1998, is a matter of considerable significance for the Hungarian left both inside and outside the HSP. Whilst the left has been dissatisfied with the party leadership's political orientation – implementing IMF policies, pursuing EU and NATO membership and so on – there has been no real electoral alternative to the HSP and although there is a plethora of minute leftist grouplets and parties, there is no real alternative political home for left-wingers.

In the period prior to the first free elections in March 1990, the HSP characterized itself as a party 'with roots in Marxism establishing a synthesis of socialist and communist basic values'[17] but attempts by the leadership to establish the HSP as a democratic socialist party did not last longer than the subsequent election defeat, after which the Left Platform, 'important but not dominant', was the only organized force which consistently argued for a democratic socialist alternative.[18]

At the first free elections, in March/April 1990 (see Table 13.1), the HSP came fourth, with 8.6 per cent of seats, behind the HDF with 42.5 per cent, the AFD with 23.8 per cent and the Independent Smallholders Party (ISP) with 11.4 per cent. The HDF formed a 'christian–national' coalition with the ISP and the Christian Democratic People's Party which had secured 5.4 per cent of the seats. By this point, the HDF had moved from its earlier position as a kind of centreground between communists and the more radical opposition groups; it had distanced itself from its more populist positions and had built up a Christian-democratic image. Korosenyi credits this shift to József Antall who was to lead the coalition government in its early years: '[Antall] shaped the Forum to be the Hungarian counterpart of the German CDU/CSU and the Austrian Volkspartei'.[19]

The Antall government focused more on political systemic change than on economic reform, which is to some extent due to the fact that, as Nigel Swain has observed, Hungarian conservatism is interventionist. Privatization legislation was also delayed partly because of the conflict of

Table 13.1   Results of Hungarian general elections, 1990–98

	1990		1994		1998	
	% votes*	seats	% votes	seats	% votes	seats
MDF	24.7	164	11.7	37	3.1	18
SzDSz	21.4	92	19.8	70	7.6	24
FKgP	11.8	44	8.8	26	13.1	48
MSzP	10.9	33	32.9	209	32.9	134
FIDESz**	8.9	21	7	20	29.48	147
KDNP	6.5	21	7.1	22		
AA	3.2	1	2.1	1		
Reserved***	n/a	8	n/a	8		
Others	12.7	10	10.6	1	13.7	15

* Percentage of votes cast for party lists
** In the 1998 election FIDESz contested in coalition with MPP
*** Fixed minority representation
MDF = Hungarian Democratic Forum; SzDSz = Alliance of Free Democrats;
FKgP = Independent Smallholders Party; MSzP = Hungarian Socialist Party;
FIDESz = Alliance of Young Democrats; AA = Agrarian Association; KDNP = Christian
Democratic People's Party.
Compiled from internet election sites.

interests over restitution between the two smaller members of the coalition government sharing power with the HDF: the ISP for peasant land, and the CDPP for church property. By the summer of 1992, a decision had been made in favour of partial recompensation versus reprivatization in kind, except for particular church properties.[20] Indeed, the Antall and (after his death) Boross governments were subject to criticism for their laggardly approach to 'modernization' and for their:

... ideological commitment to the traditional values of 'Hungarianness', to the 'Hungarian Golden Age That Never Was'. This has led to the dominance of laws of restoration over laws of modernization.[21]

However, the United States and the IMF put enormous pressure on the government to depart from this line – in much the same way as they later forced the economically nationalist and protectionist government of Iliescu in Romania to change its policies – and in spite of their reluctance they were forced to comply with free-market policies.

This shift in economic policy by the Antall and Boross governments did not bring popularity or economic success, however. The Hungarian economy entered its deepest depression since the 1930s during the

Antall/Boross governments, with the impact of IMF conditionality and World Bank structural adjustment policies being compounded by the winding up of the CMEA, the east European economic and trading organization. Taking 1989 as 100, by 1993 Hungarian Gross Domestic Product had fallen to 70–75; industrial production had fallen to around 65 and agriculture to around 60–65. Inflation was rising between 23 and 35 per cent each year and unemployment rose from around 1 per cent in 1989 to almost 15 per cent in 1993.

During the four years of the Antall/Boross governments, and its complete isolation from the government coalition and the liberal opposition parties, the HSP set about redefining itself. It was in a favourable situation in so far as it was the only parliamentary party of the left and could therefore gain support as the economic impact of the system change began to affect people's living standards. At its second party Congress in May 1990, the HSP was redefined as a 'social democratic party without a dogmatic commitment to Marxism',[22] which was organizationally developed within the party by the foundation of a social democratic platform. Gyula Horn replaced Rezső Nyers as party chairman and new leadership was introduced at all levels of the party. The HSP now reorientated itself towards the development of the image of a democratic, modern, left-wing party.[23]

One of the key issues that concerned the HSP leadership in the early period after 1990 was what stance to take towards the system change, which would determine what type of oppositional role it would play. In fact, this was resolved by the new self-identification as social democratic, which was perceived during this oppositional phase in the traditional sense. The HSP could no doubt have acquired some popular support by criticizing the structural transformation and the resulting social differentiation, but in fact the HSP opted against this approach. The HSP actively campaigned on specific legislation but did not engage in ideological criticism of the overall framework. The leadership did not wish to identify solely with the losers from the regime change – they did not want this to be their only constituency. As György Földes has observed:

... immediate and wholesale criticism would have expressed only the mood and the interests of those in the worst conditions and of those social groups which had lost their former power and social positions. Responsible Socialists saw clearly that their party should not become the political protector of only the losers, it needed a much wider support.[24]

Although this approach was criticized by elements within the HSP who would have preferred a more confrontational approach, this 'moderate' approach was pursued, and in fact, the image of modernizing professional competence, committed to national reconciliation, contrasted favourably with the rather more vengeful and moralistic attitudes of the HDF coalition. In the run up to the general election of 1994, the HSP promised improved living standards and social provision for the mass of Hungarians.

In the general election of 1994, helped by both the severe economic problems and divisions within the ruling coalition, the HSP received a third of the votes, which under the electoral system translated into 54 per cent of the seats in parliament. In spite of their overall majority, the HSP decided to form a coalition with the liberal Alliance of Free Democrats, which has been described by Hungarian economist László Andor as 'with very little exaggeration the political wing of the IMF in Hungary'.[25] Andor argues that this numerically unnecessary alliance was the result of the HSP's desire to allay any western concern about the return of postcommunist parties to power in eastern Europe, as well as the desire to share responsibility for the proposed macroeconomic austerity policies.

The concern of the HSP to demonstrate its full political transformation was also shown through its attempts to secure membership of the Socialist International, which it eventually achieved in 1996.[26] The coalition included three liberal ministers, for interior affairs, transportation and communication, and culture and education. The socialist ministers represented different political positions from within the party, but the most significant position – that of finance – was held by László Békesi, who although having held the same post in the government from 1989–90 was undoubtedly to the right, not only of the socialists, but also of many of the liberals as well:

> Békesi represented the commitment of [HSP] to austerity, and that was why his ministership, and the unchallenged acceptance of the so-called Békesi programme was an elementary pre-condition for [AFD] to make a coalition with [HSP].[27]

Although Békesi resigned in January 1995, he was succeeded by Lajos Bokros, President of Budapest Bank and of the Stock Exchange Council, and also committed to neo-liberal economic policies. He launched a controversial austerity programme in March 1995 which abolished numerous entitlements to benefits, such as family allowance and child care benefits, free higher education and so on. He was clear about the party's purpose: 'The historic task of the Socialist government is to roll back the frontiers of the welfare state.'[28] The social and economic hardship that followed in the wake of the Bokros programme was the first of two major blows that led to the loss of 300 000 votes that cost them the election in 1998. The second was the deeply damaging revelations in the autumn of 1996 of HSP corruption regarding privatization revenues. The HSP lost significant sections of support at both of these points, in 1995 to the Independent Smallholders Party and in 1996 to FIDESZ.[29]

Much of the HSP's backing for the election in 1994 had come from the organized labour movement, but as living conditions continued to deteriorate and the HSP pursued a punitive approach towards the public sector, strike waves occurred and dissatisfaction increased amongst a significant sector of the HSP's electoral base. As Robinson and Marsh commented in 1995:

> Civil servants, teachers, health workers and other public sector workers have seen their incomes fall since the collapse of socialism ... Crucially, it was their votes which brought the socialists back to power in 1994.[30]

The HSP has no formal relationship with the trade union movement – membership is on an individual rather than collective basis – but a number of cooperation agreements have operated: these ensured that where unions supported the HSP in the elections, their leaders or nominees would secure places on the party's electoral lists and have indeed sat on the HSP benches in parliament as a result. The trade union leaderships did not on the whole take firm action against the HSP austerity programme, in spite of the hardship suffered by their members, presumably because they were drawn into the electoral process by the HSP leadership. Left opposition to the policies of the HSP government, therefore, came primarily from two sources, from the Left Platform within the HSP, and from the Workers' Party.

The most comprehensive statement on the Left Platform's positions was made in its submission of a Declaration of Principles for debate at the HSP Congress in November 1995. This document outlined the Platform's position on the transformation of the world system and the left; the reasons for the collapse of state socialism and the lessons to be learnt; socialist identity; the systemic change and its consequences; and possible political demands. It describes itself as 'the only political current which has consistently represented the mixed economy, cooperatives and workers ownership.'[31] It describes the HSP in the following way:

> The HSP is the most characteristic organization of the building up of the bourgeois system, inasmuch as within it one can find the political representatives of almost all the social groups in Hungary (and this can be compared with the old Hungarian Socialist Workers Party). Bank capital, trade unions, workers, entrepreneurs, intellectuals and pensioners – all have their specific position in the HSP. However, bourgeois interests play an overwhelming role.[32]

The basic economic argument of the Left Platform is that capitalism in Hungary means the domination of multinational capital, and that this could be restricted by the government to the benefit of the Hungarian population, rather than progressing as it is and constructing a semi-periphery form of capitalism. Essentially arguing for a left social-democratic approach, the document states that:

> within the growing capitalist system the socialist party should first of all, and above all else, represent the interests of workers, the unemployed, small producers, disadvantaged women and young people starting out in life – in short, they should represent eighty per cent of society. Thus the political struggle should extend the representation of the special political interests of the workers in cooperation with the trade unions and other self-organising communities.[33]

The document concluded by suggesting that unless the HSP expresses the interests of the mass of the people, then it could easily be swept away at the 1998 general election by nationalist populism – an assessment which proved to be basically correct. The proposals, presented to the Congress by Left Platform spokesman Tamás Krausz, were fairly well-received, but overall the Congress was a triumph for Horn and Bokros, the latter receiving a huge ovation for his economic approach.[34]

The intelligentsia-based Left Alternative, which some of the Left Platform participate in outside of the HSP, has made numerous attempts to forge links with the west European left, usually through conferences, for example in 1991, 1994 and most recently in November 1997. The 1997 conference, held in Budapest, focused on alternatives to neo-liberal economic policies and attempted to link up with new European left parties, with participation from the French Communist Party and the Swedish Left Party amongst others.

It cannot be said, however, that the Left Platform has a very powerful direct impact on Hungarian politics, and it was, in fact, the Workers' Party which proved to be the greatest thorn in the side of the HSP government, over the issue of NATO membership. In the summer of 1995, the Workers' Party began a campaign to collect 100 000 signatures on a nationwide petition against Hungarian membership of NATO. By the end of the year they had collected 140 000. Under the Hungarian constitution, the collection of over 100 000 signatures on a petition necessitates a referendum and it was on the basis of this campaign that the government was eventually required to hold a referendum on NATO membership in November 1997. The turn-out was 49.2 per cent of qualified voters, of which 85.3 per cent voted yes to NATO, giving 41.5 per cent of qualified voters in favour – sufficient under the legislation to constitute a legally-binding decision.[35] Whilst the referendum found a majority for NATO membership, the Workers' Party was, nevertheless, demonstrated to have a campaigning and mobilizing capacity and found a role for itself for the first time since the system change. The Left Platform was not united in its opposition to NATO and so allowed a conscience vote in the referendum. The Left Alternative's position, however, was against NATO membership.

The core of the problem facing the HSP government from 1994–98 is well-summarized by Földes:

> ... neither the necessity of managing the economic crisis nor the tasks regarding the economic transformation offer good opportunities for a government policy based on social democratic principles. In the absence of a strong middle class and domestic bourgeoisie the costs of the crisis and transformation are paid by the salaried and the self-employed.[36]

There was an obvious contradiction between the traditional social democratic agenda on the basis of which the HSP was elected, and the transformational and austerity programmes that it actually followed, or as Ziblatt puts it: '... the HSP ...has followed a narrow path between being the social democratic protector of the welfare state as well as its most avid dismantler.'[37] This contradiction resulted in the loss of 300 000 votes at the general election in 1998 and was sufficient to lose the HSP its dominant role (see Figure 13.2).

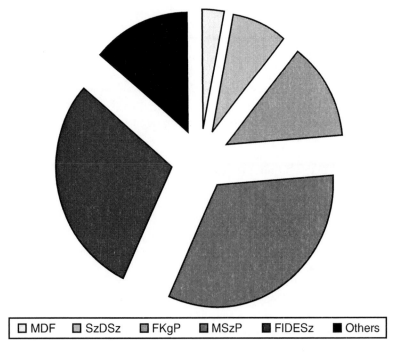

MDF = Hungarian Democratic Forum; SzDsZ = Alliance of Free Democrats;
MSzP = Hungarian Socialist Party; FIDESz = Alliance of Young Democrats.

Figure 13.2   Hungarian general election, 1998 (per cent of votes)

Many foreign observers were surprised by the HSP's defeat at the polls, for the economic record of the socialist-led government had been highly-praised by western financial institutions. The *Financial Times* described Hungary as the country 'with the strongest economic fundamentals of any post-communist country in the region'.[38] Net foreign debt was almost halved between 1994 and August 1997, from $18.9 billion to $10.9 billion. The public sector deficit was cut from 9.6 per cent of GDP in 1995 to about 5 per cent in 1997. Annual growth in GDP was about 4–5 per cent. There was a 40 per cent growth in exports in the first nine months of 1997 as against a 23 per cent rise in imports. Clearly a number of economic indicators looked good for the HSP, but many others, however, acted against them. There was a 15 per cent cut in real incomes between 1995 and 1997; 40 per cent of children in Hungary were living in poverty; unemployment was around half a million in a country of just over ten million; tuition fees were introduced in universities and colleges; mass privatizations weakened the trade union movement, and homelessness became a significant social problem.

In rejecting the effects of the HSP's neo-liberal economic policies, however, the electorate made a significant turn to the right. FIDESZ–Hungarian Civic Party (FIDESZ–HCP) under the leadership of Viktor Orbán, constructed a coalition with the ISP led by the populist demagogue József Torgyan and the Hungarian Democratic Forum, who led the ruling coalition from 1990–94 but were reduced to only 17 seats in 1998. The coalition had a small but workable majority of 213 seats out of a total of 386. This revival of the right led Tamás Krausz, one of the leaders of the Left Platform to observe: 'The new coalition is centre-right in alliance with the far right: in fact, FIDESZ is a Trojan horse for the far right. Instability is the key word in Hungary.'[39] To compound the right turn, the neo-fascist Hungarian Party of Justice and Life led by István Csurka gained 5 per cent of the vote and therefore parliamentary representation with 14 seats – the first time the extreme right has entered the Hungarian parliament since 1989.

FIDESZ–HCP, the new coalition leader, was founded in 1988 as an autonomous youth movement, the Alliance of Young Democrats. In 1989 it played a significant part in the opposition round-table which negotiated the system change. Since then it has moved steadily to the right, taking up the ground vacated by fragmenting conservative forces like the HDF, and has now emerged as the major conservative force in Hungary. FIDESZ–HCP campaigned on a 40-point programme which attacked the socialist–liberal coalition government from both left and right – for example, for the abolition of higher education fees.

With more than a third of the seats in parliament, the HSP is well-placed to conduct a strong opposition to the new government's policies over the next four years, but one of the leadership's key tasks will be to decide which orientation the HSP should pursue. There will be pressure from the Left Platform to shift the party to the left, as doubtless there will be others who think the party should shift even further into the centre-ground. This would, of course, vacate an even greater space to the left of the HSP, which, if it is not filled will lead to greater support for the far right, for there is nothing to indicate that Hungary's social and economic problems will be ameliorated in the foreseeable future.

14
Poland

The largest left party in Poland is the Social Democracy of the Republic of Poland (SdRP), the successor party to the former ruling Polish United Workers' Party (PUWP). There is some irony in this situation, for Poland was the only former communist country that had a powerful autonomous workers' movement – in the form of the free trade union, Solidarity – which was able to challenge and ultimately contribute significantly to the demise of the PUWP regime. Yet of all the political forces that have emerged from Solidarity, the left have been the least politically significant during the 1990s, and – failing to overcome the entrenched postcommunist–post Solidarity divide – have usually refused to join with the SdRP, for electoral purposes, to achieve a measure of left unity.

Whilst Solidarity was clearly a left-wing organization in its origins in the industrial struggles in Poland in the late 1970s, it moved significantly to the right during the 1980s. Smashed as a mass movement, and driven underground by the declaration of martial law by the communist government in 1981, Solidarity subsequently functioned until 1989 as a clandestine network supported by much of the western left but primarily financed by United States interests, and it thus came to play a major role in promoting the ideas of the free market right.[1] From its origins in 1980, when, in line with its programme 'The Self-Managing Republic', it pressed for free-trade-union recognition, for improved pay and conditions and for worker management, Solidarity came, by the end of the 1980s, to represent a diverse range of political perspectives, including a much-weakened left and a strong neo-liberal tendency. Under the leadership of Lech Wałęsa – himself on a very rapid rightwards-moving trajectory – it became the vehicle for capitalist restoration and the advance guard of western economic policy prescriptions.

Under such contradictory pressures, the fragmentation of Solidarity was inevitable, and during 1990 and 1991 a number of parties emerged from it. Yet the Union of Labour, based primarily on Labour Solidarity, was the only left party of any electoral significance to emerge from Solidarity, achieving 7.3 per cent of the vote in parliamentary elections in 1993. Only one of the underground leadership of Solidarity, Józef Pinior, based in Wrocław in the mining area of Lower Silesia, remained a leader of the left and active in the Union of Labour throughout the 1990s. Despite the vehement anti-communist campaign of the President, former Solidarity leader Lech Wałęsa, it was the successor party of the PUWP, leading the Democratic Left Alliance (SLD), which triumphed at the elections in 1993, in a vote against the shock therapy of the previous right-wing post-Solidarity government. As Frances Millard observed, 'Social democratic egalitarianism, and especially support for the values of the welfare state, once again became an accepted part of political discourse.'[2]

Furthermore, it was the former PUWP minister, Alexander Kwaśniewski, who defeated Wałęsa in the presidential elections of 1995. These results were a clear indication that the Polish population was not happy with the outcome of the Solidarity-led transition, with unemployment standing at sixteen percent of the labour force in 1994 and GDP still considerably lower than it had been in 1989. Thus the turn to the left was made in the direction of the former communists. Opinion polls in the early 1990s indicated that egalitarian or socialist values remained a significant factor within Polish society. As Mahr and Nagle point out:

> In a 1992 survey, 92 per cent of respondents supported maintaining the state welfare system, 82 per cent valued full employment, 80 per cent wanted to retain subsidized housing, and 70 per cent wanted cheap subsidized food to remain available.[3]

It was not surprising, then, that the SLD was elected in 1993, yet the SdRP, the main successor party in the SLD, had already undergone its own considerable transition. The SdRP had become pro-market and liberal in its economic perspective, although not completely abandoning interventionism in practice, enthusiastically supported Polish entry into NATO and the European Union, and became a full member of the Socialist International in 1996. In the general election of 1997, although it increased its percentage of the overall vote (see Figure 14.1), the SLD

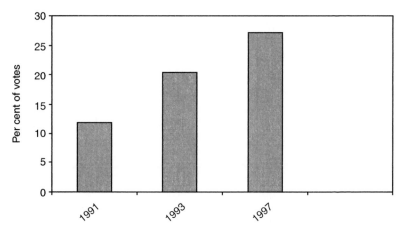

Figure 14.1　The Polish Democratic Left Alliance (SLD*) election performance, 1991–97

* This is a coalition in which the Social Democracy of the Republic of Poland is the major party.

lost to the Solidarity Electoral Alliance (AWS), a newly-formed coalition, which had managed to unify a large part of the right.

During the 1970s, Poland incurred enormous foreign debt as the government attempted to reorient its economy towards industrial production for the export market, funded by foreign loans. The downturn in the world economy and the impact of the oil price crises on the west ensured the failure of this policy, and by the mid-1970s the Polish government was spending foreign loans on subsidies to maintain the standards of living of the Polish working class. Indeed, by 1976, food subsidies constituted 12 per cent of GDP.[4] Attempts by the government to reduce subsidies and raise food prices were met with strikes and demonstrations. It was as a result of the arrests following these demonstrations that the forerunner of Solidarity was formed in September 1976 – the Committee for the Defence of the Workers. In 1980, again following strikes over price rises, government and workers – the latter represented by Lech Wałęsa – negotiated the Gdansk Accords, which legalized strikes and free trade unions. Solidarity was formed as a result, in November 1980, and rapidly attracted a membership of some millions, including many members of the ruling party.[5]

The Solidarity conference at the end of 1981 indicated the increased radicalization of the movement, and by December 1981 relations between Solidarity and the government had sufficiently broken down for party leader and Prime Minister Wojciech Jaruzelski to declare martial law in an attempt to avert Soviet military intervention. Solidarity was subsequently dissolved but continued its dissident activities as an underground organization. In 1984 the official trade unions formed the National Trade Union Accord (OPZZ) – put forward by the regime as an alternative to Solidarity – a framework for voicing economic concerns over wages and prices without playing a political role.

By 1986 the economy, which had improved in the early 1980s, had stagnated and foreign debt increased, with the situation exacerbated by western sanctions during martial law. Further strikes in August 1988 finally led Jaruzelski to attempt a dialogue with the workers and the political opposition – clearly the advent of Gorbachev had created a new political framework, and there was no longer the certainty that Soviet troops would intervene to restore political orthodoxy. Roundtable talks were conducted in April 1989, from which it was agreed to hold partially free elections in June 1989 in which Solidarity won all but one of the openly-contested seats. The PUWP now became the lesser partner in a government led by Solidarity member Tadeusz Mazowiecki.

In January 1990, the PUWP dissolved itself and two new organizations were founded. Firstly, the Social Democracy of the Republic of Poland (SdRP) led by Alexander Kwaśniewski, which established continuity of the PUWP's assets and claimed around 65 000 members. Secondly, the Polish Union of Social Democrats (PUSD) with around 3500 members, led by Tadeusz Fiszbach, which refused to have anything to do with the former ruling party's assets. Fiszbach had been provincial governor of Gdansk during Solidarity's early days there, and had very cordial relations with the union.[6] PUSD subsequently joined the Union of Labour (UP), led by Ryszard Bugaj and Zbigniew Bujak, which was formed by a merger of Labour Solidarity and the Democratic Social Movement – also from Solidarity – in 1992. The SdRP consolidated itself as the largest postcommunist party, defining itself as social democratic, although it also embraced a wide spectrum of political ideas. The other significant postcommunist party was the PUWP's ally in government until 1987, the United Peasant Party (ZSL) which transformed itself into the Polish Peasant Party (PSL).

In January 1990, Mazowiecki's Solidarity-led government introduced a shock-therapy economic programme, the Balcerowicz Plan, designed to rapidly end central planning and state subsidies and to introduce price liberalization and privatization. The emphasis was on the speed of the process and short-term pain was expected and long-term gain promised. Leszek Balcerowicz, the finance minister, dismissed any notion of a 'third way' for Poland between state socialism and capitalism, which was clearly what many Solidarity supporters were hoping for – the struggle for worker management and ownership of former state enterprises continued for several years, obstructing the privatization of large-scale enterprises.

Balcerowicz was influenced by Jeffrey Sachs and the monetarist Chicago School of economics, already out of favour in western Europe where it had become the new orthodoxy in the 1980s. GDP declined by 11.6 per cent in 1990 and unemployment rose from 0.1 per cent to 6.1 per cent in that year alone with inflation at over 500 per cent.[7] By the end of 1990, Solidarity had split, most clearly demonstrated by the fact that both Wałęsa and Mazowiecki ran as candidates in the November 1990 presidential elections. Wałęsa had voiced serious criticisms of the shock-therapy programme, realizing that it was causing considerable hardship to Solidarity's working-class voters, but this concern was clearly opportunistic as his subsequent behaviour in office demonstrated. During his campaign, he became increasingly nationalistic and conservative in his pronouncements, prompting comparisons with Pilsudski, the pre-war dictator.

Wałęsa won the contest, leading to Mazowiecki's resignation as prime minister, rightly seeing his poor electoral performance – where he was beaten into a poor third place behind Wałęsa and an unknown Polish *émigré* – as a vote of no-confidence in his policies. However, once Wałęsa was elected he dropped his criticisms of economic reform and appointed Jan Krzysztof Bielecki as prime minister. Bielecki was a member of the Liberal Democrat Congress (KLD) – the most pro-shock therapy party. As living conditions continued to deteriorate, Wałęsa and other Solidarity leaders became increasingly unpopular, and the government was fraught with tensions and divisions between Wałęsa and Mazowiecki supporters. Mazowiecki's Democratic Union (UD) was internally divided between neo-liberal and social democratic groupings.[8] Parliamentary elections were called for October 1991, leading to a clarification of the political balance of forces in Poland's first fully-free elections, albeit that only 43.2 per cent of the electorate turned out to vote and 5.6 per cent of votes cast were spoilt (see Table 14.1).[9]

The parties of the postcommunist left performed reasonably well in the Sejm elections (lower house). The SdRP had joined in the Alliance of the Democratic Left (SLD) with a number of small leftist groupings, various independents, and with the OPZZ trade union federation. The

Table 14.1 Results of Polish general elections, 1991–97*

	1991		1993		1997	
	% votes	seats	% votes	seats	% votes	seats
SLD	11.9	60	20.4	171	27.1	164
PSL	8.7	48	15.4	132	7.3	27
UD	12.3	62	10.6	74		
UP	2.12	4	7.3	41	4.8	5
KPN	7.5	46	5.8	22		
BBWR			5.4	16		
GMO	N/a	7	0.7	4		
KKW"O"	8.7	49	6.4	0		
Sol.	5.1	27	4.9	0		
PC	8.7	44	4.4	0		
KLD	7.5	37	4.0	0		
PL	5.5	28	2.3	0		
AWS					33.8	201
UW					13.4	60
Others	22.0	48	13.1	0	n/a	0

* A partially free election was held in June 1989, where only 35% per cent of the seats of
the National Assembly were contested; the Communist Bloc won 276 seats, the Catholic
Bloc 23 seats and Solidarity 161 seats.
SLD = Democratic Left Alliance; PSL = Polish Peasant Party; UD = Democratic Union;
UP = Union of Labour; KPN = Confederation of Independent Poland; BBWR = Non–Party
Bloc in Support of Reforms; GMO = German Minority Organization; KKW"O" = Catholic
Electoral Action; Sol. = Solidarity; PC = Centre Alliance; KLD = Liberal Democratic
Congress; PL = Peasant Alliance; AWS = Solidarity Electoral Action; UW = Freedom Union.
Compiled from internet election sites.

OPZZ had grown significantly since 1989 as the Solidarity trade union
lost support through its association with the post-Solidarity governments' unpopular economic policies. As Voytek Zubek observed:

> By contrast, the OPZZ was able to freely criticize the government,
> present itself as a defender of labor, and focus almost exclusively on
> workplace and bread and butter issues; its membership swelled to
> about six million members.[10]

The SLD took 12 per cent of the vote, narrowly missing being the
largest single list, and in fact the SdRP became the largest single party
after the UD split towards the end of 1992.[11] The left peasant list, the
PSL's Programme Alliance, polled 8.7 per cent. The most pro-reform
parties, Mazowiecki's UD and Bielecki's KLD polled respectively
12.3 per cent and 7.5 per cent, just under the combined total for the

former communist parties. Catholic and christian democratic parties made a reasonable showing, with the Centre Alliance, associated with Wałęsa, polling 8.7 per cent and the Catholic Electoral Alliance polling 8.7 per cent. The catholic and christian democratic parties coming out of Solidarity dominated the new governing coalition, under the leadership of Jan Olszewski of the Centre Alliance. Olszewski's intention was to end the recession in the Polish economy by easing up on the austerity measures and stimulating demand. The plans were rejected by the Sejm, and also opposed by Wałęsa, who had the backing of the IMF. Olszewski reverted to the previous reform approach, which was of particular significance if IMF funding were to be restored – it had been withdrawn in September 1991 after Poland had missed its June debt-interest repayment and had failed to meet a number of its loan conditions. Olszewski's government was short-lived, followed by a brief tenure by Pawlak, and then that of Hanna Suchocka, which returned to a policy of tax increases and spending cuts, eventually regaining IMF funding in 1993. Suchocka's government fell in May 1993 in the face of increasing industrial unrest and a refusal to increase the pay of striking workers.

The left was now well-placed for the 1993 general election, as both liberals and conservatives had been discredited in government in a very short space of time, and the social welfare image of the former communists was very appealing in the harsh economic climate. The SLD's campaign, based around the slogan 'We don't have to go on like this',[12] was critical of the economic reforms, socially progressive – supporting women's rights and abortion, the legal access to which the Suchocka government had severely limited – and against the increasing clericalization of society. On the economic front, SdRP leader Alexander Kwaśniewski called for 'greater state intervention in the economy, a slowing down of the privatization program ... and higher subsidies for state industries to ease them through the transition'.[13]

It was clear, however, that the SLD was not opposed to the transition process. It stressed rather the importance of capitalism 'with a human face', building up its profile as a social democratic party and supporting welfare provision in the fields of health, education, pensions and so on. Its core constituency was those who had lost out in the transition process including the unemployed and pensioners, but also small business people who found free market capitalism an insecure business environment.[14] The SdRP, in particular, also attracted what Vojtek Zubek terms 'nomenclatura-turned-capitalists',[15] for the SdRP was the successor to the PUWP's reformist wing, which gave rise to the nomenklatura capitalist phenomenon. Indeed, because of this, Zubek points out, 'it was the post-communist SdRP that began to enjoy the greatest and most consistent support from the business community.'[16] The PSL's constituency was mostly drawn from the more conservative and religious Polish farming community, especially individual smallholders, who were badly affected by the removal of state subsidies to agriculture; the PSL offered support to the farmers, for example through preferential credits, and promised increased protection, through tariffs, from the influx of cheap imported agricultural products subsidized by the EU's Common Agricultural Policy.

During the campaign, the SLD was also joined by the Polish Socialist Party (PPS), under the leadership of Piotr Ikonowicz. The PPS was founded in November 1987 as an initiative of Solidarity's left wing, split in 1988 and subsequently linked up with *émigré* and pre-war PPS groupings.[17] The participation by the PPS – despite its numerical smallness – in the SLD helped to give the alliance a political image which was broader than just the parties of the previous regime.

In September 1993, the SLD and PSL together took two-thirds of the seats in the Sejm, the SLD taking 20.4 per cent of the vote and the PSL 15.4 per cent. Mazowiecki's Democratic Union took 10.6 per cent and the Solidarity left-wing Union of Labour (UP) took 7.3 per cent. Overall, the post-solidarity parties were fragmented – preoccupied with their own fratricidal quarrels – unpopular and performed badly.

Following the elections, the SLD sought the UP's cooperation as a potential coalition partner in an attempt to broaden the coalition – it did not want, as Mahr and Nagle point out, 'to be viewed as reconstituting the old system'.[18] The UP's condition for participation was the ending of the mass privatization plan – a condition with which the SLD would not comply, for the SLD had committed itself to the privatization plan as part of the IMF's conditions for funding. In fact, the UP was not predisposed towards working with the SdRP, and liked to portray itself as 'a party of socialists with "clean hands" and with a socialist past which could not unite itself with the SdRP, the party of a sordid and opportunistic past', although in fact it had many members formerly from the PUWP.[19] It identified itself as a party of the social democratic left, and its programmatic features placed it in the framework of traditional statist west-European social democracy. It favoured greater state intervention in the economy than the SLD and advocated a more gradual transition to avoid increased social inequality. The SLD developed more along the lines of the Hungarian Socialist Party –

towards being a socialist party of the new type embracing neo-liberal economic policies, but facing the same contradiction – being simultaneously a party of a section of the new capitalist class whilst relying electorally on the losers in the economic transition.

The elections left Poland with a difficult political cohabitation between the rabidly anti-communist and increasingly demagogic President Wałęsa, and a former communist government. The first two years of the PSL/SLD coalition government were dominated by the conflict with President Wałęsa who was bitterly opposed to the government – he portrayed it as the restoration of unreconstructed communists, vetoed its bills and threatened to dissolve parliament.

The new coalition government, under the leadership of Pawlak, the leader of the Polish Peasant Party, included five SLD and eight PSL deputies. The government indicated its commitment to continuity in both economic and foreign policy, whilst stressing the importance of a more gradual and egalitarian approach to the economic reforms. In fact, Pawlak consistently delayed the mass privatization programme that had been agreed in April 1993 which would transfer six hundred state firms to investment funds – in preparation for flotation – in which shares could be bought for a nominal sum. The SLD was opposed to the obstruction of privatization but although Pawlak approved a third wave of privatization in October 1994, this issue was not really resolved until Pawlak was replaced as prime minister in March 1995 by the SLD Sejm speaker, Józef Oleksy, and was finally completed by 1996. Whilst the government's mass privatization scheme had been hesitant, however, other forms of privatization had developed more rapidly, for example, the so-called 'privatization through liquidization'.[20] In this process, the state company was dissolved and taken over by its former employees, in some cases with outside investors and in other cases without. About three quarters of the 977 enterprises privatized by the end of 1993 had been privatized through this method.[21]

The Polish economy showed consistent growth from 1992 – 6 per cent and over from 1994 to 1996 – and by 1996 had achieved the level of real GDP of 1989 – the first in the region to do so. Inflation, which hit 618 per cent in 1990 had come down to 27.8 per cent in 1995.[22] This steady growth reflected positively on the government and was a factor in the presidential election campaign of 1995 which favoured the SLD candidate, Alexander Kwaśniewski. Lech Wałęsa's campaign was primarily based on anti-communism – 'I will smash communism', he pledged in an interview in *Życie Warszawy*.[23] Kwaśniewski campaigned under the slogan 'Let's Choose the Future' and refuted Wałęsa's accusations:

> I know ... what kind of accusations are levelled against me. Code words like 'People's Republic of Poland Mark II' or 'post-Communist' or 'aggressive anticlerical' are used. I am sure it is also said that Kwaśniewski is dreaming of a return to the disreputable practices of real socialism and that he is just waiting for a chance. I have the right to ask on what evidence these charges are based? They are very handy for loud-mouthed lying demagogy.[24]

Kwaśniewski also stressed his desire to be the 'guardian of fundamental national values', and as president to represent the whole of the Polish nation, not just one section of it, to build a tolerant, just and democratic society, and to ensure continuity in economic policy and foreign affairs. He reiterated his support for Poland's membership of NATO and the European Union – Poland had joined NATO's Partnership for Peace in February 1994 and had applied to join the European Union in April 1994. In reality, there was very little fundamental difference between Wałęsa's and Kwaśniewski's basic policy approaches: they both supported economic reform, EU and NATO membership, which were the key issues. Aside from that, the differences were mainly related to their approaches to social policy questions such as abortion, secularization and so on.

The result of the elections was a narrow victory for Kwaśniewski, in spite of the fact that Cardinal Glemp, the leader of the Roman Catholic church in Poland had 'described the election as a stark choice between Christian and "neo-pagan" value systems'.[25] In round one, Kwaśniewski polled 35.1 per cent and Wałęsa 33.1 per cent. Thirteen other candidates shared the remaining votes of which the highest was 9.2 per cent for Jacek Kuroń – the former Solidarity intellectual with a youthful left-wing record from the 1960s, who had become economically and socially liberal by the early 1980s, and had twice been minister of labour in Solidarity coalition governments since 1989.[26] Kuroń was the candidate for the strongly pro-market Freedom Union, a party formed in April 1994 from the merger between the post-Solidarity Democratic Union and the post-Solidarity Liberal Democratic Congress. The Freedom Union was not united in his support, however, as many members considered Kuroń to be too left-wing and secular.[27] Waldemar Pawlak of the Polish Peasant Party polled 4.3 per cent, and Tadeusz Zielinski, the candidate for the Union of Labour and the

Polish Socialist Party, polled 3.5 per cent. In the second round, Kwaśniewski scored 51.7 per cent and Wałęsa 48.28 per cent.[28]

In defeat, Wałęsa refused to accept the legitimacy of the election results and attempted to overturn the outcome in the supreme court, which subsequently confirmed the election result. He also encouraged allegations that the Prime Minister, Józef Oleksy, had worked for Soviet, and then Russian, intelligence from the early 1980s right up to 1995. Although not proven, this resulted in Oleksy being replaced as prime minister by Włodzimierz Cimoszewicz, who had been the SLD candidate for the presidency in 1990.

Problems also continued within the governing coalition itself – the Peasant Party continued to try and slow the privatization process – and the inherent contradiction within the SLD began to manifest itself as the social costs of the SLD's economic policies began to have a serious impact on their constituencies of support. Previously almost a silent partner, the parliamentary grouping of the OPZZ (trade union) sector of the SLD, under the leadership of Ewa Spychalska, now demanded that their rights within the coalition be clearly defined. The OPZZ deputies were becoming increasingly 'unhappy with the strongly pro-market and pro-capitalist orientation of the [SLD]',[29] for although the Polish economy has performed well according to a number of macro-economic indicators, the introduction of capitalism had also had a considerable social cost and caused wide extremes of wealth and poverty. By December 1994, unemployment had reached 2.8 million, or 16 per cent of the workforce, and excluding agriculture the figure was over 26 per cent.[30] As David Holland pointed out in 1996, 'Real wages retain only 75 per cent of the purchasing power that they had in 1989 and there is a chronic housing shortage, reflecting the collapse in the construction of social housing, which is down to levels not seen since the 1940s.'[31]

Food price rises in the first half of 1996, combined with continuing inflation at around 25 per cent and high unemployment resulted in a drop in support for the government. Opinion poll data showed that whereas in January 1996, 26 per cent of the population thought that the economic situation was bad, by June 1996 this had risen to 45 per cent. As the *Eastern Europe Newsletter* observed at the time, 'The "feel good" factor which helped Kwaśniewski win the presidency and allowed the SLD to ride out the storm over the "Oleksy Affair" is beginning to disappear.'[32] This was bad news for the SLD, as Poland was effectively in the run up to a general election, which was scheduled for autumn 1997.

Support increased for the right-wing parties who were now making strenuous efforts to learn the lessons of the previous general election and form an electoral coalition to end their fragmentation and defeat the SLD. A new right-wing populist group, the Movement for Polish Reconstruction (ROP), founded after the presidential elections to take leadership of the right away from Wałęsa, and led by former prime minister Jan Olszewski, very rapidly rose to 16 per cent by mid-1996. The Solidarity union, under the leadership of Marian Krzaklewski, and in many respects politically similar to the ROP, also polled about 16 per cent which put them at roughly the same level of popular support as the SLD–PSL coalition. Polls also indicated that the liberal–centrist Freedom Union was losing support, as was the left-wing Union of Labour.[33]

During the autumn of 1996, Krzaklewski began to consolidate a broad grouping called Solidarity Electoral Action (Akcja Wyborcza Solidarnosc – AWS), which drew together 37 small and medium-sized right-wing parties around the core of Solidarity.[34] Two issues further polarized politics in the spring of 1997, both of which sharpened the secular/clerical divide in Polish society. The first was the new constitution which was to be put to a popular referendum. The constitution had been co-authored by the SLD, the PSL, the Freedom Union and the Labour Union. The AWS and ROP argued for a rejection of the constitution on the basis that it did not give sufficient weight to the catholic church and did not include the right to outlaw abortion. The second was the issue of the Concordat with the Vatican, signed by Hanna Suchocka's Freedom Union government in 1993, and still requiring parliamentary ratification. The SLD, Union of Labour and a minority of the Freedom Union had, up until then, resisted ratification, insisting that it undermined the secular nature of the state. During the spring of 1997, however, Kwaśniewski sought a pledge from the catholic church that it would not misuse the privileges enshrined in the Concordat, and on this basis he would then proceed to seek its ratification by parliament. In this way Kwaśniewski hoped that he would be able to ensure the neutrality of the church in the forthcoming election and defuse some of the right's anti-secular rhetoric but he did not, ultimately, succeed in securing the ratification of the Concordat.

Clear tensions were now emerging within the SdRP itself. Kwaśniewski, in addition to making overtures to the church which were deeply unpopular with the majority of the SdRP members, was also trying to appease forces like the Freedom Union by approving legislation that would force communist period intelligence personnel to reveal their intelligence records if they wanted to hold state or political office. Kwaśniewski was, presumably, attempting to prepare the ground for a possible SLD-Freedom Union coalition after the elections. There was considerable logic within this approach, for Kwaśniewski was indeed a neo-liberal secular modernizer, as was the Freedom Union – the most pro-free market party, and this would probably have been the favoured option of the IMF and most western governments and institutions. The SLD had experienced an increasingly fractious relationship with the PSL, its governing coalition partner from 1993–9, primarily over differing attitudes towards privatization and economic reform. Over many issues the PSL – as a conservative, interventionist peasant party with strong catholic links – had more in common with the right-wing post-Solidarity parties than with the SLD and Kwaśniewski would clearly have preferred a coalition with the neoliberal Freedom Union. Not only was this unpopular with the Freedom Union, however, it was also unpopular with the majority of the SdRP, under the leadership of Jòzef Oleksy, who were not prepared to conciliate with the church and the extreme free-marketeers.

However, the election results ensured that the SLD was not in a position to form the new government (see Figure 14.2). The SLD, which conducted a lacklustre campaign on the themes 'We kept our word' and 'A good today, a better tomorrow', actually increased its vote, polling over 700 000 more votes (over 6 per cent) than in 1993, with 27.1 per cent. However, the AWS, campaigning on the theme of 'Finishing the Solidarity Revolution', did even better and emerged as the largest group, with 33.8 per cent, polling almost 400 000 more votes than the sum of its parts in 1993. The PSL dropped massively from 15.4 per cent to 7.3 per cent, failing on this occasion to broaden its appeal beyond a section of the rural electorate and, indeed, losing its pre-eminence in that sector. The Union of Labour, with 4.7 per cent, failed to pass the electoral threshold of 5 per cent. As Aleks Szczerbiak observed, this 'represented a historic defeat for the ambitious project to build a Polish social-democratic party which did not have its roots in the previous communist system.'[35] The key player was now the Freedom Union which polled 13.4 per cent and effectively held the balance of power.

A new government was sworn in at the end of October, uniting the AWS with the Freedom Union under the premiership of the AWS member and Solidarity economic advisor Jerzy Buzek. The new coalition had the support of 261 out of 460 seats in the Sejm. Leszek Balcerowicz, the leader of the Freedom Union who was responsible for the shock-therapy programme in the early 1990s, became minster of finance.

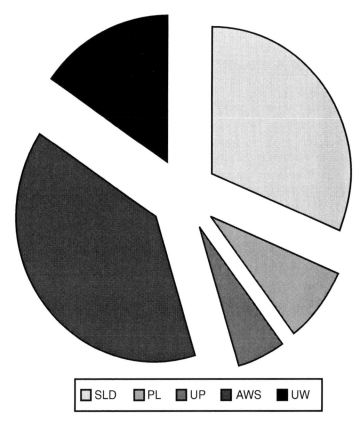

SLD = Democratic Left Alliance; PL = Peasant Alliance; UP = Union of Labour;
AWS = Solidarity Electoral Action; UW = Freedom Union.

Figure 14.2   Polish general election, 1997 (per cent of votes)

A number of problems faced the new government which were made
more difficult by differences, not only between the AWS and the
Freedom Union, but between the numerous parties which constituted
the AWS, and there were two small splits from it. The issue of the pace
of reform was again raised, for Balcerowicz was determined to speed up
the process, particularly privatization, the cutting of industrial subsidies
and tightening of domestic demand to reduce inflation and keep in line
with IMF requirements.[36] AWS's trade union supporters, however,
would undoubtedly be opposed to further privatization and the reduction of demand would have a negative impact on living standards and

therefore social harmony. Indeed, as a result of Balcerowicz's policies, prices rose by 3.2 per cent in January 1998, leading to a rapid slump for the government in the opinion polls.

Balcerowicz's economic policies continued to be a source of conflict between the coalition partners throughout 1998. In November, many AWS deputies voted against the government in the Sejm in favour of extra child benefits, ensuring a defeat for the government. As a result, Balcerowicz and the Freedom Union threatened to withdraw from the coalition and the impasse was only resolved by a pledge from AWS party whips that they would, in future, impose discipline on AWS deputies.[37] Balcerowicz's policies were also causing dissatisfaction amongst the voters. In April 1998, the OPZZ trade union federation – part of the SLD – organized a mass demonstration in Warsaw against government policies, and opened what it called a 'general dispute' with the government, presenting a list of 16 'systemic demands' to the government on pay, consultation, welfare reforms, employee share ownership, foreign investment, pensions, utility prices and a minimum wage, as well as demands about specific industrial sectors and plants.

The local elections of October 1998 – the first in which national political groupings dominated rather than local coalitions – were an interesting test of public opinion, one year after the general election. Notwithstanding a level of public dissatisfaction, AWS's national share of the vote had stabilized at 33 per cent – less than 1 per cent down on its general election performance; the SLD was 4.4 per cent up at 31.5 per cent; the Social Alliance, a newly-formed electoral alliance which unites the PSL, the Union of Labour and the Polish Pensioners' Party, took 11.9 per cent; and the Freedom Union was beaten into fourth place, down nearly 2 per cent with 11.6 per cent.[38] As Alexander Szczerbiak has pointed out, however, the AWS' economic reforms had still to have their full effect, and will only make their real mark during 1999. If dissatisfaction with the government further increases, then it is likely that support for both the SLD and the Social Alliance – within which the PSL is the strongest partner – will grow. If the SLD were to emerge as the largest single bloc at the next general election, but without an overall majority, then a coalition between these two blocs would be a possibility.

Conclusion

The NATO bombing campaign against the Federal Republic of Yugoslavia, which began in March 1999, further confirmed the political character of the new European left. NATO's intervention in Yugoslavia marked a new landmark in the post-Cold War international political order. Illegal under international law, not having being endorsed by the Security Council of the United Nations and involving a military attack on a sovereign state, it was also launched outside of the terms of NATO's own Charter, which specified that military action can only be taken in defence of one of its member states.

The profound implications of this action were confirmed by the 50th anniversary meeting of NATO leaders in Washington DC on 24 April 1999. This adopted a new 'Strategic Concept' drafted by the United States, which committed NATO to 'out of area' – that is, offensive – operations in a geographical area extending far beyond the borders of the military alliance's member states. It said that the future field of NATO operations would extend to the whole of western Europe, eastern Europe and the former Soviet Union. A suggestion, reportedly by France, that such operations should require the authorization of the United Nations was rejected.

In these circumstances, polls which showed that more than 90 per cent of the population of Russia were opposed to NATO bombing of Yugoslavia were understandable. Quite apart from the real sympathy which exists in Russia for the Serbs, there was also an overwhelming perception that if NATO can unilaterally decide to wage war upon a sovereign state, outside of any framework of international legality, then it is quite possible, and even probable, that NATO intervention into the former Soviet Union could follow at some point. As a result all politicians in Russia were under intense popular pressure to oppose

NATO's action, and the pro-Western parties already deeply discredited by the catastrophic results of IMF-influenced free market economic reforms saw their support spiral further downwards.

Similarly, in China, the communist government also saw the bombing as setting a precedent of by-passing the United Nations which could, in the future, be used to justify military intervention in Asia or even China itself. As a result, having already acted jointly with Russia to condemn the US-led bombing of Iraq at the beginning of the year, the two countries became even more united in the stridency of their denunciations of the bombing of Yugoslavia. The Cuban government took an even more vigorously anti-NATO position. The NATO intervention also reinforced the political division between the new European left, which, in its greater majority opposed the bombing of Yugoslavia, and the majority leaderships of the social democratic parties which through Tony Blair, Lionel Jospin and Gerhard Schröder vigorously supported it.

Opposition to NATO bombing was most pronounced in southern Europe and the Balkans. In Greece there were mutinies in the Navy, threats of industrial action by railworkers, massive demonstrations and majority public condemnation of NATO's attacks. In Italy, the Party of Communist Refoundation led mass opposition to the bombing. In the Czech Republic, the communists – the third largest party – threatened to block railways carrying NATO troops. In Poland, a majority of the MPs of the Democratic Left Alliance signed a statement, initiated by the Polish Socialist Party, opposing the bombing. In Russia, the communist-dominated lower house of parliament called upon the government to supply arms to Yugoslavia.

Elsewhere in Europe, virtually every party of the new European left opposed the NATO action, seeing it as an ominous destruction of the post-war international order structured through the United Nations and its replacement by a kind of new colonialism – whereby the United States uses military violence where other means do not suffice to extend its hegemony into eastern Europe, the Balkans and ultimately the former Soviet Union.*

---

* Thus, opposition to NATO's bombing of Yugoslavia started to bridge the gap between the non-social democratic left in western and eastern Europe. This was reflected in the decision of the New European Left Forum to invite parties like the Communist Party of the Russian Federation, the Polish Socialist Party and the Communist Party of Bohemia and Moravia to discuss security in Europe at the 16th NELF meeting in Madrid on 17 July 1999.

Within the social democratic parties, significant minorities also opposed the NATO action. As well as figures like Tony Benn MP and Alice Mahon MP on the left wing of the British Labour Party, this also included Oskar Lafontaine in Germany.

These events have confirmed the character of the new European left as a clearly demarcated, and distinct, political current from social democracy, and also as one whose politics continues to find an echo within the left wing of the social democratic parties and the sectors of the electorate and labour movements upon which they are based. In addition, these parties are also attractive to that part of the voting base of the Green parties which has been horrified by the role of the Green Party foreign minister in Germany in attempting to justify German participation in bombing Yugoslav cities.

That this is part of an overall process, of a left wing crystallizing in opposition to the adoption of monetarism and support for US-led wars by the majority of European social democracy, was illustrated by the battle over economic policy in Germany and the European Union at the beginning of 1999. Oskar Lafontaine picked a fight, which he ultimately lost, not only with German big business over taxation, but more fundamentally with the European Central Bank over the entire direction of economic policy with the European Union. He called for a break with monetarism and threatened to increase public spending to reflate the German economy if the Central Bank refused to cut interest rates. Lafontaine lost, but it is symptomatic that it subsequently became clear that he was also unhappy with NATO bombing Yugoslavia and with the German SPD's hostility towards coalitions with the German PDS.

The combination of the defeat of Lafontaine on the economic and social field and the almost unanimous backing of European social democratic majority leaders for the bombing of Yugoslavia, has crushed the widely-canvassed hope that the accession of social democratic governments to power in the majority of the EU states would signify the reassertion of a Keynesian economic agenda and a stance critical of US strategic dominance via NATO. The demise of Lafontaine means that, for the moment at least, there is no prospect of European social democracy becoming a vehicle for a counter-thrust to the new world order which emerged after 1989–91. That does not mean that the large proportions of voters – from a quarter to more than a half according to the polls – opposed to NATO bombing of Yugoslavia will disappear. Neither does it mean that the large sections of the European labour movement opposed to Euro-monetarism will go away. It does mean that in western Europe, with the exception of the particular situation of the British Labour left, in most cases these large minorities of the population will continue to provide the basis upon which the new European left consolidates itself: as a growing factor in the mainstream of European politics.

Notes

1 1989–99: crisis, splits, renewal and revival – introduction

1. E. J. Hobsbawm (1995) *Age of Extremes* (London: Abacus), p. 56.
2. See F. Fukuyama (1992) *The End of History and the Last Man* (London: Penguin).
3. *Wall Street Journal*, 10 April 1995.
4. See P. Nolan (1995) *China's Rise, Russia's Fall* (London: Macmillan).
5. Parliamentary Report to 1997 Labour Party Conference.
6. A. Giddens (1998) *The Third Way* (Cambridge: Polity Press), p. 24.
7. *Wall Street Journal*, 6 October 1998, p. 2.
8. P. Theuret, 'A la gauche de la social-démocratie', *Futurs*, forthcoming.
9. *Ibid.*
10. See D. Sassoon (1996) *One Hundred Years of Socialism* (London: I. B. Tauris).
11. D. Sassoon (ed.) (1997) *Looking Left* (London: I. B. Tauris), p. 2.
12. *Ibid.*, p. 4.
13. L. Elliott and D. Atkinson (1998) *The Age of Insecurity* (London: Verso), p. 221–2.

2 The European left before 1989: Washington, Moscow and Brussels

1. See *Documents of the First International* (1967) (Moscow: Progress).
2. Quoted in E. Mandel (1978) *Stalinism and Eurocommunism* (London: NLB), p. 9.
3. This argument is developed in M. Silberschmidt (1972) *The United States and Europe: Rivals and Partners*.
4. G. Ross, *The Great Powers and the Decline of the European States System, 1914–45* (Harlow: Longman, 1983) p. 7.
5. A. B. Ulam, *Expansion and Coexistence: Soviet Foreign Policy 1917–73*, second edition, (New York: Praeger, 1974) p. 158 (f.n.).
6. K. van der Pijl, *The Making of an Atlantic Ruling Class* (London: Verso, 1984), p. 55.
7. J. Ross, in *Profils de la social-democratie européenne* (Paris: La Brèche, 1982) p. 45.
8. *Ibid.*
9. G. Kolko (1969) *The Politics of War* (London: Weidenfeld and Nicolson), p. 252.
10. *Ibid.*, p. 249.
11. S. E. Ambrose (1976), *Rise to Globalism*, revised edition (Harmondsworth: Penguin), p. 18.
12. M. Schaller, *The American Occupation of Japan* (Oxford: OUP, 1985) pp. 87–8.
13. S. E. Ambrose, *op. cit.*, p. 154.
14. P. Anderson (1996) 'Under the Sign of Interim', *London Review of Books*, 4 January.

15. For more details of the economics of this process see the series of *Socialist Economic Bulletin*, in particular 'Behind the Fall of the Dollar', April 1995.
16. P. F. della Torre, E. Mortimer and J. Story (eds) (1979) *Eurocommunism: Myth or Reality?* (Harmondsworth: Penguin), p. 10.
17. *Ibid.*, p. 332.
18. *Ibid.*, p. 337.

3 Eastern Europe: the road to 1989

1. R. Overy, *Russia's War* (London: Allen Lane, 1997) sleeve note.
2. The feasibility of using US possession of the atomic bomb as a means to pressure the Soviet Union was carefully assessed by US planners at the beginning of the Cold War, but finally dropped as the rational Soviet response would be to over-run western Europe. See D. Horowitz, *From Yalta to Vietnam* (Harmondsworth: Penguin, 1965).
3. See P. Anderson, *Passages from Antiquity to Feudalism* (London: Verso, 1974) and *Lineages of the Absolutist State* (London: Verso, 1974).
4. P. Anderson, *Passages from Antiquity to Feudalism, op. cit.*, p. 252.
5. D. Horowitz, *op. cit.*, p. 285.
6. J. Williamson, *The Economic Opening of Eastern Europe* (Washington, DC: IEE, 1991), p. 7.
7. D. Lane, *The Rise and Fall of State Socialism* (Cambridge: Polity, 1996) p. 42.
8. *Socialist Economic Bulletin*, 'Lessons of the Economic Reform in China', London, 1990.
9. J. Williamson, *op. cit.*, p. 4.
10. All of these issues had been extensively debated in the Soviet Union in the 1920s, the key protagonists being Stalin, Trotsky and Bukharin. For the classical critique of socialism in one country, see Trotsky's *The Third International After Lenin*.
11. *Socialist Economic Bulletin*, 'Behind the Fall of the Dollar', London, April 1995, p. 4.
12. Marx and Engels Collected Works, Vol. 6, p. 519.
13. F. Halliday, *The Making of the Second Cold War* (London: Verso, 1983) p. 162.

4 Russia: an undecided outcome

1. United Nations Development Programme (UNDP), *Human Development under Transition: Europe and CIS* (New York, 1997) p. 180.
2. *Ibid.*
3. *Ibid.*, p. 181.
4. *Ibid.*
5. *Ibid.*, p. 182.
6. Interfax News Release, Moscow, November 1998.
7. D. Kotz and F. Weir, *Revolution From Above* (London: Routledge, 1997) p. 4.
8. P. Gowan, *Socialist Register* (Halifax: Merlin, 1998) pp. 134–5.
9. Argued in Kotz and Weir, *op. cit.*
10. J. Barth Urban and V. D. Solovei, *Russia's Communists at the Crossroads*, (Oxford: Westview, 1997) p. 1.
11. Kotz and Weir, *op. cit.*, p. 167.

12. *Ibid.*, p. 162.
13. J. Steele, *Eternal Russia* (London: Faber and Faber, 1994) p. 378.
14. *Ibid.*, p. 382.
15. J. Lester, 'Overdosing on Nationalism: Gennadii Zyuganov and the Communist Party of the Russian Federation', in *New Left Review*, 221, 1997, p. 37.

5   The recomposition of the West European Left since 1989 – introduction

1. E. Hobsbawm, *Age of Extremes* (London: Abacus, 1995) p. 69.
2. L. Weinberg, *The Transition of Italian Communism* (New Brunswick, NJ: Transaction, 1995) p. 55.
3. *Socialist Campaign Group News*, May 1997.
4. *Financial Times*, 5 February 1999.
5. *Financial Times*, 17 November 1988.
6. European Community, 1991–2 Annual Report.
7. *Wall Street Journal*, 10 April 1995.
8. M. Itoh, *Socialist Register*, 1992, p. 197.
9. R. Blackburn (ed.), *After the Fall* (London: Verso, 1991) p. 192.
10. *Links*, 4 (1995).
11. D. Sassoon, *One Hundred Years of Socialism* (London: I. B. Tauris, 1995), p. 627.
12. P. Camiller, 'Spain: The Survival of Socialism?', P. Anderson and P. Camiller (eds) *Mapping the West European Left*, (London: Verso, 1994) p. 250.
13. R. Gillespie (1990) 'Realignment on the Spanish Left', *Journal of Communist Studies*, 6 (3), p. 119.
14. T. Abse (1994), 'Italy: A New Agenda', in P. Anderson and P. Camiller (eds), *op. cit.*, p. 205.
15. D. Sassoon, *op. cit.*, p. 752.
16. S. Gundle (1993), 'The Italian Communist Party', in D. S. Bell (ed.), *West European Communists and the Collapse of Communism* (Oxford: Berg), p. 27.
17. R. East and J. Pontin (1997), *Revolution and Change in Central and Eastern Europe*, revised edition (London: Pinter), p. 144.
18. G. Fagan (1992), 'The Party of Democratic Socialism', *Labour Focus on Eastern Europe*, 41, p. 30.
19. *Ibid.*, p. 33.
20. H. Bortfeldt and W. C. Thompson (1993), 'The German Communists', in D. S. Bell (ed.), *op. cit.*, p. 145.
21. D. F. Ziblatt (1998), 'The Adaptation of Ex-Communist Parties to Post-Communist East Central Europe', *Communist and Post-Communist Studies*, 31 (2), p. 129.
22. D. S. Bell (1993) 'French Communism's Final Struggle', in D. S. Bell (ed.), *op. cit.*, p. 65.
23. S. Wilks, 'New Left Parties in Scandinavia', *Contemporary Political Studies*, 3, (1996) p. 1842.
24. Interview with Johan Lönnroth, 15 January 1999.
25. 'For a World in Solidarity', Party Programme, Swedish Left Party, 1996, p. 5.
26. Election Platform 1998, Swedish Left Party, p. 8.
27. S. Wilks (1996) *op. cit.*, p. 1846.

28. Finnish Left Allliance web site: http://www/vasemmistolitto.fi/english.htm
29. H. Beekers (1998) 'Dutch Labour on the Spot as Voters Swing to Left', *Spectre*, 4, p. 23.

6   France

1. G. Ross and J. Jenson (1994) 'France: Triumph and Tragedy', in P. Anderson and P. Camiller (eds), *Mapping the West European Left* (London: Verso) p. 167.
2. *Ibid.*, p. 162.
3. D. S. Bell (1993), 'French Communism's Final Struggle', in D. S. Bell (ed.), *Western European Communists and the Collapse of Communism* (Oxford: Berg), p. 57.
4. *Ibid.*
5. G. Ross and J. Jenson (1994) *op. cit.*, p. 170.
6. Interview with J. Jancovich, 29 December 1998.
7. D. S. Bell (1993) *op. cit.*, p. 58.
8. *Ibid.*, p. 59.
9. D. S. Bell, 'Twenty-Fifth Congress of the French Communist Party: Saint-Ouen, 6–10 February 1985', *Journal of Communist Studies*, 1, 2, (1985) p. 213.
10. *Ibid.*, p. 215.
11. *Ibid.*, p. 214.
12. S. Hopkins, 'The Twenty-Seventh Congress of the French Communist Party: Saint-Ouen, 18–22 December 1990', *Journal of Communist Studies*, 7, 1, (1991) p. 265.
13. Interview with J. Jancovich, *op. cit.*
14. D. S. Bell (1985) 'Twenty-Fifth Congress of the French Communist Party', *op. cit.*, p. 216.
15. A. F. Knapp (1987) 'Towards Self-Liquidation? The French Communist Party in 1987', *Journal of Communist Studies*, 3 (2), p. 198.
16. D. S. Bell (1993) 'French Communism's Final Struggle', *op. cit.*, p. 60.
17. S. Courtois (1988) 'The French Communist Party: An Historic Decline?', *Journal of Communist Studies*, 4 (4), p. 164.
18. Quoted in D. S. Bell (1993) 'French Communism's Final Struggle', *op. cit.*, p. 64.
19. A. F. Knapp (1987) *op. cit.*, p. 199.
20. S. Courtois, *op. cit.*, p. 164.
21. *Ibid.*, p. 166.
22. S. Hopkins, *op. cit.*, pp. 268–9.
23. Interview with J. Jancovich, *op. cit.*
24. D. S. Bell, 'The French Communist Party in the 1992 Departmental and Regional Elections', *Journal of Communist Studies*, 8 (3), p. 135.
25. *Ibid.*, p. 137.
26. S. Hopkins (1993) 'The French Communist Party in the Legislative Elections (21 and 28 March 1993)', *Journal of Communist Studies*, 9 (3), p. 282.
27. *Ibid.*, p. 279.
28. *Ibid.*
29. Interview with J. Jancovich, *op. cit.*
30. D. S. Bell (1998) 'The French Communist Party in the 1990s', *Journal of Communist Studies*, 14 (3), p. 130.

31. *Espaces Marx Bulletin*, November 1998.
32. *Ibid.*
33. Speech by Robert Hue at press conference, Paris, 15 January 1999.
34. *Appel Commun*, launched by thirteen European left parties, Paris, 15 January 1999.
35. *Ibid.*

7 Italy

1. For further details, see Chapter two.
2. *Correspondances Internationales – nouvelle epoque*, Summer 1997, p. 16.
3. J. L. Newell and M. Bull (1997) 'Party Organisations and Alliances in Italy in the 1990s: A Revolution of Sorts', *Journal of West European Politics*, 20 (1), p. 84.
4. *Correspondances Internationales – nouvelle epoque, op. cit.*, p. 16.
5. P. Daniels (1992) 'The Democratic Party of the Left and the 1992 Italian General Election', *Journal of Communist Studies*, 8 (3), p. 130.
6. J. L. Newell and M. Bull (1997), *op. cit.*, p. 84.
7. *Ibid.*
8. L. Maitan, *Inprecor*, 15 October 1998.
9. *Ibid.*
10. 'The Debate in Communist Refoundation – A Selection of Materials', *Links*, 8 (1997), p. 68.
11. T. H. Behan, '"What's in a name?" Italy's Communist Refoundation', unpublished paper.
12. J. L. Newell and M. Bull (1997) *op. cit.*, p. 85.
13. L. Maitan (1998) *op. cit.*
14. *Correspondances Internationales – nouvelle epoque, op. cit.*, p. 17.
15. J. L. Newell and M. Bull (1997) *op. cit.*, p. 101.
16. T. H. Behan, *op. cit.*
17. *Ibid.*
18. J. L. Newell and M. Bull (1997) *op. cit.*, p. 103.
19. S. Hellman (1997) 'The Italian Left After the 1996 Elections', in R. D'Alimonte and D. Nelken (eds), *Italian Politics: The Center-Left in Power* (Oxford: Westview Press), pp. 84–5.
20. L. Maitan (1998) *op. cit.*
21. S. Hellman (1997) *op. cit.*, p. 89.
22. 'The Debate in Communist Refoundation – A Selection of Materials', *op. cit.*, p. 69.
23. *Ibid.*, p. 91.
24. *Ibid.*, p. 92.
25. T. Gill (1998) 'Tragic Split for the Italian Left', in *Morning Star*, 20 October, p. 10.
26. L. Maitan (1998) *op. cit.*
27. *Ibid.*
28. *Financial Times*, 6 October 1998, p. 3.
29. T. Gill (1998) *op. cit.*, p. 10.
30. *Ibid.*
31. L. Maitan (1998) *op. cit.*

8 Spain

1. P. Theuret (1995) 'Izquierda Unida: 10 Années d'Experience', in *Correspondances Internationales*, 20, p. 33.
2. J. Amodia, 'Requiem for the Spanish Communist Party', in D. S. Bell (ed.), *West European Communists and the Collapse of Communism* (Oxford: Berg, 1993) pp. 117–18.
3. K. Medhurst (1986) 'The Partido Comunista de España (PCE) and the Referendum on Spain's Continuing Membership of NATO', *Journal of Communist Studies*, 2 (3), p. 297.
4. *Ibid.*
5. R. Gillespie (1990) 'Realignment on the Spanish Left', *Journal of Communist Studies*, 6 (3), p. 120.
6. *Ibid.*, pp. 121–2.
7. R. Gillespie (1988) 'Spain: Crisis and Renewal in the PCE', *Journal of Communist Studies*, 4 (3), p. 337.
8. J. Amodia (1993) *op. cit.*, p. 112.
9. P. Theuret (1995) *op. cit.*, p. 10.
10. Quoted in R. Gillespie (1992), 'Spain: Centrifugal Forces in the United Left', *Journal of Communist Studies*, 8 (4), p. 310.
11. P. Theuret (1995) *op. cit.*, p. 17.
12. *Ibid.*
13. *Ibid.*
14. *Correspondances Internationales – nouvelle epoque*, Summer 1997, p. 9.
15. P. Theuret (1995) *op. cit.*, p. 9.
16. *Ibid.*
17. D. Toledano (1997) 'A Liberating Rupture', *International Viewpoint*, 295, p. 15.
18. P. Baker (1998) 'Conflict in Spain's United Left', *Labour Focus on Eastern Europe*, 59, p. 97.
19. D. Toledano (1997) *op. cit.*, p. 14.
20. *Ibid.*
21. J. Pastor (1997) 'A Necessary Rupture?', *International Viewpoint*, 295, p. 13.
22. P. Montes and J. Albarracín (1998) 'A Balance Sheet of the 5th Federal Assembly', *International Viewpoint*, 297, p. 12.
23. *Ibid.*, p. 13.
24. Interview with P. Theuret, 29 January 1999.
25. P. Theuret (1995) 'Izquierda Unida', *op. cit.*, p. 11.
26. *Correspondances Internationales – nouvelle epoque*, *op. cit.*, p. 65.
27. *Ibid.*, p. 67.
28. *The Guardian*, 23 June 1997.

9 Germany

1. See, for example, H. Bortfeldt and W. C. Thompson (1993) 'The German Communists', in D. S. Bell (ed.), *West European Communists and the Collapse of Communism* (Oxford: Berg), p. 156.
2. For further details on the ending of SED state power, see Chapter 5.
3. G. Fagan (1992) 'The Party of Democratic Socialism', *Labour Focus on Eastern Europe*, 41, p. 33.

4. *Correspondances Internationales – nouvelle epoque*, Paris, Summer 1997, p. 6.
5. F. Oswald (1996) 'The Party of Democratic Socialism: Ex-Communists Entrenched as East German Regional Protest Party', *Journal of Communist Studies and Transition Politics*, 12 (2), p. 177.
6. H. Bortfeldt (1991) 'The German Communists in Disarray', *Journal of Communist Studies*, 7 (4), p. 523.
7. G. Fagan (1997) 'The German PDS and EU Expansion', *Labour Focus on Eastern Europe*, 56, pp. 98–101.
8. PDS Peace and International Policy Working Group (PIPWG) Newsletter (1997) 3, p. 5.
9. *PDS PIPWG Newsletter*, 3 (1998), p. 1.
10. W. C. Thompson (1996) 'The Party of Democratic Socialism in the New Germany', *Communist and Post-Communist Studies*, 29 (4), p. 436.
11. F. Oswald (1996) *op. cit.*, p. 184.
12. PDS National Executive, *Five Years of German Unification* (Berlin: PDS, 1995) pp. 12–3.
13. *Ibid.*, p. 13.
14. *Ibid.*
15. H.-G. Betz and H. A. Welsh (1995) 'The PDS in the New German Party System', *German Politics*, 4 (3), p. 99.
16. *PDS PIPWG Newsletter*, 3 (1994), p. 1.
17. *PDS PIPWG Newsletter*, 5 (1994), p. 1.
18. A. Klein (1994) 'The PDS goes West', *Labour Focus on Eastern Europe*, 49, p. 102.
19. *Ibid.*
20. *PDS PIPWG Newsletter*, 3 (1994), p. 1.
21. A. Klein, *op. cit.*
22. *Ibid.*
23. *Ibid.*
24. *PDS PIPWG Newsletter*, 8 (1994), p. 3.
25. L. McFalls, 'Germany and the Return of the Communists', in M. Kraus and R. D. Liebowitz (eds), *Russia and Eastern Europe After Communism* (Oxford: Westview Press, 1996) p. 256.
26. F. Oswald (1996) *op. cit.*, p. 187.
27. *Ibid.*, pp. 187–8.
28. *PDS PIPWG Newsletter*, 7 (1994), p. 2.
29. E. Jesse (1997) 'SPD and PDS Relationships', *German Politics*, 6 (3), p. 90.
30. *Ibid.*, p. 92.
31. J. Olsen (1998) 'Germany's PDS and Varieties of "Post-Communist" Socialism', *Problems of Post-Communism*, 45 (6), p. 51.
32. E. Jesse (1997) *op. cit.*, p. 97.
33. *Ibid.*, p. 96.
34. J. Olsen (1998) *op. cit.*, p. 50.
35. *Ibid.*
36. *PDS PIPWG Newsletter*, 1 (1995), pp. 9–10.
37. J. Olsen (1998) *op. cit.*, p. 50.
38. PDS Website press release on elections, 27 September 1998.
39. Interview with Sylvia-Yvonne Kaufmann, 15 January 1999.
40. PDS press release, *op. cit.*

41. *Ibid.*
42. *PDS PIPWG Newsletter*, 4 (1998), p. 1.
43. *Ibid.*, pp. 1–2.
44. Interview with Sylvia-Yvonne Kaufmann, *op. cit.*
45. *Ibid.*
46. *Ibid.*
47. *PDS PIPWG Newsletter*, 5 (1998), p. 5.
48. *Ibid.*, p. 5.
49. *Ibid.*, p. 3.
50. *Appel Commun*, Paris, 15 January 1999.
51. Interview with Sylvia-Yvonne Kaufmann, *op. cit.*

10 Postcommunists in power in Central and Eastern Europe – introduction

1. Quoted in *Wall Street Journal*, 7 June 1996.
2. European Bank of Reconstruction and Development, *Transition Report update April 1998* (London: EBRD, 1998).
3. *Ibid.*
4. *The Observer*, Business section, 6 December 1998, p. 4.
5. P. Gowan (1997), 'The post-communist socialists in Eastern and Central Europe', in D. Sassoon (ed.), *Looking Left: European socialism after the Cold War* (London: I. B.Tauris), p. 156.
6. *Wall Street Journal*, *op. cit.*
7. P. Gowan (1997) *op. cit.*, p. 153.
8. K. Henderson (1998) 'Social Democracy Comes to Power: the 1998 Czech elections', *Labour Focus on Eastern Europe*, 60, p. 7.
9. P. Gowan (1998) 'The Passages of the Russian and East European Left', in L. Panitch and C. Leys (eds), *Socialist Register 1998*, p. 130.
10. F. Millard (1994) 'The Polish Parliamentary Election of September, 1993', *Communist and Post-Communist Studies*, 27 (3), p. 310.
11. L. Andor (1994) 'The Hungarian Socialist Party', *Labour Focus on Eastern Europe*, 48, p. 58.
12. A. Robinson and C. Bobinski, 'Future Forged in the Past', *Financial Times*, 21 November 1995, p. 19.
13. See, for example, L. Szamuely (1994) 'Privatization in a Transforming Central and Eastern Europe', *Privatization in the Transition Process* (Geneva: United Nations), p. 25.
14. European Bank of Reconstruction and Development, *Transition Report 1995*, (London: EBRD, 1995).
15. P. Gowan (1995) 'The Passages of the Russian and East European Left', *op. cit.*, p. 136.
16. This analysis was developed in G. Földes, 'The Position and the Problems of Hungarian Social Democracy', unpublished paper, Budapest, 1997, p. 7.
17. *Financial Times*, 'Hungary survey', 21 November 1995, p. I.
18. *Ibid.*, p. II.
19. *Ibid.*, p. I.
20. B. Lomax (1994) 'Elections in Hungary: Back to the Future or Forward to the Past', *Journal of Communist Studies and Transition Politics*, 10 (4), p. 93.

21. D. F. Ziblatt (1998) 'The Adaptation of Ex-Communist Parties to Post-Communist East Central Europe', *Communist and Post-Communist Studies*, 31 (2), p. 132.
22. Bill Lomax also makes this point in 'Elections in Hungary', *op. cit.*, p. 96.
23. V. Zubek (1995) 'The Phoenix out of the Ashes', *Communist and Post-Communist Studies*, 28 (3), p. 299.
24. 'The Activity and History of the Left Alternative', paper published by the Left Alternative, Budapest, 1994, p. 1.

11 Bulgaria

1. P. Gowan (1997) 'The post-communist socialists in Eastern and Central Europe' in D. Sassoon (ed.), *Looking Left* (London: I. B. Tauris), p. 155.
2. L. Andor and M. Summers (1998) *Market Failure* (London: Pluto), p. 66.
3. *Ibid.*, p. 81.
4. B. Kassayie (1998) 'The Evolution of Social Democracy in Reforming Bulgaria', *Journal of Communist Studies and Transition Politics*, 14 (3), p. 109.
5. *Ibid.*, p. 110.
6. *'Nezhna' Kontrarevolutsia e Otgovornostta* (Sofia, 1994).
7. O. Pishev (1991) 'The Bulgarian economy: transition or turmoil', Ö. Sjöberg and M. L. Wyzan (eds), *Economic Change in the Balkan States* (London: Pinter), p. 107.
8. *Ibid.*, p. 108.
9. A. Andreev (1996) 'The Political Changes and Political Parties', in I. Zloch-Christy (ed.), *Bulgaria in a Time of Change* (Aldershot: Edward Elgar), p. 31.
10. *Eastern Europe Newsletter*, 3 (23) (1989), p. 4.
11. *Ibid.*
12. Andreev (1996) *op. cit.*, pp. 32–3.
13. R. Daskalov (1998) 'A Democracy Born in Pain: Bulgarian Politics, 1989–1997', in J. D. Bell (ed.), *Bulgaria in Transition* (Boulder, Colorado: Westview), p. 11.
14. M. L. Wyzan, 'The Bulgarian economy in the immediate post-Zhivkov era', in *Economic Change in the Balkan States, op. cit.*, p. 83.
15. *Ibid.*, p. 84.
16. *Ibid.*
17. *Ibid.*, p. 95.
18. *Ibid.*
19. R. East and J. Pontin (1997), *Revolution and Change in Central and Eastern Europe*, Revised edition, (London: Pinter), p. 195.
20. Kassayie (1998) *op. cit.*, p. 112.
21. P.-E. Mitev, 'The Party Manifestos for the Bulgarian 1994 Elections', *Journal of Communist Studies and Transition Politics*, 13, 1 (1997) p. 87.
22. Kassayie (1998) *op. cit.*, p. 112.
23. East and Pontin (1997) *op. cit.*, p. 195.
24. *Ibid.*, p. 196.
25. Kassayie (1998) *op. cit.*, p. 114.
26. Programme quoted in Kassayie (1998) *op. cit.*, p. 113.
27. *Ibid.*, p. 115.
28. *Ibid.*, p. 116.

29. *Ibid.*, p. 117.
30. East and Pontin (1997) *op. cit.*, p. 195.
31. P. Gowan (1997) in *Looking Left, op. cit.*, p. 160.
32. *Ibid.*, p. 167.
33. Kassayie (1998) *op. cit.*, p. 121.
34. G. Karasimeonov (1993) 'Sea-changes in the Bulgarian Party System', in *Journal of Communist Studies*, 9 (3) p. 276.

12   Romania

1. M. Rady (1992) *Romania in Turmoil* (London: I. B. Tauris), p. 124.
2. P. Gowan (1997) 'The post-communist socialists in Eastern and Central Europe', in D. Sassoon (ed.), *Looking Left* (London: I. B. Tauris), p. 160.
3. *Ibid.*
4. S. D. Roper (1994) 'The Romanian Revolution from a Theoretical Perspective', *Communist and Post-Communist Studies*, 27 (4), p. 408.
5. A. Teodorescu (1991) 'The future of a failure: the Romanian economy', in Ö. Sjöberg and M. L. Wyzan (eds), *Economic Change in the Balkans* (London: Pinter), p. 70.
6. D. N. Nelson (1988) 'The National Conference of the Romanian Communist Party', *Journal of Communist Studies*, 4 (3), p. 332.
7. D. Deletant (1995) *Ceausescu and the Securitate* (London: Hurst), p. 329.
8. D. N. Nelson (1988) *op. cit.*, p. 331.
9. S. D. Roper (1994) *op. cit.*, p. 407.
10. M. Rady (1992) *op. cit.*, p. 69.
11. P. Ronnas (1991) 'The Economic Legacy of Ceauşescu', in Sjöberg and Wyzan, *op. cit.*, p. 48.
12. *Ibid.*, p. 49.
13. *Ibid.*
14. M. Rady (1992) *op. cit.*, p. 23.
15. *Ibid.*, p. 125.
16. P. Ronnas (1991) *op. cit.*, p. 62.
17. *Ibid.*
18. Quoted in A. Teodorescu (1991) *op. cit.*, p. 78.
19. M. Rady (1992) *op. cit.*, p. 167.
20. P. Camiller (1990) 'After University Square', *Labour Focus on Eastern Europe*, 2, p. 40.
21. M. Rady (1992) *op. cit.*, p. 183.
22. R. East and J. Pontin (1997) *Revolution and Change in Central and Eastern Europe*, revd edn, (London: Pinter), p. 184.
23. *Ibid.*, p. 162.
24. *Ibid.*, p. 165.
25. *Eastern Europe Newsletter*, 'Romania Country Survey' (1995), p. 2.
26. *Ibid.*
27. European Bank for Reconstruction and Development, *Transition Report 1997* (London: EBRD, 1997) p. 192.
28. *Ibid.*
29. *Eastern Europe Newsletter*, 'Romania Country Survey', *op. cit.*, p. 2.
30. EBRD *Report 1997, op. cit.*, p. 192.

31. T. Gallagher (1998) 'Romania's desire to be normal', *Contemporary Politics*, 4 (2), p. 114.
32. *Eastern Europe Newsletter*, 10 (23) (1996), p. 6.
33. T. Gallagher (1998) *op. cit.*, p. 118.
34. *Eastern Europe Newsletter*, 11 (14) (1997), p. 5.
35. *Eastern Europe Newsletter*, 11 (16) (1997), p. 1.
36. European Bank for Reconstruction and Development, *Transition Report Update – April 1998* (EBRD: London, 1998) p. 62.
37. *Financial Times*, 24 November 1998.
38. *Eastern Europe Newsletter*, 12 (12) (1998), p. 10.
39. *Economist*, 23 January 1999.
40. *Ibid.*

13 Hungary

1. A. Àgh, 'Bumpy Road to Europeanization', in A. Agh (ed.), *The Emergence of East Central European Parliaments: The First Steps* (Budapest: Hungarian Centre of Democracy Studies, 1994) p. 72.
2. R. L. Tőkés (1996) *Hungary's Negotiated Revolution* (Cambridge: Cambridge University Press), p. 178.
3. *Ibid.*, p. 179.
4. L. Antal, L. Bokros et al., 'Fordulat és reform', *Kozgazdasagi Szemle*, June 1987. Translated by M. Makai.
5. T. Mikes, 'Opposition in the 1980s', *Eszmelet*, Selected Essays (Budapest, 1997), pp. 143–4.
6. R. L. Tőkés, *op. cit.*, p. 297–8.
7. A. Korosenyi (1992) 'The Decay of Communist Rule in Hungary', in A. Bozoki, A. Korosenyi and G. Schöpflin (eds), *Post-communist Transition: Emerging Pluralism in Hungary* (London: Pinter), p. 3.
8. Hungarian Ministry of the Interior Website: www.valasztas.hu.
9. Interview with G. Földes, Director of Institute of Political History, Budapest, June 1997.
10. A. Bozoki, 'Post-communist transition: political tendencies in Hungary', in A. Bozoki et al., *op. cit.*, p. 18.
11. P. H. O'Neil (1998) *Revolution from Within: The Hungarian Socialist Workers' Party and the Collapse of Communism* (Cheltenham: Edward Elgar), p. 174.
12. L. Andor (1994) 'The Hungarian Socialist Party', *Labour Focus on Eastern Europe*, 48, p. 60.
13. 'The Activity and History of the Left Alternative', paper published by the Left Alternative, Budapest (1994) p. 1.
14. A. Bozoki (1992) *op. cit.*, p. 20.
15. G. Földes, 'The Position and Problems of the Hungarian Social Democracy', unpublished paper, Budapest, 1997.
16. This issue is discussed in László Andor's forthcoming work *Transition in Blue: Hungary on the Road to the European Union*.
17. Party programme quoted in D. F. Ziblatt (1998) 'The Adaptation of Ex-Communist Parties to Post-Communist East Central Europe: a Comparative Study of the East German and Hungarian Ex-Communist Parties', *Communist and Post-Communist Studies*, 31 (2), p. 132.

18. *Ibid.*
19. A. Korosenyi (1992) *op. cit.*, p. 73.
20. A. Àgh (1994) *op. cit.*, p. 75.
21. *Ibid.*
22. Congress statement quoted in D. F. Ziblatt (1998) *op. cit.*, p. 133.
23. G. Földes (1997) *op. cit.*
24. *Ibid.*
25. Interview with economist László Andor, June 1995.
26. This issue is discussed in L. Andor, *Transition in Blue, op. cit.*
27. *Ibid.*
28. *Financial Times*, Hungary survey, 21 November 1995, p. II.
29. L. Andor (1998) 'Nationalists Strike Back', *Spectre*, 5, p. 16.
30. *Financial Times*, Hungary survey, *op. cit.*, p. I.
31. HSP Left Platform. 'Declaration of Principles', Budapest (1995) p. 7.
32. *Ibid.*
33. *Ibid.*, p. 8.
34. *Eastern Europe Newsletter*, 9 (24), (1995) p. 6.
35. Hungarian Ministry of the Interior Website, *op. cit.*
36. G. Földes (1997) *op. cit.*
37. D. F. Ziblatt (1998) *op. cit.*, p. 135.
38. *Financial Times*, 9 December 1997.
39. Interview with Left Platform leader Tamàs Krausz, May 1998.

14   Poland

1. D. Holland, 'The Polish Left and European Union Enlargement', conference paper, University of North London, November 1996.
2. F. Millard (1994) 'The Polish Parliamentary Election of September, 1993', *Communist and Post-Communist Studies*, 27 (3), p. 295.
3. A. Mahr and J. Nagle (1995) 'Resurrection of the Successor Parties and Democratization in East-Central Europe', *Communist and Post-Communist Studies*, 28 (4), p. 400.
4. R. East and J. Pontin (1997) *Revolution and Change in Central and Eastern Europe*, Revised edition (London: Pinter), p. 14.
5. K. Jasiewicz (1993) 'Polish Politics on the Eve of the 1993 Elections: Toward Fragmentation or Pluralism?', *Communist and Post-Communist Studies*, 26 (4), p. 388.
6. D. Holland, 'Poland in Transition', *Labour Focus on Eastern Europe*, June 1991, p. 17.
7. European Bank of Reconstruction and Development, *Transition Report 1995* (London: EBRD, 1995) p. 203.
8. G. Sanford (1993) 'Delay and Disappointment: The Fully Free Polish Election of 27 October 1991', *Journal of Communist Studies*, 9 (2), p. 116.
9. *Ibid.*, p. 115.
10. V. Zubek (1995) 'The Phoenix Out of the Ashes: The Rise to Power of Poland's Post-Communist SdRP', *Communist and Post-Communist Studies*, 28 (3), p. 291.
11. F. Millard (1994) *op. cit.*, p. 297.
12. A. Mahr and J. Nagle (1995) *op. cit.*, p. 401.

13. *Ibid.*
14. *Ibid.*
15. V. Zubek (1995) *op. cit.*, p. 283.
16. *Ibid.*
17. From an article in *Nowa Lewica*, a Union of Labour publication, which appeared in translation in *Labour Focus on Eastern Europe*, 52, (1995) p. 24.
18. A. Mahr and J. Nagle (1995) *op. cit.*, p. 396.
19. V. Zubek (1995) *op. cit.*, p. 296.
20. G. Swain and N. Swain (1998) *Eastern Europe since 1945* (Basingstoke: Macmillan), p. 206.
21. *Ibid.*
22. D. Holland (1996) 'Dirty Politics in Poland', *Labour Focus on Eastern Europe*, 53, p. 50.
23. D. Holland (1995) 'Presidential Elections in Poland', *Labour Focus on Eastern Europe*, 52, p. 4.
24. A. Kwaśniewski (1995) 'Programmatic Declaration', translated from *Gazeta Wyborcza*, in *Labour Focus on Eastern Europe*, 52, p. 12.
25. F. Millard (1996) 'The 1995 Polish Presidential Election', *Journal of Communist Studies and Transition Politics*, 12 (1), p. 105.
26. *Ibid.*, p. 102.
27. *Ibid.*
28. Election results published in *Labour Focus on Eastern Europe*, 52, (1995) p. 40.
29. D. Holland (1996) 'Dirty Politics in Poland', *op. cit.*, p. 50.
30. G. Weclawowicz (1996) *Contemporary Poland* (London: UCL Press), p. 144–5.
31. D. Holland (1996) 'Dirty Politics in Poland' *op. cit.*, p. 51.
32. *Eastern Europe Newsletter*, 10 (13), p. 6.
33. *Ibid.*, p. 5.
34. *Eastern Europe Newsletter*, 10 (21) (1996), p. 3.
35. A. Szczerbiak (1998) 'Electoral Politics in Poland: The Parliamentary Elections of 1997', *Journal of Communist Studies and Transition Politics*, 14 (3), p. 76.
36. *Eastern Europe Newsletter*, 11 (24) (1997), p. 5.
37. *Eastern Europe Newsletter*, 12 (12) (1998), p. 10.

Index